A NATION IN TURMOIL

A NATION IN TURMOIL

Nationalism and Ethnicity in Pakistan, 1937–1958

YUNAS SAMAD

Sage Publications
New Delhi/Thousand Oaks/London

in association with
The Book Review Literary Trust
New Delhi

Copyright © Yunas Samad, 1995

First published in 1995 by

Sage Publications India Pvt Ltd
M-32 Greater Kailash Market, I
New Delhi 110 048

Sage Publications Inc
2455 Teller Road
Thousand Oaks, California 91320

Sage Publications Ltd
6 Bonhill Street
London EC2A 4PU

Published by Tejeshwar Singh for Sage Publications India Pvt Ltd, lasertypeset by Print Line, New Delhi and printed at Chaman Enterprises, Delhi.

Library of Congress Cataloging-in-publication Data

Samad, Yunas. 1951–
    A nation in turmoil: nationalism and ethnicity in Pakistan, 1937–1958 / Yunas Samad.
    p.   cm.
Includes bibliographical references and index.
1. Nationalism—Pakistan—History.   2. Ethnicity—Political aspects—Pakistan
3. India—Politics and government—1919–1947.   4. Pakistan—Politics and government.   I. Title.
DS382.S35   954.9103'5—dc20   1995   94-45239

ISBN: 0-8039-9214-9 (US-hb)
           81-7036-442-6 (India-hb)

Sage Production Editors: Deepika Ganju and Indiver Nagpal

CONTENTS

LIST OF ABBREVIATIONS

AICC	*All-India Congress Committee*
AIML	*All-India Muslim League*
APML	*All-Pakistan Muslim League*
BPC	*Basic Principles Committee*
BPML	*Bengal Provincial Muslim League*
CID	*Criminal Investigation Department*
Cmd	*Command Papers*
CPI	*Communist Party of India*
CPP	*Communist Party of Pakistan*
CRO	*Commonwealth Relations Office*
CSP	*Civil Service of Pakistan*
DSF	*Democratic Students Federation*
FO	*Foreign Office*
IOR	*India Office Records*
JAML	*Jinnah Awami Muslim League*
JUI	*Jamiat-ul-Ulama-i-Islam*
MEDO	*Middle East Defence Organization*
NAP	*National Archives of Pakistan*
NAUS	*National Archives of the United States*
NDC	*National Documentation Centre*
NWFP	*North West Frontier Province*
PPML	*Punjab Provincial Muslim League*
PRO	*Public Records Office*
PRODA	*Public Representatives Offices (Disqualification) Act*
PWA	*Progressive Writers' Association*
QAA	*Quaid-i-Azam Academy*
QAP	*Quaid-i-Azam Papers*
RG	*Record Group*
SEATO	*South-East Asia Treaty Organization*
SHC	*Shamsul Huq Collection*
UP	*United Provinces*
UPML	*United Provinces Muslim League*

Note on Spelling: Diacritical marks have not been used. Old English spelling (such as Dacca instead of Dhaka) has been used throughout, except in quotation form. Similarly, no attempt has been made to standardize proper names. I have simply followed the spelling used by the person in question.

ACKNOWLEDGEMENTS

This book is based on my doctoral thesis at Oxford University. During my research I accumulated many intellectual and personal debts. My foremost thanks go to my supervisor, Tapan Raychaudhuri, whose wisdom, scholarly rigor and warm friendship inspired and sustained me throughout this investigation. I am also indebted to Gowher Rizvi, Valerian Rodrigues, Hamza Alavi and Iftikhar Malik who, at different stages of my research, have made incisive comments and encouraged me. I am grateful for the cooperation and help that I have received from librarians of the India Office Library, the Public Records Office, the Bodleian Library, the School of Oriental and African Studies Library, the Library of Congress, the National Archives, Washington DC, the National Archives of Pakistan, the Quaid-i-Azam Academy, the National Documentation Centre, the Nehru Memorial Museum and Library, the Jamia Millia Islamia Library and the Dhaka University Library. I am also grateful for the assistance and friendship of Harun-or-Rashid who was of invaluable help to me in Dhaka. The entire research was dependent on the generosity of the British Academy, which awarded me a scholarship and a travel grant from the Beit Fund and made it possible for me to research in the South Asian subcontinent. I am also indebted to my colleagues in the Department of Social and Economic Studies, in particular, Stephen Collins and Yasmin Hussain, for supporting and encouraging the publication of this book. Finally, I must thank Josefina for, without her support, this project would have never been completed, and Jamil who helped in his own way.

INTRODUCTION

T he withdrawal of the British from India marked an early phase in the wave of decolonization which followed the end of the Second World War. However, as elsewhere, transfer of power to a single successor state did not take place, and out of the angst and trauma of partition emerged two states — India and Pakistan. With hindsight it becomes clear that there were two strands present in the decolonization process. Two imagined communities were forged: one distinct, based on Indian nationalism, and the other more ethereal, formed around Islam. The Congress Party representing a tripartite consensus between the English educated élites, business magnates and dominant peasants provided a viable coalition until the 1980s, which was responsible for establishing stable government and consolidating civil society. However, Pakistan as a sovereign state was not a stable entity. The Muslim League, a loose amalgam of élite and popular forces, proved to be incapable of fulfilling its historic role of becoming the natural party of government. It was also a poor guardian of the democratic process and unable to prevent military interventions. Unlike India, authoritarian rule has become the leitmotif of Pakistani politics. This, in turn, has precipitated challenges to the state, some successful, by sub-nationalist currents. In 1971 Pakistan was torn apart by civil war, leading to the emergence of Bangladesh. Later, the remnant of the Pakistani state was severely tested by the Baluchistan rebellion in the mid-1970s and by the Sind uprising in the mid-1980s.

The very substantive body of research and publications on South Asia's Muslims in modern times, however, fails to account for this divergence. One reason is that the denouement is generally accepted as a discontinuity that divides the literature into either studies on colonial India or concentrates on Pakistan. The main body of historiography focuses on Muslim nationalism but fails to throw light on post-partition dilemmas, while the research on contemporary issues tends to be ahistorical. The general thrust of the historical enquiry, quite naturally, is to focus on the rise of Muslim separatism, which culminated in the demand for Pakistan. This started with the debate among Muslims over the compatibility between Islam and liberal democracy. The concern of majoritarian domination led some Muslims in the direction of separatism,[1] a development encouraged by the introduction of constitutional reforms. Dyarchy created new vistas, which facilitated the rise of Muslim separatism in the Muslim-majority provinces.[2] Much has been written on the remarkable achievements of the great Quaid-i-Azam Mohammad Ali Jinnah,[3] but the role of Islam in mobilizing the Muslim masses in 1946 has only been partially explained.[4] There was, however, nothing inevitable about partition, and a substantial number of Muslims remained steadfastly loyal to the Congress.[5] This point is reinforced by research that emphasizes the instrumental character of Islam[6] and the deeply entrenched feeling of regional identity in many areas, such as the North West Frontier Province.[7] Complementing this argument are the analyses that point to the role of economic factors which undermined the Unionist citadel in the Punjab[8] and in Bengal, and the role they played in fuelling communal polarization which invalidated the Krishak Proja Party's secular approach.[9] Finally, the revisionist thesis of Jalal casts a long shadow over whether Jinnah actually intended to lead Muslims out of India to the promised land of Pakistan. She has suggested that Jinnah preferred alternative strategies whereby Muslims would remain, but that these did not come to fruition due to the Congress' opposition and exigent circumstances.[10]

When one turns to the body of literature dealing with Pakistan, the most striking feature is the relegation of Muslim identification to the background. Arguments based on this allegedly 'primordial' loyalty are generally absent from explanations of the political developments. For a country that was ostensibly created in the name of the Two-Nation theory, Islam was quickly marginalized from the main debates in Pakistani politics. This was at least true until the 1980s, when General Zia brought religion back to the centre stage with his maladroit endeavours to Islamicize the state in an attempt to legitimize his rule. There was, instead, an increasing preoccupation with ethnic mobilization, which emerged in opposition to authoritarian rule. The traditional perspective on early Pakistani history maintains that the leadership crisis was the main factor responsible for the failure of parliamentary democracy. The inability to find men of calibre to replace the founding fathers, Mohammad Ali Jinnah and Liaquat Ali Khan, was the cause of the Muslim League's collapse. Concomitant with this decline, ethnic politics, particularly in Bengal, attempted to fill the vacuum and their failure only exacerbated the confusion and chaos. In order to stabilize the situation, the military-bureaucratic oligarchy stepped in.[11] This view has been questioned by institutional approaches which maintain that national security imperatives led to the rapid expansion of the state at a time when a political vacuum was emerging, thus resulting in a shift of power.[12] Developments coincided with a changing global scenario, where cold war compulsions (made all the more urgent by regional developments, particularly in Iran) led the United States to look to the Pakistan state as an ally. The resulting cooperation was to further tilt the balance in favour of institutional domination.[13] Another position argues that the League's leadership, lacking any roots in Pakistan, turned to the institutions for support and became enthusiastic supporters of a strong centre. The ensuing tussle between 'in' and 'out' groups crystallized into tensions between the centre and the periphery.[14] Compounded with the structural imbalances, it became the source of friction which led to the politicization of ethnicity in Bengal[15] and minority provinces in erstwhile West Pakistan.

There is little research on the historical continuities that influence contemporary issues in Pakistan. This work explores these links in terms of a new hypothesis: there is an element of continuity in the tension between centrifugal and centripetal forces between pre-independence and post-partition Muslim politics. This provides a useful framework for the exploration of both historical and thematical Muslim political responses to efforts at centralization. This book examines the dominant concerns of Muslim politics in British India, focusing on the United Provinces and the Muslim-majority provinces: Bengal, the Punjab, Sarhad and Sind, and analyses how imperfectly Muslim nationalism had subsumed regional identification in these areas. Independence, however, marks the widening of difference between nationalism and ethnicity, and these circumstances eventually lead to the replacement of constitutional democracy with military dictatorship. The thrust of the analysis is to understand the historical determinant of Pakistani politics.

The object of this book is to explore South Asian Muslim politics as a continuum from the colonial to the post-partition period in Pakistan and to examine the tension between overarching Muslim unity and regional identity.

The first three chapters investigate the process leading to the establishment of the basic parameters of Muslim politics: weak all-India parties and strong provincial ones. But, after the 1937 elections, the Muslim League became influential due to the opportunities created by the Raj–Congress conflict and the increasing influence of the Pakistan slogan. Hence, by the mid-1940s, the League was able to achieve partial unity of all Muslims under the Pakistan banner. Only with the failure of the Simla Conference and the emergence of economic nationalism was the League able to make major advances in many majority-Muslim provinces. However,

Jinnah remained under pressure from regionalist forces within the party and from pro-Congress groups. The opposition collapsed when communal fury engulfed northern India and the Congress accepted partition partly as a result of the riots.

The Muslim League leadership in Pakistan was convinced for various reasons that the country, and they themselves, could survive politically only if a strong centre was established. But they went about this task in an authoritarian way. The result was that the fragile unity which had been created by Muslim nationalism was broken up and strong centrifugal forces re-emerged in reaction to the efforts at centralization. However, the military-bureaucratic oligarchy pressed ahead and implemented a constitution which was designed to increase Karachi's control over the provinces. When it became clear that the anti-centre opposition would come to power and dismantle the unitary structures, the military-bureaucratic oligarchy imposed martial law. Thus the tension between centripetal and centrifugal forces was a continuous theme in South Asian Muslim politics which contributed to political instability.

This research is based on a wide range of archival sources listed in the bibliography. Most of these have been used very little up to now. *Inter alia*, I have drawn upon the CID records in the National Documentation Centre, Lahore, which describe in minute detail the events occurring on the ground in the Punjab, Sind and Sarhad, thereby providing new information essential for understanding the rise of Muslim nationalism in the 1940s. Similarly, the material examined in the National Archives, Washington DC, and the Public Records Office offers new insights into the political processes in Pakistan. By examining hitherto unexplored evidence in a new hypothesis that traces the roots of Pakistan's politics to the colonial era, I have tried to push the frontiers of enquiry in this subject beyond its familiar limits.

NOTES

1. F. Shaikh, *Community and Consensus in Islam: Muslim Representation in Colonial India, 1860-1947* (Cambridge, 1989).
2. David Page, *Prelude to Partition: The Indian Muslims and the Imperial System of Control, 1920-32* (New Delhi, 1982).
3. Sharif al Mujahid, *Quaid-i-Azam Jinnah* (Karachi, 1981); K.B. Sayeed, *Pakistan: The Formative Phase, 1857-1948* (London, 1963); S. Wolpert, *Jinnah of Pakistan* (Oxford, 1984).
4. D. Gilmartin, *Empire and Islam: Punjab and the Making of Pakistan* (London, 1988).
5. Mushirul Hasan, *Nationalism and Communal Politics in India, 1916-28* (New Delhi, 1979).
6. P.R. Brass, *Language, Religion and Politics in North India* (Cambridge, 1974).

7. S.A. Rittenberg, *Ethnicity, Nationalism and the Pakhtuns: The Independence Movement in India's North-West Frontier Province* (Durham, 1988).
8. Ian Talbot, *Punjab and the Raj, 1849-1947* (Delhi, 1988).
9. S. Bose, *Agrarian Bengal: Economy, Social Structure and Politics, 1919-1947* (Cambridge, 1986).
10. A. Jalal, *The Sole Spokesman: Jinnah, the Muslim League and Demand for Pakistan* (Cambridge, 1985).
11. L. Ziring, *Pakistan: The Enigma of Political Development* (Kent, 1980); M.R. Afzal, *Political Parties in Pakistan, 1947-1058* (Islamabad, 1986); K.B. Sayeed, *The Political System of Pakistan* (Boston, 1967).
12. A. Jalal, *The State of Martial Law* (Cambridge, 1990); H. Alavi, 'Authoritarianism and Legitimation of State Power in Pakistan', in S. Mitra, ed, *The Post-Colonial State in Asia* (London, 1990).
13. H. Alavi, 'The Origins and Significance of the Pakistan–US Military Alliance,' in S. Kumar, ed, *Year Book on India's Foreign Policy* (New Delhi, 1991).
14. G. Rizvi, 'Pakistan: The Domestic Dimensions of Security,' in B. Buzan and G. Rizvi, eds, *South Asian Insecurity and the Great Powers* (Basingstoke, 1986).
15. R. Jahan, *Pakistan: Failure in National Integration* (New York, 1972).

1

THE CONSTITUTIONAL PROCESS AND THE FORGING OF POLITICAL IDENTIFICATIONS

Indian Muslims in the early twentieth century were not a monolithic entity. Primordial identifications based on languages, sect and region, as well as class interests, competed with each other for their loyalty. Opposing these were factors such as nationalism, both the Indian and the Muslim variant, which sought to counter the primordial pulls and class conflicts by imposing an overarching unity based on confessional faith or participation in the imagined community of the Indian nation. Another factor that affected the emergence of political identifications was the introduction of constitutional reforms. In the inter-War years, the parameters of Indian politics, and its Muslim component in particular, were defined by Dyarchy. A striking feature of this development was that certain cultural referents of identity acquired crucial political significance because they were recognized as the basis for demarcating constituencies in the new legislatures. The interplay of these factors forged political identifications, which determined the course of the subsequent political process.

His Majesty's Government, on 20 August 1917, made the declaration that steps would be taken for 'the progressive realization of responsible government in India'.[1] Britain's ultimate intention regarding India's status, however, remained obscure and it was not until the Second World War that the vague promises on devolution of power gave way to unambiguous declarations of intent. Britain's position was Janus-faced.

Constitutional advance was not designed to hasten her departure from India but to realign the structure of collaboration and control and thus ensure the flow of advantages. Edwin Montagu's August statement was an attempt to rally 'moderates' behind the Raj at a time when the Empire needed war-time allies.[2] The Reform Acts of 1919 and 1935 which later followed from this initiative, encouraged interest groups to compete for collaboration with the Raj and thus help shield the administration from the onslaught of the nationalist movement. Consequently, this exacerbated the divisions in India between the princely states and British provinces and between non-Congress parties and the Indian National Congress.

The India Act of 1919 set in motion centrifugal forces that were responsible for deflecting Indian politics away from the all-India stage to the provinces. There was no responsible government at the centre and the Governors retained control over the reserved subjects. But the provincial councils were expanded, the number of elected members increased and matters concerning the provincial government and socio-economic development were transferred to ministers responsible to the legislature. The exclusion of the princely states from the reform process demonstrated their separateness and, by the late 1920s, it became clear that India had bifurcated into two political entities — British India and the princely states. The princes had become strong advocates of autonomy. They wanted to minimize British interference in their affairs and wanted assurances that paramountcy would not be transferred to an Indian dominated central government.[3] The Raj, by firmly retaining its grip at the centre, treated the Indian states separately; and by giving some power to the provinces generated a pull, as intended, towards the periphery.

The devolution of power to the provinces also contained built-in biases. To ensure the loyalty of the provinces, the government insisted on 30 per cent of the seats in each council being reserved for nominated and special interests. There was no province where the largest elected group could command a majority in the legislature, except for the Central Provinces. The consequence was that, without a Hindu-Muslim accord, the balance of power lay with the government. The implication was clear. Constitutional success was only possible through cooperation with the government. This combined with the old policy, formulated in the Morley-Minto Reforms of 1909, of deliberately offsetting the urban politicians against the rural lobby. The English-educated professionals, politically the most active, were excluded from operating the new constitution.[4] The councils were packed with the 'landed aristocracy' who were considered 'the natural and acknowledged leaders in country areas,' with members from 'the smaller landed gentry' held in reserve.[5]

The centrifugal tendency was reinforced by the incorporation of separate electorates and reserved seats into the Reforms of 1919. Separate electorates were first conceded to Muslims in the Morley-Minto Reforms and later extended to Sikhs and others by the Lord Southborough Committee on franchise. The consequence of recognizing separate constituencies for some communities and specific interests (such as landowners and universities), was to atomize the political world into smaller particles. Thus, the building blocks of constitutional politics provided a number of foci for centrifugal tendencies. They manifestly fostered communitarian politics and mutually conflicting groupings based on vested interests. The mere fact that Muslims and Sikhs were granted separate electorates, and non-Brahmins and Marathas were conceded reserved seats, encouraged political formations to take place along cleavages based on community at the expense of Indian nationalism. The logic of such arrangements was to encourage further divisiveness. The alleged monolithic unity of Muslims was shown to be false when the Anjuman-i-Islam Ahle-Sunnat-ul-Jamat [sic] demanded the extension of separate electorates for Sunnis so as to maintain their distinction from Shiahs.[6] However, what made the system most destructive for political unity was the increase in communalism. Between 1923 and 1927, approximately 450 lives were lost in communal riots between Muslims and non-Muslims. Communal friction, however, was not restricted to relations between the two major communities. In Bombay and the south, tension developed between Brahmins and non-Brahmins, Marathas and non-Marathas and Untouchables and higher castes.[7]

The most significant impact of the Montagu-Chelmsford Reforms on Muslim politics was the shift of power and influence from the Muslim minority provinces to the Muslim majority provinces. Before the introduction of Dyarchy, all-India Muslim organizations were dominated by the Western-educated élite of the United Provinces, Bihar and Bombay. Dyarchy, however, shifted the political focus from the urban to the rural politicians. In the United Provinces, the rural-agrarian constituencies were dominated by big *talukdars* and zemindars. Out of the twenty-nine Muslim seats in the legislature, twenty-four were held by landholders.[8] They now eschewed all-India politics and became involved in regional affairs. To gain power they had to ally themselves with their Hindu counterparts and emphasize their common class interest. They were very successful in this and were well rewarded for it. Between 1923 and 1928, the Nawab of Chhatari rose steadily from the office of a minister to that of Home Member, and finally ended up as Acting Governor of the province. Another prominent Muslim, Nawab Yusaf, acted as a minister from 1926 to 1937. Their success, however, on the provincial level debarred them from the leadership of Muslim Indians as a whole.[9]

In the Punjab before Dyarchy, political activity was concentrated in the large towns of the province, mainly in the Lahore and Jullundur divisions. With the 1919 Reforms, the political focus shifted to the Muslims of the rural areas. Out of a total of thirty-two seats, twenty-seven were allocated to the Muslim-majority districts of western Punjab. Thus the landlords and agriculturists benefited from the constitutional advance at the expense of the urban interests; and the powerful Muslim zemindars of the Rawalpindi and Multan areas became dominant in the council. They formed a major centre of centrifugal politics among Muslims. The Punjab Muslims, with a strong home base, were able to exploit the devolution of power to its hilt and became the most vocal advocates of provincial autonomy. Similarly in Bengal, thirty-three out of the thirty-nine seats allocated to Muslims were for rural areas, mainly in the eastern districts of Bengal.[10] Unlike their counterparts in the Punjab, the Muslims were too disunited to take full advantage of the Reforms. The grip of communal parties also retarded the emergence of regionalism in the province. However, once regionalism became a powerful factor by the early 1930s, it influenced Bengal Muslim politics quite decisively.

The overall effect of Dyarchy was to produce strong foci of political power that were based on region and community. Thanks to separate electorates, the Muslims in the provinces where they were in the majority, as in Bengal and the Punjab, enjoyed ministerial power. Hence by 1929, when the decennial review of the Montford constitution was in progress, Muslims in these provinces had become strong advocates for the maximum extension of provincial autonomy. Their political agenda favoured a weak federal structure, with weightages for Muslims in the federal government and separate electorates. This was in direct opposition to the Congress Party's policy as expressed in the Nehru Report, where a strong unitary state and the replacement of separate electorates by joint electorates were demanded. This formula was also rejected by the princes who had no desire to be associated with a Congress-dominated unitary government in British India.

The opportunity for the Muslims and the princely states to follow their preferred trajectories came when the Congress refused to cooperate with the Raj. The deadlock over the demands for immediate *swaraj* and majority representation at the negotiations led to the Congress boycotting the Round Table Conference. This allowed Muslims and the princes a free hand in influencing the constitution-making process of the 1930s in their favour. The India Act of 1935 reconfirmed and consolidated the centrifugal developments initiated explicitly or implicitly by the Reforms of 1919. It envisaged an India Federation to be composed of the princely states and the provinces of British India, and a legislature in which the representatives of the majority of Indians would be permanently in a minority. There was no devolution of power at the centre: the Governor-General had exclusive authority over defence, foreign affairs and ecclesiastical matters, and was advised by ministers nominated by him. The Act also suited the princes who could decide how and when to federate, and they were assured that the centre would remain in British hands. The anti-Congress Muslims were also satisfied, for it granted the provinces full responsible government free from central control, except in certain crucial matters. The province of Sind was formed and the North West Frontier Province was granted full provincial status. The position of the Muslims was further reinforced by the Communal Award, which gave them separate electorates and weightages. The consequence of the constitutional advance from the Reforms of 1919 to the India Act of 1935 encouraged, in the Muslim-majority provinces, powerful centrifugal forces based on community and regional identity.

Opposing the centrifugal effect of the Montford Reforms was the centralizing influence of Indian nationalism. The most explicit manifestation of this centripetal tendency was the Khilafat and Non-cooperation Movement. The demonstration of Hindu-Muslim solidarity on such a grand scale, however, was to be the exception rather than the rule. The Muslim involvement with the Indian National Congress steadily decreased during the inter-War period. The number of Muslim supporters that Indian nationalism could command in the 1937 elections was a mere handful in comparison with the number of Muslims involved in the common struggle of the early 1920s. A testimony to the decline of Muslim support for the Congress was Jawaharlal Nehru's unsuccessful Muslim Mass Contact Campaign of 1938. The break-up of the Hindu-Muslim alliance was partly due to the contradictions inherent in the strategy of using religious and cultural symbols to mobilize the respective communities. Muslim commitment to Indian nationalism was partly undermined by the disappearance of the Khilafat issue. It is argued that the suspension of the joint struggle directed political energies into communal channels. These weaknesses, amplified by Dyarchy, reduced centripetal Muslim politics — especially its involvement in shared national goals — to a pale shadow of its former glory.

The first evidence of effective political cooperation between Hindus and Muslims came when the separate electorates, awarded by the Morley-Minto Reforms of 1909, was exploited for the purpose of unity in the Lucknow Pact of 1916 agreed between the All-India Muslim League and the Congress. This effectively blurred the divisions between the two organizations. Later in 1919, the *ulama* entered politics, overwhelmed the Muslim League and founded the All-India Khilafat Committee. Initially, the Khilafat Movement included collaborators as well as nationalists. Even staunch loyalist *talukdars* from Awadh (such as the Raja of Mahmudabad) and urban professionals from the Punjab and Bengal (such as

Fazl-i-Husain and Fazlul Huq) were involved. The Raja of Mahmudabad acted as a benefactor to many aspiring politicians, and had given financial support to the Ali brothers, Khaliquzzaman and Raj Ghulam Husain, amongst others.[11] Fazl-i-Husain, a lawyer supported by Barkat Ali and Zafar Ali Khan, both journalists, and Omar Hayat Khan Tiwana, a zemindar, were responsible for establishing Khilafat committees in the Punjab. In Bengal, Fazlul Huq, Abdul Kasem and Mujibur Rahman Khan, all men with legal backgrounds, and Akram Khan, a journalist, convened the first Khilafat meeting. However, when the Montford constitution was promulgated, the centrifugal effects of the Reforms pulled away support from the movement. The lure of office was irresistible for Fazl-i-Husain and Fazlul Huq, and they became involved in council politics.

The departure of the loyalists was hastened by the extra- parliamentary dimension that the opposition was developing. Religion had entered politics and the movement was turning into a confrontation with British colonialism. However, for the *ulama* to have a substantial impact, they had to be united. The difficulty was that the theologians were divided by doctrinal, educational and personal differences. There was, however, a thin thread binding them together, which was the shared educational experience of the *Dars-i-Nizamia*: the curriculum they had all gone through at the different seminaries. Abdul Bari, supported by some of the Delhi *ulama* (such as Mufti Kafayatullah, *maulanas* Ahmad Said and Hakim Ajmal Khan, Daud Ghaznavi of the Punjab, Akram Khan from Calcutta, the *pirs* of Sind and a Bombay Shiah, Hakim Abu Yusaf Ispahani) formed the original nucleus around which the Jamiat-ul-Ulama-i-Hind grew.[12] Later in 1920 the Deoband *ulama* joined and, in March 1921, the Shiah *mujtahid* of Lucknow, Sayed Yusaf Husain, issued a *fatwa* in favour of non-cooperation for Shiahs as well. Ahmad Raza Khan, the leading divine of the Bareilly seminary, however, abstained from the Khilafat agitation;[13] only Abdul Halim of Mainpuri participated from that seminary. As the cohesion among the *ulama* increased, the agitation became more influential among non-literate peasants, artisans and weavers in the rural areas.

Abdul Bari, besides leading the Madrasa Nizamia at Firangi Mahal, was also a respected Qadiri *pir* and, therefore, was able to win over the Sindi Qadiri and Naqshbandi *sajjada-nashins*, such as Pir Ghulam Mujaddid Sirhindi of Matiari; and from Larkana, Pir Turab Ali Shah Rashdi and Pir Ali Anwar Shah. Moreover, many of Bari's *murids* (such as the Ali brothers, Shaukat and Mohammad, Dr Mukhtar Ahmad Ansari, Mian Mohammad Chotani and Mushir Husain Kidwai) became actively involved in the Khilafat Movement. Other *murids*, such as the Rani of Jehangirabad, assisted by raising funds.[14] The Non-cooperation Movement, however, was suspended by Gandhi on 5 February 1922 in response to the serious riot at Chauri Chaura. The *ulama* were disappointed and angry at the suspension of non-cooperation. Hasrat Mohani and Abdul Bari had been arguing for the extension of non-cooperation to civil disobedience; instead it was called off. This was a major setback for the divines and struck at the central rationale of their active involvement in nationalist politics. Now the only way the divines could defend the caliphate and the holy shrines was through exhortations to the faithful in the name of the Koran and *sharia*. However, once the political debate shifted to questions of council entry, the *ulama* became superfluous. Within a year Abdul Bari was complaining that 'those who pretended to be our friends at one time and made a cat's-paw of the *ulama* now seem anxious to get rid of them'. By early 1924 Bari severed connections with the Congress and advised the *ulama* to return to their *madrasas* and *maktabs* and not to trust Hindus.[15]

The other result of calling off the Non-cooperation Movement was the break-up of the Jamiat-ul-Ulama-i-Hind. Most of the divines returned to their seminaries, and old loyalties reasserted themselves. The Shiahs left the Jamiat and reactivated the Shiah Political Conference. The Deoband, amongst other schools, became preoccupied with the *tabligh* and *tanzim* movements, which emerged due to increased communal tension in the aftermath of the Khilafat. As for the Firangi Mahal, its influence in the Jamiat was greatly reduced after the death of Bari in 1926. From then on, the Jamiat became an organization dominated by Deobandis. However, not all the divines returned to their seminaries. Some of the *ulama* (such as Azad from Calcutta, Mohani from Kanpur, Hakim Ajmal Khan from Delhi and Daud Ghaznavi and Ataullah Shah Bokhari of the Punjab) remained involved in nationalist politics.

The Khilafat Movement was at death's door, and it finally collapsed when Mustafa Kamal Pasha abolished the caliphate in March 1924. The remaining Khilafatists, mainly urban professionals, were now divided between 'no-changers' and swarajists. Tassaduq Sherwani and Choudhry Khaliquzzaman served as secretaries of the Swaraj Party from 1923. In Bengal, the participation by Khilafatists (such as Akram Khan, Abdul Karim, Mujibur Rahman Khan and Wahid Husain), provided a strong base for the Swaraj Party among Calcutta Muslims, and in the Chittagong and Rajshahi regions. Swarajists, however, had little support in the Punjab due to the hold of the Unionists, and in Sind due to the withdrawal of the *pirs*. Those who were against council entry (such as Hasrat Mohani, the Ali brothers, Saifuddin Kitchlew and Zafar Ali) had to find new issues to justify their political roles. Their extensive use of Islamic idioms and metaphors led them to first become involved in the *tanzim* and *tabligh* movement and later in communal politics. Mohammad Ali now accused Gandhi of being under the influence of Lajpat Rai and Malaviya, and he moved away from the Congress. Finally, in 1925, in protest against these developments, M.A. Ansari resigned from the Khilafat organization and concentrated on working only with pro-Congress Muslims.

The differences emerging among the Khilafatists reached a breaking point in the late 1920s. The all-White composition of the Simon Commission caused great moral outrage, and the nationalists responded by producing their own recommendations for a new constitution. However, instead of reviving the Hindu-Muslim alliance, the Nehru Report of 1928, polarized relations between the two communities. Jinnah's earlier demands, elaborated in the Delhi proposal of 1927, were only partially met. His view that a third of the seats in the Central Legislature should be reserved for Muslims was rejected. Ultimately, the Nehru Report represented the maximum concessions that Hindu revivalists (such as Lajpat Rai, Dr Moonje, M.R. Jayakar and M.M. Malaviya) were willing to make. Motilal urged Gandhi to concentrate on getting the Mahasabha to accept one-third representation, as even Azad, Ansari and Sherwani favoured this concession.[16] However, at the All-Parties' National Convention at Calcutta in December that year the Nehru Report was ratified, despite Jinnah raising new objections. The shift in Jinnah's position was a recognition that he had little support among the Muslims, and he was forced to fall in line with the All-India Muslim Conference to survive. The differences between the Congress and non-Congress Muslims essentially revolved around two major issues — the nature of the central government and the electorate. The Nehru Report recommended a unitary structure at the centre and the replacement of separate electorates by weightages for minorities, with joint electorates and reserved seats. Thus, the ultimate implication of the report was to take back all the concessions that the Muslims had gained since 1909 without giving anything in return. Consequently, Muslim opinion rallied around the All-India Muslim Conference — an organization articulating the interests of the regional parties that had emerged under Dyarchy. The Conference demanded the retention of separate electorates and a federal centre with residuary powers vested in the provinces.

Ansari's response to the failure of the convention was to rally pro-Congress Muslim opinion around the All-India Nationalist Muslim Party, which he formed in July 1929. The main organizers of the party were Khwaja Abdul Majid, Azad, Khaliquzzaman, T.A.K. Sherwani, R.A. Kidwai, Asaf Ali, Sayed Abdullah Brelvi, Ghaffar Khan, Dr Mohammad Alam, Dr S. Kitchlew and Sayed Mahmud. The party, however, was not successful and fell between two stools. Shaukat Ali lambasted Ansari for cooperating with the Congress Party, which he claimed was 'an adjunct of the Hindu Mahasabha'.[17] The Hindu communalists (like B.S. Moonje) saw the Nationalist Muslim Party as an attempt to put a large number of Muslims into the Congress so as to manipulate it.[18] It made little headway among the Muslims, existed only in newspapers, and could not establish an independent identity as it was 'backed by the Hindu Sabha press'.[19] Its lack of influence among the Muslims was amply demonstrated by the limited Muslim involvement in the Civil Disobedience Movement. Only in Calcutta and the Pakhtun areas of the Frontier were a significant number of Muslims involved in the agitations. In the Punjab, Sind and Bombay there was little enthusiasm; and in the United Provinces, the organizers of the Civil Disobedience Movement deliberately minimized propaganda work in areas of high Muslim concentration in order to avoid a possible conflict.[20] Some UP Muslims, such as Mohani and Sherwani, and some of the Deobandis, did participate in the agitation. Despite the precautions, the movement triggered off a communal reaction in UP, Assam, Bombay and Dacca. This negative effect on the National Muslim Party resulted in defections from its ranks. On 4 May 1931, the Majlis-i-Ahrar-i-Islam was founded by a breakaway group from the Nationalist Muslim Party. It was organized by Daud Ghaznavi, Ataullah Shah Bokhari and Mazhar Ali. Zafar Ali was a sympathizer, but later went on to establish the Ittihad-i-Millat.[21] These groups cooperated with the Civil Disobedience campaign but were also involved in purely Muslim issues, such as the Shahidganj agitation, which precipitated communal tensions. By 1933 the Nationalist Muslim Party was defunct, and nationalist Muslims received another setback when Ansari died in 1936.

The Congress scored an impressive victory in the 1937 provincial elections, but among the Muslim constituencies its results were not so good. Excepting the Sarhad, it could not claim to have any substantial following among the Muslims. In the United Provinces, Kidwai was defeated by an unknown Muslim Leaguer and, in recognition of the Congress' unpopularity, Khaliquzzaman stood on a League ticket. Even pro-Congress organizations (such as the Jamiat-ul-Ulama-i-Hind, Majlis-i-Ahrar, Ittihad-i-Millat and the Shiah Conference) put up separate candidates.

Another group of Muslims, an even smaller one, which also emerged from the Khilafat Movement and associated with the Congress were the Muslim communists and socialists. A small number of *muhajirin* — those involved in the *hijrat* to Afghanistan — came under Bolshevik influence and went on to Tashkent in the Soviet Union. Some of them (such as Shaukat Usmani) turned to socialism. In the mid-1920s, the *muhajirin* returned, came into contact with small pockets of socialists that included Muslims, and established workers' and peasants' parties and trade unions mainly in Bengal, the Punjab and the United Provinces. The Labour-Swaraj Party was founded by Qutubuddin Ahmad, Qazi Nazrul Islam and Shamsuddin Ahmad in Calcutta, and its general secretaries at various times were Abdul Halim, Muzaffar Ahmad and Abdul Razzak. They organized the substantial migrant Muslim population into various unions (such as the Khansamas' Union, the Seamen's Union and the Bengal Jute Workers' Association). In the Punjab, socialist Muslims were responsible for organizing various unions, and Abdul Majid, Gauhar Rahman Darveshi and Ferozuddin Mansur were elected to important positions on the Punjab Labour Research Bureau. Majid was later involved with Bhagat Singh and others in forming the Naujawan Bharat Sabha, while Darveshi and Mansur were elected to the leadership of the Kirti-Kisan Party. In the United Provinces, Shaukat Usmani became involved with the All-India Trade Union Congress and later, in 1928, he worked with Habib Ahmad Nasim in setting up the Oriental Information and Publicity Bureau.[22]

Associated with the Congress Socialist Party was another current of Muslim socialists that emerged from a different heritage. Many Indian students from prosperous families in the 1920s studied in Europe. Some of them came into contact with the Communist Party of Great Britain at university. Students such as Sajjad Zaheer, Mahmudul Zafar, and Mian Iftikharuddin from Oxford University, Muhammad Din Taseer from Cambridge University and Dr Z.A. Ahmad, Hajra Begum and briefly Dr K.M. Ashraf from London, became involved in study circles organized by Ralph Fox and Clemens Dutt, both leading members of the Communist Party. By 1936 Sajjad Zaheer and Mulk Raj Anand founded the Progressive Writers' Association of India. Its purpose was to urge writers 'to consciously help, through their writings, the forces of enlightenment and progress'. It attracted intellectuals and students such as Faiz Ahmad Faiz from Amritsar, and Sibte Hasan, Akthar Raipuri, Hayat Allah Ansari, Dr K.M. Ashraf and Dr Abdul Alim from Aligarh. Their influence, however, was small due to personal differences, communalism and the intervention of the security forces. The Meerut Conspiracy trial weakened the socialist movement, and socialists channelled their efforts into the youth leagues and the Congress in order to survive. Even this little advantage was denied to them when the Indian Government, in 1934, banned the Communist Party of India, the Naujawan Bharat Sabha and all its affiliated bodies. A new organization was then established within the Congress — the Congress Socialist Party — so that some non-clandestine work could continue. The change in direction was facilitated by Nehru's leaning towards socialism. Abdul Alim joined the executive committee of the Congress Socialist Party. Nehru appointed Z.A. Ahmad and K.M. Ashraf to the Economic and Political Department of the Congress, Sajjad Zaheer to lead the UP Provincial Congress Committee and made Mahmudul Zafar, one of his private secretaries. This, however, had the unforeseen effect of denuding the Communist Party of most of its Muslim membership.[23]

The other organization that orientated Muslim politics in a pan-Indian direction, as opposed to local ends or sectarian courses, was the Muslim

League. The League, however, suffered even more than the Congress from the forementioned changes, and could not claim to be the representative of the majority of the Muslims. The decline in the fortune of the premier Muslim party began, ironically, with the Lucknow Pact of 1916. The nationalist wing of the League led by Jinnah, along with Wazir Hasan, Mazharul Huq and the Raja of Mahmudabad, wanted to reach an understanding with the Congress. The League, however, became divided and the loyalist wing, comprising the UP landowners, dissociated themselves from this development. Many Bengali Muslims also resisted the pact, as it under-represented Bengal, and demanded a revision of the terms. The accord reflected the interests of the Muslim élites of the Muslim-minority provinces. The United Provinces, Bihar and Bombay received greater representation than their population justified, while the Punjab and Bengal received less. Consequently, the Hindu-Muslim concordat created dissension within the Muslim League.

These divisions were exacerbated by the centrifugal impact of the Montagu-Chelmsford constitution. The Muslim League lost the support of extremely influential yet conservative landlords of the United Provinces who were tempted away by the Reforms of 1919. Their tergiversation from the leadership of all-India politics weakened the Muslim League. The negative impact of the Reforms on the Muslim League was compounded by the emergence of the Khilafat and Non-cooperation Movement. This time the nationalist wing of the League split on the issue of constitutional as opposed to agitational politics. Having been released from prison, the Ali brothers, Azad and Hasrat Mohani, joined hands with the *ulama*, led by Abdul Bari, to overwhelm the League's opposition to satyagraha.

Jinnah, along with Sayed Raza Ali and Mohammad Yaqub, was among the few all-India Muslim politicians who refused to participate and were therefore bypassed by the Khilafat Movement. These politicians had to mark time and could only become active in constitutional politics when the agitation was over. However, the handful who were not prepared to wait, such as Mazharul Huq, accepted the fatal option of working with landlord politics. By the mid-twenties Huq had no choice but to retire from politics completely. The only alternatives left were to work in the UP government or in the Indian States. The Raja of Mahmudabad and Wazir Hasan served as Home Member in the UP government and as Assistant Judicial Commissioner of Awadh respectively. Sir Ali Imam and Samiullah Beg opted out of British India for Hyderabad. Ali Imam became the Nizam's Prime Minister and later became his Chief Justice.[24]

By 1926 Jinnah's position was considerably marginalized by the various negative developments. He continued focusing on all-India issues and formed the Independent Party in the Imperial Legislative Council.

But it was not a Muslim party and there were only two Muslims in it including himself. The controversy over the Simon Commission presented him the opportunity to make a comeback. However, by agreeing to boycott the Commission with the Congress, Jinnah lost further support. The Muslim League split into the Shafi and Jinnah League over this issue. With an even smaller power base, Jinnah attempted to re-establish his position on the all-India stage. The Delhi Proposal of 20 March 1927 demonstrated his willingness to revive Hindu-Muslim solidarity by trading-off separate electorates in exchange for the extension of full provincial status to Sind, the NWFP and Baluchistan, and conceding to Muslims a third of the seats in the Central Legislature. This offer was rejected by the right wing of the Congress, and Jayakar was quick to point out that Jinnah did not speak for the bulk of the Muslims.[25]

Most Muslims, especially from the Muslim-majority provinces, were adamant that they would not surrender separate electorates and rallied around the All-India Muslim Conference. Jinnah was now a voice in the wilderness spurned by all sides. To boost his position, he reunified the two branches of the Muslim League and searched for an alternative strategy. His Fourteen-Point proposal of March 1929 was a desperate attempt to avoid political oblivion. It accepted the Conference's position that the centre should be federal, but left open the option of replacing separate electorates with a joint electorate. The All-India Muslim Conference, however, was never a true centralist party. Its primary function was to present a united Muslim opinion at the Round Table Conference in order to extend the advantages gained by the Muslim-majority provinces. In composition, it was an uneasy amalgam of conflicting interests. The conservative nationalists, represented by the rump of the Central Khilafat Committee and the Jamiat-ul-Ulama-i-Hind, had to join hands with the arch loyalists — the princes and landlord parties — as well as various other organizations, such as the heterodox Ahmadiyya Association.[26]

Fazl-i-Husain's role as the driving force behind the All-India Muslim Conference, organizing propaganda and maintaining unity between the different factions, was crucial. The Agha Khan, President of the Muslim Conference, led the Muslim delegation, and Fazl-i-Husain put pressure from within and outside the Executive Council to ensure that Muslim delegates followed the Conference line. His concern about Jinnah's presence in the delegation was that if 'Jinnah starts...expressing his views' they might be accepted as the opinion of Muslims. To prevent Jinnah jeopardizing his carefully laid plans, he put forward Shafaat Ahmad Khan and Zafrullah Khan who were ready to cut Jinnah down to size if he got out of hand. Moreover, Fazl-i-Husain persuaded Lord Irwin not to nominate the Congress candidate, Dr Ansari, as a member of the delegation.[27] With this support he used the Conference to exert his authority on the constitutional developments that were taking place in the 1930s, and moulded it in the shape desired by the Punjab.[28] At the Round Table Conference, the Muslim delegation followed a two-pronged strategy of demanding the retention of separate electorates and the maximum extension of provincial autonomy. Implicit in this strategy was the calculation that any initiative from the majority community had to be sufficiently attractive to tempt Fazl-i-Husain into reconsidering his current position. However, if there was no *quid pro quo* from the Hindus, he would be unwilling to surrender separate electorates.[29]

When it appeared that the Labour Government, along with Shafi, the Nawab of Bhopal, Sultan Ahmad, Fazlul Huq and Jinnah were causing trouble by trying to reach an agreement over joint electorates,[30] Fazl-i-Husain was quick to react. He wrote to the delegation admonishing them for betraying the Conference's position and instigated the Muslim press and Muslim organizations to protest at this development. This was enough for the waverers to fall in line and, and the Agha Khan reinforced the action by repudiating Jinnah and Shafi.[31] Similarly, Fazl-i-Husain responded in a determined fashion when he found out that the Muslim Conference (represented by Shaukat Ali, Shafi, Shafee Daoodi and Iqbal) met Congress Muslims (Sherwani, Ansari and Khaliquzzaman) in order to reach a settlement before the second session of the Round Table Conference. What Fazl-i-Husain did not want was to surrender separate electorates in a deal that would satisfy the Muslim-minority provinces at the expense of the Punjab and Bengal, as had happened before with the Lucknow Pact. The deadlock forced the British to concede to Fazl-i-Husain what the Congress had refused as the price for his continued support. Both the Punjab and Bengal emerged from the Communal Award of 1932 in a stronger position. They had, now, more seats in the council than any other community. In the Punjab, the Muslims had 49 per cent of the reserved seats, and in Bengal 48, as well as separate electorates.[32]

The announcement of the Communal Award cleared the way for the rest of the reforms. The other key issue left for Fazl-i-Husain and the Agha Khan was the question of federation. The Muslim princes were concerned that such a constitutional arrangement would undermine their sovereignty by establishing a unitary structure. The Agha Khan argued for a 'United States of Southern Asia' — a federation that would give the greatest amount of autonomy to its constituent units. The aspirations of the princes dovetailed with those of the Muslim-majority provinces. The Punjab and Bengal wanted to maximize provincial autonomy, and the NWFP and Sind wanted provincial status as well. Fazl-i-Husain's activities ensured that the Government of India Act of 1935, which eventually emerged, would give the Muslim-majority provinces the maximum autonomy.

However, the demand that residual powers should be vested in the provinces was not conceded; these remained with the Governor-General to be used at his discretion.

Once the All-India Muslim Conference had served the Punjab's purpose, and there was nothing on its agenda except the maintenance of status quo, Shafaat Ahmad Khan wrote to Fazl-i-Husain:

The Muslim Conference programme has been exhausted. It is empty of content. I have been scratching my head in vain for the last two years in a vain search for a new programme for Muslim India.... You alone can do it. It will serve as a beacon to all of us.[33]

Fazl-i-Husain bluntly replied that taking on the status of an all-India leader was 'suicide', and told the élites of UP to find their own leader. He turned his back on all-India politics, returned to Lahore to reorganize the Unionist Party and called on his colleagues in UP and other provinces to follow his lead and form agriculturalist parties cutting across communal boundaries.[34]

The ploy for a weak centre by both the princes and the majority provinces left little room for Jinnah's centripetal strategy. His hostility to federation was well known.[35] He realized that the new constitutional arrangement would be dominated by an array of collaborators determined to hem in the Congress. In this vista there was no scope for an alternative Muslim strategy. Jinnah remained in Britain after the Conference, and for all practical purposes had retired from politics. He practised in the Privy Council and tried to get nominated to it. His lack of success, however, made him amenable to returning to India, in March 1934, at the urging of Liaquat Ali Khan.[36]

Why did some Muslims, especially those from the United Provinces, turn to Jinnah? Fazl-i-Husain's refusal to accept the all-India mantle, combined with the leadership crisis in UP, were important factors. By 1934, the British Indian Association and the Agra Province Zemindar Association were responsible for the establishment of the National Agricultural Party of Awadh and the National Party of Agra respectively. Both organizations were reduced to ineffectiveness by personality clashes, desultory organization and by the increase in communal pressure. The Hindu *talukdars* became associated with the Awadh Liberal League and the Muslims joined the Muslim Conference or the League.[37]

Jinnah returned hesitatingly to revive the moribund League. He united the Aziz and Hidayat factions into which the League had split, and attempted to reassert the old centralizing strategy based on cooperation with the Congress. Again, the nationalist approach was opposed by pusillanimous sycophants based in the provinces, who preferred special privileges under the Raj's protection. A short-lived revolt was led by Hafiz Hidayat Husain and supported by Fazl-i-Husain and the Nawab of Chhatari. They formed the 'Parliament Majlis,' but it collapsed on Hidayat's death.[38] On 23 June 1935, Jinnah entered negotiations with Rajendra Prasad on the thorny issue of separate electorates, which he was willing to surrender in return for other safeguards. There was some support for this move among the Muslims of east Bengal. During the negotiations, however, Jinnah kept raising the stakes, first asking for clear majorities in the Punjab and Bengal, and finally insisting that the terms had to be accepted by the *bhadralok* of east Bengal, the Sikhs, the Hindu Mahasabha and Malaviya. Eventually the Jinnah-Prasad talks broke down due to the implacable hostility of the *bhadralok* to the Communal Award, but it became clear during the discussions that 'Jinnah is humbugging the Congress'.[39] This clearly exposed the weakness of Jinnah's position. He was only acting as a broker between the Congress and the regional Muslim parties and Fazl-i-Husain was unwilling to negotiate, especially with Jinnah as an intermediary.

Resistance to Jinnah's efforts to reorganize Muslim politics around a central body began to crumble just before the elections in 1936. The All-India Muslim Conference in March that year withdrew from the elections and postponed the decision to merge with the Muslim League, leaving the question to be decided by those elected to the provincial legislative assemblies.[40] This left the field clear on the all-India level for Jinnah and in April, at the Bombay session of the Muslim League, he again argued for minimum cooperation with the Congress. This move was again blocked by the regionalist leaders. At this session, however, preparations for the elections were made, and Jinnah was allowed to preside over the formation of the Central Parliamentary Board. He hoped that the tentacles of the Board would enable him to assert the League's leadership over Muslims. Fazl-i-Husain's death in June removed his greatest rival from within the Board and, after consultations with prominent members, he nominated Mohammad Iqbal, Liaquat Ali Khan, Shaheed Suhrawardy, Ismail Chundrigar, Mirza Abul Hassan Ispahani and the young Raja of Mahmudabad, Mohammad Amir Ahmad Khan.

With the establishment of the Central Board, Jinnah's next move was to establish provincial counterparts. In Bengal he was able to get the United Muslim Party, led by Khwaja Nazimuddin and Suhrawardy, to merge with the League. Fazlul Huq at first dallied with the idea, but eventually rejected it. In the Punjab, Sikander Hayat bluntly told Jinnah not to meddle in the affairs of the provinces.[41] Only a handful of urban politicians (such as Mohammad Iqbal, Khalifa Shujauddin, Sheikh Sadiq Hasan and Barkat Ali) supported the League. The situation in Sind and the Frontier was even worse. In both provinces, the Muslims were totally absorbed in local factional politics and ignored Jinnah's call to join him. Jinnah, however, was more successful in the United Provinces. In 1933 the Muslim Unity Board was formed by merging the Muslim Conference and nationalist Muslims. The Board consisted of men such as the Raja of Salempur and Mahmudabad, Nawab Ismail Khan, Shaukat Ali, Maulana Husain Ahmad Madani, Ahmad Said, Liaquat Ali Khan and Choudhry Khaliquzzaman. By promising them a majority on the UP Parliamentary Board, Jinnah was able to persuade them to join the League. The move towards the League was helped by the ambiguous relationship between the League and the Congress. A 'number of Muslims...drifted gradually to the League side under the vague impression that it was much [*sic*] a curious affair'.[42] The Jamiat also supported the League, thinking that there was little difference between the two organizations and that they would cooperate with each other after the elections.[43] Significantly, the Rajas of Salempur and Mahmudabad and Liaquat Ali fought the elections as independents and not on League tickets. The Muslim League, however, made a poor show in the elections of 1937. It had been rejected by the regionalist parties in the Muslim majority provinces, and its only arena of influence was among the urban Muslims mainly from the United Provinces.

The analysis so far demonstrates that in relation to the aggregate Muslim population, only a handful of Muslims were members of or supported the centralist parties. Neither the Congress nor the Muslim League could claim to have a substantial following among the Muslims. A major reason for this development was the centrifugal effect of the Montford constitution. The devolution of power to the provinces reinforced strong sub-nationalist groupings that were keen to consolidate and expand provincial autonomy. In areas that were not Governor's provinces, strong regionalist pressures were created for the duplication of devolution. While Bengal and the Punjab wanted an increase in provincial autonomy, the North West Frontier Province and Baluchistan wanted upgrading to full provincial status, and Sind separation from the Bombay Presidency, which would then allow them to enjoy the fruits of autonomy. In each of these areas, however, the evolving centrifugal forces had their distinct and separate concerns and moved in different directions. Consequently, the mix between regional and Muslim identity and the class composition of the regionally orientated forces varied from area to area, and over time.

The Punjab National Unionist Party — an agriculturalist organization formed in 1923 — was an expression of Punjabi ethnicity as well as the class interests of local landed classes reacting to the constitutional advance. It was a political combination formed in the council by the merger of the Punjab Muslim Association, representing Muslim landholders supporting Fazl-i-Husain, and the Punjab Zemindar Central Association, which represented Sikh and Hindu Jat supporters of Chaudhuri Chhotu Ram. Under Fazl-i-Husain's leadership, the Unionist Party was to become the most successful constitutional party in India. The well spring of Muslim support for the Unionists came from the zemindars and *pirs* of western Punjab who prospered under British rule. The Raj had co-opted them into the colonial structure so as to utilize their *biraderi* networks and to make them perform demi-official functions as honorary magistrates, *zaildars* and *lambardars*. Apart from this, western Punjab became the major recruiting ground for the British military machine in India, providing half its recruits.[44] The Raj rewarded the Punjab amply for being the 'sword-arm of the British Empire' in various ways. The canal colonies opened in the newly irrigated areas were used to reward the large landlords and peasants from the recruiting areas of western Punjab with land grants.[45] Taxation was kept as low as possible and, in 1901, the Land Alienation Act was passed to protect the interests of the agriculturalists from the urban Hindu *bania*.

Rural Muslim politics broke down, not into an array of large individual landlords but into family blocs. The role of *biraderi* was a significant factor in giving the fractious zemindars a degree of cohesiveness in the political arena. The position of the leading families was strengthened by the hold over their tenants through *biraderi* links, recruitment to the army and, in the case of the *sajjada nashins*, a spiritual hold over their *murids*. A few families dominated Punjab politics — the Hayats of Wah, the Noon and Tiwana families of Shahpur and the Daultanas of Mailsi. The other important families were the Legharis and Pirs of Taunsa Sharif of Dera Ghazi Khan, the Pir of Makhad from Campbellpur, the Multan Qureshis, Gardezis and Gilanis, the Baghbanpura Mians, the Mamdot family from Ferozepur and the Mokul and Qizilbash clans from the Lahore districts.[46] These families, however, had long-standing feuds originating from cattle rustling and property disputes, and these differences were behind their political rivalry.

With the introduction of Dyarchy, Fazl-i-Husain was able to bring together the Hayat, Noon, Tiwana and Daultana families, despite their rivalries, into the Muslim group, which then allied itself with the Jat agriculturalists of the Ambala division. Together they worked the 1919 Reforms in a way that undermined the position of the centralist parties. Fazl-i-Husain claimed that he simply carried out the Congress programme more successfully than the Congress had done elsewhere in India.[47] There is no doubt that he had introduced reforms favouring the agriculturalists in general, and especially the Muslims. Legislations were enacted introducing compulsory primary education and the construction of schools and dispensaries in rural areas, which benefited the rural community generally. However, quotas for Muslims in education and health facilities and the terms of the Municipal Amendment Act were designed, specifically, to benefit Muslims at the expense of urban Hindus. As a result, Punjabi regionalism, based on an alliance of agriculturalist and Muslim communitarian interests, effectively blocked the advance of all-India politics in the province; both the Congress and the Muslim League were restricted to the urban areas, making little headway in the countryside.

With this strong provincial base, Husain was able to play a major role in influencing the Round Table Conference in the Punjab's favour. Patently, by holding on to the Punjab line, he rejected the alternatives based on Muslim identity. Iqbal's call for a separate Muslim state and Choudhary Rahmat Ali's Pakistan scheme were ignored or dismissed. Similarly, the Sikh's proposal — made at the second session of the Round Table Conference — that Sind should be joined with the Punjab, minus Ambala division, was rejected. Fazl-i-Husain realized that the Sindis, who were clamouring for the separation of Sind from the Bombay Presidency, were suspicious of Punjabis and would not be prepared to be bundled into a 'Muslim Empire' dominated by the Punjab. A more serious objection, however, was raised by Fazl-i-Husain himself, who pointed out that Sind was a deficit province and that amalgamation would threaten the financial viability of the Punjab as well.[48] Fazl-i-Husain only encouraged Muslim unity around the Conference as long as it suited the Punjab's interests. Once his aims had been accomplished, he was happy to sacrifice Muslim unity and was prepared to make a deal with the Hindus and Sikhs. The Unionist Party could only exploit the reforms if it cooperated with the non-Muslim communities, and Fazl-i-Husain was quite willing to negotiate away separate electorates; but neither the urban Muslims nor the Hindus and Sikhs were willing to pay the necessary price. Despite this setback, the India Act of 1935 was a triumph for the Punjab. It incorporated the Communal Award and extended provincial autonomy, and still allowed the formation of a cross-communal rural bloc.[49]

Fazl-i-Husain returned to the Punjab and, despite his precarious health, reorganized and reconstituted the Unionist Party. His concern was that if the Punjab was not to become India's Ulster, the three communities should work together on the basis of 'a definitely liberal and socialistic programme' and work for 'the uplift of the Indian masses'. Therefore, he refused to support openly the Kashmir and Shahidganj agitations because of their divisive nature. He saw communal tensions not as religious but as economic and political conflict.[50] Consequently, the Punjab perspective was bound to conflict with Jinnah's resuscitated centralist approach. When Jinnah established a Central Parliamentary Board, Fazl-i-Husain opposed it. He considered the very concept of a central party organ as political centralization and the antithesis of provincial autonomy. Moreover, associating with the League would prevent cooperation with

Hindu and Sikh agriculturalists and stoke the fires of communal tension. Clearly, he was not prepared to witness Jinnah undoing what he had persevered so hard to establish, and was intolerant of any interference in the Punjab. Jinnah visited the Punjab in 1936 to establish a Punjab Parliamentary Board but had little success. When he left he said, 'I shall never come to the Punjab again. It is such a hopeless place.'[51] Fazl-i-Husain's policies, after his death in 1936, were continued by Sikander Hayat and, in the elections of 1937, the Unionists won seventy-five seats, of which a very large proportion were rural seats.[52] Originally, two League candidates were successful, Raja Ghazanfar Ali and Barkat Ali, but Ghazanfar Ali was tempted by the lure of office to join the Unionist Party. The election results were a clear victory for Punjabi regionalism over all-India Muslim politics.

Bengal's Muslims pursued a strategy similar to that of Fazl-i-Husain. Bengali Muslim society, however, was deeply divided. The *ashraf-ajlaf* dichotomy was reinforced by other divisions that emerged in colonial Bengal. The weakness of the Bengal Muslim élite and their lack of cohesion meant that they were not able to take full advantage of the Montford Reforms and exploit numerical superiority at either the provincial or the all-India level. The *ashraf* status groups — Sayed, Pathan, Mughal and Sheikh — represented a small minority of the Muslim population and were confronted by the *ajlaf* majority who were originally low caste Hindu converts. The *ashraf-ajlaf* polarity was reinforced by the *ashraf's* contempt for the Bengali language and preference for Arabic, Persian or Urdu. The chasm between élite and popular Muslim culture greatly weakened the *ashraf's* influence over the *ajlaf*.[53] It was, however, partly bridged by the proliferation of *anjumans* and communal associations, such as the Central National Mohammedan Association, which established an ideological link between the *ashraf* and *ajlaf*.[54] The *ashraf* élite's position was further undermined by the Permanent Settlement of 1793. Only a small group of powerful zemindars, such as the Nawabs of Murshidabad, Bogra and Dacca, survived the upheaval. Other rural *ashraf* families (such as those of Nawab Abdul Latif, Obaidullah al-Obaidi Suhrawardy and Moulvi Abdul Jabbar) came to terms with the new colonial reality and acquired a western education. Thus two strands emerged from the surviving *ashraf* families — the western-educated professional and the landed élite.

The other major influence on the development of all Bengalis was the overwhelming domination of the metropolis over the *mofussil*. Calcutta's magnetic attraction dominated the social, cultural and economic life of the Bengali Muslim élite. The spoils of patronage and power to be gained in the metropolis undermined the importance of the isolated districts. The preoccupation of the Calcutta élite with the politics of the city, and the class interests of the Muslim zemindars, meant that the leadership of the *proja* movement fell to the weak and disorganized Bengali-speaking Muslim middle class. The movement was led by *jotedars* and supported by peasants and the rural proletariat. In the divisions of Dacca, Chittagong and parts of Rajshahi, where Muslims were predominant, the principal antagonism was between the Hindu landlords and Muslim tenants over *abwabs*, interest rates, indebtedness and rent. Typically, as most trading caste Hindus were simultaneously landlords, moneylenders and traders, class conflict at times took the shape of communal riots.[55]

Politically, the *proja* movement emerged at the Kamariarchar *proja* conference at Mymensingh in 1914, which was attended by Fazlul Huq, Abul Kasem, Akram Khan, Maniruzzaman Islamabadi, Rajibuddin Tarafdar and Alimuzzaman Choudhry. By 1923, Proja Samitis were organized in the districts of Noakhali, Tippera, Dacca, Mymensingh, Pabna and Bogra, and to a lesser degree in Bakarganj, Rangpur, Dinajpur and Murshidabad. However, the leadership that organized the *samitis* were the supporters of Chittaranjan Das. Following his death and the Calcutta riot of 1926, the Calcutta-based leadership of the Congress reasserted its control over the provincial Congress organization, repudiated the Bengal Pact between the Hindus and Muslims, and removed the district leadership that had emerged with the Non-cooperation Movement. Many Muslims (such as Akram Khan and Tamizuddin Khan) left the Congress at this stage. The final blow to Hindu-Muslim solidarity came when the amendment to the Bengal Tenancy Act, passed in 1928, was opposed by the Congress. From now the emerging political solidarity of Bengali Muslims was to develop outside the ambit of Indian nationalism.

The next stage in the development of their political solidarity came when the Calcutta élite decided to woo the support of the rural Muslim population they had ignored until then. Muslim politics in the legislative council had reached an impasse by the late 1920s. Muslims had demonstrated that their greatest enemy was their own disunity. However, in order to demonstrate that the Nehru Report had little credibility among Bengali Muslims, it was not enough for the élite to be united. They had to demonstrate that they had support in the rural areas. Thus in 1929, the Nikhil Banga Proja Samiti — a rural tenants' association — was formed with the cooperation of the Calcutta élite.[56] The leadership included loyalist conservatives as well as nationalists such as Abdur Rahim, Fazlul Huq, Abdullah Suhrawardy, Abdul Momin, Abdul Karim, Mujibur Rahman, Akram Khan, Shamsuddin Ahmed and Tamizuddin Khan. The Nikhil Banga Proja Samiti was a turning point in Bengal politics. It was the first regional organization drawn along class lines. The leadership was exclusively Muslim, though it did have support from the *namasudra proja*. Its class composition, however, was repugnant to A.K. Ghaznavi, the Nawab of Dacca, Habibullah, and other Muslim zemindars, who refused to be associated with it. The urban professionals of the metropolis saw the Nikhil Banga Proja Samiti only as a political symbol, and the organization remained inactive until 1932 when it began to function as an affiliating body. At the grass-roots level, however, the peasant movement was very active in the 1930s. The slump in agricultural prices due to the Depression exacerbated relations between tenants and landlords. There was a rapid increase in the number of *proja* and *krishak samitis* in the eastern districts, and the *krishak samitis* showed signs of socialistic influence.[57]

The antagonism between the Urdu speaking *ashraf* élite and the Bengali speaking peasantry explains the subordinate role of Bengal in the Muslim Conference. Fazlul Huq backed separate representation because he considered it the only way a backward community could be adequately represented. However, for many from east Bengal, the issue of separate or joint electorates was not so important. The District Boards already elected members on the joint electorates. Muslim ineffectiveness was due to lack of experience and factionalism but, by the 1930s, these disadvantages had been overcome.[58] Fazlul Huq's support for the Conference's strategy was also informed by economic issues. He used the Round Table Conference to attack the Meston Award which, by removing the jute tax from the provincial to the central list, left the finances of the province in shambles. On this point all Bengalis concurred — Hindus, Muslims and government officials. The effect of the taxation was aggravated by the Depression of the 1930s, and it severely limited state patronage in matters such as expenditure on health and education. The jute-growing districts worst affected by the jute tax provided Huq with his most vocal *proja* support. Eventually, the Otto Niemeyer Report redressed the situation by assigning 62 per cent of the jute export-tax to Bengal.[59]

The short-lived unity of Bengali Muslims, however, broke down when Abdur Rahim resigned the presidentship of the Nikhil Banga Proja Samiti in 1934. The Samiti split between two factions — west Bengal backing Abdul Momin and east Bengal backing Huq and Shamsuddin Ahmed for the leadership. The east-west split was also coterminous with the Urdu-Bengali division in the organization's leadership. Later, at the Mymensingh conference of 1935-36, a bitter squabble followed, which finally forced Akram Khan, Momin and other west Bengal leaders to drop out of the *proja* movement leaving Huq in control. Under the leadership of younger and more radical men from the eastern districts, the organization changed its name to the Krishak Proja Party (Peasants' and Tenants' Party), so as to widen its appeal, and prepared for the elections of 1937.

The *ashraf* élite also reorganized themselves in preparation for the hustings. In 1932, the Calcutta merchants, led by Ispahani, had formed the New Muslim Majlis and later, in 1936, H.S. Suhrawardy and Khwaja Nazimuddin organized the United Muslim Party. These two organizations merged with the Muslim League to form the Muslim League Parliamentary Board. Fazlul Huq was also involved in negotiations but insisted on the abolition of zemindari without compensation, while Jinnah favoured abolition with compensation. The Krishak Proja Party and the Bengal Muslim League entered the elections as opponents. Huq, championing the aspirations of rural Bengal, fought the campaign on the slogan *dal-bhat* (rice and lentils, that is, adequate food), the abolition of zemindari and free primary education. The Bengal Muslim League, on the other hand, could only stress Muslim solidarity and depended on influence and on *pirs* to win seats. Their distance from the rural population was highlighted by the fact that, except for Akram Khan, no member of the League felt at home addressing a Bengali-speaking audience. The Bengal Muslim League won thirty-nine seats in the elections and the Krishak Proja Party secured only thirty-six, but Huq was hoping to enter into an alliance with the Bengal Congress Party. The All-India Congress Working Committee, however, was unmoved by the pleas from the Bengal Congress that it should be allowed to form a coalition. Finally, the Muslim League offered Huq the premiership to prevent him from cooperating with the Congress.[60]

In Sind, the development of regional nationalism took a different course from that of the Punjab and Bengal. The movement for separation brought partial unity among the élite and forced them to raise the issue at the all-India level together with the centralist parties. However, once Sind was established as a separate province, the élite lost interest in all-India politics and became preoccupied with regional issues only. As a result, the movement for separation established Sindi regional concerns and ethnic identity as the major force in the politics of the province.

Sind's Muslim politics was dominated by large landholders, and they were the bedrock of the British administration. Power in the rural areas was in the hands of Baluchi *jagirdars* (such as Mir Ali Murad Talpur and Ghaili Khan Chandio) and Sindi *waderas* belonging to the Bhutto, Junejo and Soomro families. Some of these large landholders were also *pirs*, such as Pir Ali Shah and Pir Abid Shah from Ghotki. They combined temporal and spiritual authority, which gave them tremendous social influence. Many *pirs* were Sayeds, and they formed a separate influential grouping in Sind politics. Together, the *waderas, pirs*, Sayeds and *mirs* formed the traditional channel of authority through which government authority affected the rural masses. Symbols of honour (such as chairs at *darbars, lunghis* and other awards that enhanced their prestige) were used to secure the collaboration of *waderas* and *pirs. Izzat* conferred status and power, helping *jagirdars* and *waderas* to compete for influence over the small zemindars and *haris*. Similarly, *pirs* needed to enhance their prestige to compete for *murids*.[61] There were further divisions along ethnic lines between Sindis and Baluchis, which formed the basis of their factional groupings. The towns were not politically powerful and their little influence was further weakened by divisions between Hindus and Muslims. The Hindus belonged for the most part to the Bhaiband mercantile communities and the Amil administrative caste. Among the Muslims, the most important groups were Memons, Khojas and Bohras concentrated in Karachi and Hyderabad. The Muslim middle class consisted almost entirely of these groups.[62] From the urban groups several provincial leaders emerged. Among these were Abdullah Haroon, a Memon, Hatim Alavi, a Bohra, and Mohammad Hashim Gazdar from Karachi.

The first phase of Sindi regionalism was characterized by Hindu-Muslim solidarity and the process of defining regional nationalism. Hindus were more active than Muslims on the issue of separation. Harchandrai Vishindas and Ghulam Mohammad Bhurgiri worked in conjunction to press the Sindi demand for autonomy. Both were members of the Indian National Congress and, in 1913, Vishindas raised the question of separating Sind from Bombay as a new province at the Karachi session of the Congress. Sind, it was argued, was geographically, ethnographically, linguistically, economically and administratively self-contained and distinct from the rest of the Bombay Presidency. The region's distinctive identity was also expressed in its opposition to the Punjab. The settlement of Punjabis in the Jamrao Canal colony generated apprehension among Sindis that they would be absorbed by its larger neighbour.[63] However, the Sind Muhammadan Association, a landlord organization, petitioned Lord Montagu on his trip to India in 1917 that they wanted a separate province composed of Sind and Baluchistan.[64] This ambiguity in identification reflected the significant number of Baluchi tribes in Sind and the prominence of their leaders, the *mirs*, in the Association. Constitutional advance, however, had been rejected for Baluchistan and it was to remain under direct rule from the centre, which resulted in the proposal being dropped.[65]

Sind remained with the Presidency under the Act of 1919, and the demand for separation became more vociferous. In the early twenties, Bhurgiri and Vishindas argued that the devolution of power that Dyarchy introduced was vitiated by the special status of the Commissioner of Sind. His autocratic position minimized the benefits of reform and strengthened the argument for separation. But Bhurgiri's death in 1924 coincided with greater Muslim involvement in regionalism and increasing Hindu opposition to the idea of a separate province. The Khilafat Movement threw up new leaders, such as Sheikh Abdul Majid Sindhi, Noor Mohammad Vakil and Abdullah Haroon. Sheikh Abdul Majid took over from his mentor Bhurgiri and concentrated on turning the demand for separation into an all-India issue. He raised the question with the All-India Khilafat Committee and the All-India Muslim League. He also gained the support of the young leaders who emerged with the Non-cooperation Movement, such as Mohammad Ayub Khuro, Ghulam Mohammad Sayed, Sayed Miram Mohammad Shah, Allah Buksh Soomro and Ali Mohammad Rashidi. Sir Shah Nawaz Bhutto, however, was against separation as he had close links with Bombay and had all-India aspirations.

The communal polarization that followed the collapse of the Khilafat and Non-cooperation Movement also affected Sind. The Larkana communal riots of 1927 widened the rift between the two communities, and the Hindus now actively opposed the demand for separation. Dr H.L. Chablani's main argument was that the province was economically unviable. This argument was quite fallacious and had already, in 1918, been disputed by the Hindu dominated Sind Provincial Conference.[66] Undaunted, the anti-separationists enlisted the support of the Hindu Mahasabha and influenced the Nehru Report's position on the question of separation. The Report introduced a proviso that separation had to meet economic and administrative criteria.

The demand for separation was adopted by the All-India Muslim Conference and incorporated into the Muslim demands raised at the Round Table Conference. The Hindus, led by Hirand Kensingh and G.T. Hingorani, intensified their activities and organized a vocal anti-separationist campaign. In reaction, Muslim opinion gathered momentum around an informal organization established in 1932 — the Sind Azad Conference. This platform gave a semblance of unity to Muslim politics which, up to then, had been dominated by factionalism. However, the central government was nervous about Sind emerging as a deficit province due to the heavy expenditure made on the Sukkur Barrage. At the Round Table Conference in London in 1932, following discussions and two investigations into the financial arguments, it was agreed to separate the province, and subventions equivalent to a capital grant of twenty crore rupees were allocated to help the new province.[67]

The temporary unity, however, between the rural élites and the middle class professionals and merchants that emerged in the quest for regional autonomy collapsed once provincial status was granted. Now the tenuous links that Sindi regionalists had formed with all-India Muslim politics were allowed to wither away. Three parties based on the rural élites emerged from the Sind Azad Conference to contest the 1937 elections. In reality they were just conglomerations of factions that lacked any organization. The Sind Azad Party was formed when the Karachi Khilafat Committee, the Sind Hari Association and the Jamiat-ul-Ulama Sind merged. Led by Abdul Majid Sindhi, it established ties with the Muslim League to improve its electoral chances. Otherwise, it was exclusively a regional grouping uninterested in all-India matters. Jinnah, when he visited the province in 1936, attempted unsuccessfully to persuade Sindhi to join the League. His failure meant that he was unable to establish a parliamentary board. The main local party was the Sind United Party that was established by Abdullah Haroon along the lines of the Unionist Party. Although no Hindu joined the party, there was some contact with the Congress. The personality clash between Ghulam Mohammad Hidayatullah and Shah Nawaz Bhutto divided the party and Hidayatullah left to form the Sind Muslim Party, an exclusively Muslim organization. Later, the Sind Muslim Party was joined by M.A. Khuro and Mir Bandeh Ali Talpur. It also gained the support of the Junejo and Jatoi families.[68]

The polls simply confirmed the domination of the *waderas, pirs*, Sayeds and *mirs* and expressed their exclusively regional concerns. The only party claiming an all-India outlook, the Azad Party, did badly in the polls. However, the success of the United Party at the polls was vitiated by the defeat of its leading personalities, Bhutto and Haroon. The Governor, Sir Lancelot Graham, added to the confusion by nominating Hidayatullah as premier. The consequence was large scale defections from the United Party, forcing it to sit on the opposition benches under the leadership of Allah Buksh Soomro. With the tenuous link with all-India politics broken after the separation of Sind, Muslim politics in the province became totally absorbed with provincial affairs.

The North West Frontier Province was formed in 1901, by separating the five Political Agencies and the adjoining districts from the Punjab and incorporating them into a new province. It was a novel approach to security as the region was controlled directly by Delhi and not, as previously, by the provincial government in Lahore. Security considerations dominated the administration's perspective on the province, and none of the moves towards responsible government were implemented. Here, political development was not along the road charted out by the Morley-Minto and Montford Reforms. The lack of political advance, combined with Sarhad's specific topography, was responsible for a more turbulent political evolution.

The major division in the North West Frontier Province was between the Pakhtun and non-Pakhtun populations. In the 'settled' districts — Peshawar, Kohat, Bannu, Hazara and Dera Ismail Khan — the urban-rural divide coincided with the religious division in the province. The Hindus and Sikhs made up 8 per cent of the population and were a substantial minority in Dera Ismail Khan. Non-Muslims were mainly traders and merchants and also dominated the professions and the higher ranks of the bureaucracy. On the other hand, the Muslims of the 'settled' areas were mainly rural, and were not an ethnically unified entity. The Pakhtuns were a minority comprising only 37 per cent of the total Muslim population. The non-Pakhtun population, mainly Awans and Jats, comprised 55 per cent of the total and were in an overwhelming majority in Hazara district.[69] But, despite being in a minority, the Pakhtuns were the dominant ethnic group in the region and the only one that traditionally owned land. The exception were the *pirs*, the only non-Pakhtuns who were traditional landholders. This gave them the necessary material prerequisite to compete for political dominance. The advantage of the *sajjada nashins* (such as Pir Khels of Kohat, the Jadun Pirs of Rajuya, the Kaka Khel Mians, the Gilani Pirs of Kohat, and the Manki Pirs) over the *khani* élite was that their influence transcended tribal loyalties. However, in the 'tribal' areas, Pakhtuns were in an overwhelming majority. In these agencies — Malakand, Khyber, Kurram, North Waziristan and South Waziristan — the tribes were conceded a degree of autonomy in the running of their internal affairs in return for loyalty to the British. They were regulated by the *jirgas*, which dispensed justice according to their custom of *pakhtunwali*. The British administration maintained loose control over these semi-autonomous enclaves through a combination of subsidies and punitive expeditions.[70] The consequence of this policy was that the tribal social structure was left intact and became the vehicle for centrifugal tendencies. Typically, their particularism was combined with anti-colonialism and resulted in a series of revolts led by religious leaders, such as the Faqir of Ipi, Mirza Ali Khan.[71]

Among the Pakhtuns of the 'settled' districts, the British ruled with the collaboration of the large *khans* (such as the Nawab of Hoti, Sir Akbar Khan and the Nawab of Teri, Arbab Sher Ali Khan). However, the introduction of civil administration resulted in the withdrawal of executive and judicial powers from the leading chiefs, and they became increasingly dependent on the British. The extension of the Punjab Land Alienation Act to the Frontier in 1904 further undermined their authority. The Act's main beneficiaries were the small *khans* who were closer to the land than the big *khans*. As a result, the landlord moneylenders acquired more land, and a large number of people were reduced to the position of tenants. The hold of the landlords, mostly small *khans*, over the petty proprietors also increased and this shift in power resulted in the smaller *khans*, who were not dependent on the British, acquiring increased importance in Pakhtun society. The upshot was that the loyalist big *khans* suffered a decline in their power and were challenged by the small *khans* supported by tenants and *kamins*.[72]

It was from this milieu that Pakhtun ethnicity emerged. Leaders such as Ghaffar Khan and Dr Khan Sahib were minor chiefs, and their supporters were tenants and *kamins* from the Peshawar and Mardan districts where landlord-tenant relations were tense. Their influence, however, was weakened by the interlocking of party politics with *tarburwali* (rivalry between close kin). Politically, the roots of regionalism can be traced to the combination of three factors — the Third Afghan War of 1919 and the rise of King Amanullah, the Azad schools movement started by Ghaffar Khan, and the Khilafat Movement. After the failure of the *hijrat*, Ghaffar Khan formed the Anjuman-i-Islah-ul-Afghania to initiate cultural reform in Pakhtun society and later, in 1928, started a Pushtu journal called *Pakhtun*. By then, the residue to the Khilafat Committee, the Frontier Congress, the Afghan Jirga and its sister organization, the quasi-military Khudai Khidmatgars, began to work together in the Civil Disobedience Movement. Once the movement started, the ranks of the Afghan Jirga became dominated by new members, which explains the decentralized character of the agitation. However, the robust repression of the civil disobedience campaign was met with fierce resistance that culminated in the *de facto* control of Peshawar by the Congress and serious unrest in the Political Agencies. Ghaffar Khan was arrested and the agitation was forcefully crushed. The rebellion continued for the next few years and was finally suppressed after the deployment of reinforcements and by the extensive use of air power.[73]

From this point onwards Pakhtun ethnicity became a significant force. The Khudai Khidmatgars spread mainly to the villages in the Peshawar and Mardan districts, and organized the tenants and artisans against the *khani* élite by combining a resolute nationalist posture with vague demands for the reduction of revenue assessment. The peasantry was seriously affected by the depression, and relations between landlords and tenants were tense. The agitation, however, was divided by agnatic rivalry and had little influence in the non-Pakhtun areas due to the uncompromising position of Ghaffar Khan who said, 'This country belongs to a Pathan [*sic*] and Pathans will rule over it, and nobody else has the right to govern it'.[74] Despite this drawback, he was able to consolidate his position by leading the Afghan Jirga and Khudai Khidmatgars to join the Congress in 1931. Initially there was a factional dispute between the urban, non-Muslim Congressmen and the rural Pakhtun orientated Afghan Jirga. The All-India Congress Committee, however, sided with Gaffar Khan. The result was that the Frontier Congress was captured by Pakhtun ethnicity, rather than Indian nationalism, and the All-India Central Committee accepted this state of affairs so as to claim that it had support in the province.

Among the big *khans* and loyalists there was a weaker current of regionalism, which was articulated on the constitutional plane. The Frontier administration was totally against any constitutional advance in the province. Even the Simon Commission found the strategic and defence considerations to be so important that they could not consider any form of responsible government for the region. To press their claim, they became associated with the All-India Muslim Conference. Sahibzada Abdul Qaiyum Khan was a member of its Working Committee and Abdul Aziz, Azizullah Khan of Toru, Fateh Mohammad Khan Khattak and Nawab Khaliqdad Khan Bhaya were also associated. Fazl-i-Husain's regionalist strategy naturally appealed to Abdul Qaiyum and, at the Round Table Conference, he projected the argument that the North West Frontier Province should have full provincial status in a weak federation.[75] Despite the unanimity between the Congress, Muslim League and the Muslim Conference on this issue, the Indian Government refused to budge. The latter, however, was forced to concede reforms, partly because of the Peshawar Disturbance. It was admitted by officials that the disturbances could have been avoided had constitutional means to express grievances existed.[76] Thus it was a direct consequence of the Civil Disobedience Movement that the constitutional reforms, in operation in the rest of India, were applied to the Frontier. With the operation of Dyarchy, the *khani* élite's interest in regionalism subsided and they became absorbed in factional rivalry. There were three groups in the legislative council — Malik Khuda Buksh's Azad Party, Nawab Hamidullah Khan of Toru's Liberal Party and Ghulab Rabani Khan's Progressive Party. The Minority Party represented the Sikhs and Hindus, and there were a series of acrimonious disputes between the Muslims and non-Muslims in the council over the communal composition of the administration, the re-placement of Sanskrit by Urdu and English in government schools and the various agricultural legislations.

When elections were announced for 1937, the polarization that took place in Sarhad politics was between the loyalist landholders on the one hand, and the Pakhtun nationalists backed by tenant farmers on the other. The big *khans* were divided by agnatic rivalry, but some Hazara *khans* formed a bloc around Sahibzada Abdul Qaiyum Khan. However, his past disdain for the *khani* élite and his modest family background made him an anathema to many *khans*. They turned to the Nawab of Hoti, Akbar Khan, and formed another loose group around him. In 1936, Jinnah tried to revive the provincial Muslim League but the one Muslim body that could have provided a constituency had been pre-empted by the Congress. Jinnah was forced to turn to urban professionals, such as Pir Buksh and Malik Khuda Buksh of the Azad Party, and Allah Buksh Yusafi and Rahim Buksh Ghaznavi of the Peshawar Khilafat Committee, and co-opt them to the All-India Muslim League Parliamentary Board. Most of the members, however, deserted to the Congress and the remainder fought the elections as Azad Party candidates. The Frontier Congress benefited from the divisions in the opposition and was the most successful party in the elections. Its success was due to its link-up with Pakhtun ethnicity. This duality was accepted by the AICC as it gave some substance to its claim of representing Muslims as well as non-Muslims.

Community consciousness was the other cultural identification that was politicized by Dyarchy. Sometimes identifications based on class, region and nation became subordinate to confessional awareness. Muslim labourers under particular political conditions came to see themselves first as Muslims and then as workers. This influence subsumed communalism — that is, an attitude of aggressive intolerance *vis-à-vis* non-Muslims. 'Communal conflicts were an articulation of community consciousness...but were not a necessary attribute of community consciousness'.[77] The dividing line between urban groups which were communitarian, and those that were communal, was thin at times. With the introduction of the Montford Reforms, Muslim identification had acquired a political edge. It became the basis for competition with non-Muslim élites for power and patronage. Friction between the communities increased as some politicians deliberately exacerbated communal tensions to get access to the institutions of power. This reinforced the tendency of all political parties to exploit Muslim identification.

Muslim identification was inextricably intertwined with the complexities of town politics. The urban areas were dominated by competing factions led by the *rais* who exerted influence on the politics of the *mohallahs*. The local 'neighbourhood leadership' itself depended on the shifting alliances between the *ulama*, petty merchants and 'bazaar factions'.[78] In Calcutta, the Muslim élite was composed of the *ashraf* stratum backed by mercantile families from the Kutchi Memon, Dawoodi Bohra and Ismaili sects. Despite the participation of Azad, Huq and others in the Khilafat, communalism was always simmering below the surface. Bazaar faction leaders (such as Hakim Rehat Hussain), who were rabid communalists, kept the Khilafatists under constant pressure. Later the friction between communities over *korbani* and music before mosques was aggravated by the emergence of the *shuddhi* and *sangathan* movement and their Muslim counterpart, the *tanzim* and *tabligh*.[79] The only groups to remain independent of the Khilafat leadership and also free from communal influence were the migrant labourers from Bihar and the Punjab who had become unionized. The radicalized labour unions refused to support the élite leadership because their primary interest was economic.

The emergence of nationalism and the radicalization of labour caused consternation in government circles and among conservative Muslims. The Bengal administration aided and abetted the arch communalist Abdur Rahim's efforts to sabotage the Das Pact, and thus countered developments they feared.[80] Shaheed Suhrawardy, originally a supporter of Das, was influenced by his father-in-law, Abdur Rahim, and became deeply involved in communal politics. In the spontaneous Calcutta riots of 1926, Suhrawardy and Y.C. Ariff stoked the fires of sectarianism among up-country merchants and artisans. Fazlul Huq and Mujibur Rahman were forced to bend to communal pressures from below but were more restrained. The net result of the riots was that Hindu-Muslim solidarity broke on the rocks of communalism. Rahim and Suhrawardy emerged with the largest bloc of Muslim supporters in the city, composed mainly of migrant labour from Bihar and north India. Moreover, the radicalization of the Muslim working class was aborted and Suhrawardy formed the National Labour Federation, in 1927, to which most Muslim workers became affiliated.[81] Communalism, however, was only used as a means to gain power and as a source of electoral support. The fact that Rahim formed a short-lived coalition ministry with Byomkesh Chakravarti showed that communalism was just another tool in Dyarchic politics. The communalist groups merged with the Muslim League in 1936.

In urban Punjab, the Ahrar's political practices not only widened the gap between Muslims and non-Muslims, but also attempted to redefine Muslim identification. The Ahrar's support was mainly concentrated among the lower middle class of urban Punjab, and led by urban professionals and the reformist *ulama*. They came to prominence in 1931 with their opposition to the Kashmir State's appropriation of mosques, Muslim graveyards and other holy places. The Ahrar became involved in a tussle for the leadership of the All-India Kashmir Committee which included, among others, Dr Iqbal and the Ahmadiyya leader, Mirza Bashir-ud-Din Mahmud Ahmed. The political rivalry that revolved around the latter's insistence on using constitutional methods was compounded by doctrinal differences between orthodox Sunnis and the Ahmadiyyas. The Ahrar's successful civil disobedience campaign enhanced the prestige of the organization and widened their support. The issue transcended the limits of the Kashmiri *biraderi* to become a concern of all Muslims in India. The success led them to declare themselves an all-India organization in 1932 — the Majlis-i-Ahrar-i-Hind. Their involvement, however, in an exclusively Muslim issue did not mean that they had become a communal organization. Despite their differences with the Congress, the Ahrar wanted to incorporate demands on Kashmir into the Congress campaign. They participated in the Civil Disobedience Movement and were suspected of accepting Congress funds.[82]

The Ahmadiyyas had emerged in the *tanzim* movement as champions of Islam against the Arya Samaj, but were considered by the orthodox Muslims to be heretics. In 1933 their heterodox character became an issue among Muslims when they became more assertive and were involved in a dispute with the Mubahila group in their stronghold in Qadian.[83] The Ahrar, already hostile to the Ahmadiyyas over the Kashmir agitation, supported the Mubahila attacks against them. The anti-Ahmadiyya campaign took off and the Ahrars, joined by Zafar Ali, reached the height of their power. However, they made a tactical error in handling the Shahidganj agitation that was just beginning in July 1935. The Muslims claimed that Shahidganj was a mosque, while the Sikhs claimed it to be a gurdwara. The Ahrars decided to leave the matter to the Anjuman-i-Tahaffaz-i-Masjid for several reasons. They did not want to deflect attention from the anti-Ahmadiyya campaign, lose the support of the Congress in becoming involved in an overtly communal issue and, finally, were unwilling to go to jail just before the elections. They hoped to convert their street popularity into electoral support and become influential in the provincial assembly.[84]

The Ahrars became divided over Shahidganj, and their opponents, such as the Khaksars, attempted to replace them. Zafar Ali now became hostile to the Ahrars and established the Ittihad-i-Millat. Pir Jamaat Ali Shah was declared head of the Blue Shirts, and invoked the support of other rural *pirs*. Support for the Shahidganj movement spread from the urban to the rural areas. Sufi *pirs*, however, were subject to influences from the government, and the collaborators hesitated in calling for civil disobedience on the issue. Jamaat Ali Shah was now under pressure, especially from the reformist *ulama*. To shore up his position, he temporally enlisted the support of the Khaksars but repudiated the alliance over doctrinal differences. However, due to Jamaat's vacillation and the proximity of the elections, the agitation died down and was reactivated only after the hustings. Zafar Ali was elected to the Central Assembly and the Ittihad-i-Millat won two seats in the provincial legislature. The Ahrar Party's loss of prestige was reflected in its poor showing in the poll. They won only two seats in the Punjab and three in Bihar.[85]

The Montford Reforms reinforced the centrifugal tendency among urban Muslims trying to organize on the basis of religious identification, and their aspirations became interlocked with the political rivalry between communities. Appeal to communal identity became the channel to power in the legislative council for urban politicians. The use of religious and cultural emblems had a varying impact, depending on the context. In a heterogeneous metropolis such as Calcutta, only those religious and cultural artefacts that stressed Muslim unity were employed. To unify Muslims, schismatic differences had to be temporally relegated to the background by using Islamic idioms and metaphors that only highlighted differences with non-Muslims. The conservatives exploited communalism to break the nationalist hold over Muslims. The Ahrars had similar aspirations, but their willingness to cooperate with the Congress meant that they could not adopt an uncompromisingly communal stance. In fact, they redefined Muslim identity to exclude the Ahmadiyya from the fold of Islam. This shows that the Muslim position could sometimes be flexible. Some symbols relating to the basic precepts of Islam (such as the *ummah* and Koran) were primordial in character and appealed to all Muslims. But, clearly, the process of selecting the symbols to be used was subject to political exigencies.

The Montagu-Chelmsford Reforms set in motion centrifugal forces that deflected Indian politics away from the all-India level to the provinces. The Act's in-built biases in favour of the rural lobby at the expense of the urban professionals, and the retention of separate electorates, combined to create a strong pull to the periphery. Separate electorates also fostered communitarian politics and, implicitly, communalism. By the time of the decennial review, Muslim-majority provinces became strong advocates for greater provincial autonomy, a weak federal centre and for the retention of separate electorates. The Congress' boycott of the Round Table Conference allowed the Muslims to put their imprint on the Government of India Act of 1935, which reinforced political groupings based on religion and region and discouraged nationalist politics.

The AICC's centralizing influence was able to neutralize the centrifugal impulses among its non-Muslim constituency, but the Congress lost the support of the Muslims. There was a steady decline in Muslim support following the giddy days of the Khilafat Movement. On the eve of this movement itself, loyalists were quick to depart so as to participate in council politics. Later they were joined by the *ulama*, after Gandhi called off the non-cooperation campaign. The remaining Khilafatists also lost their unity, joining the 'no changers' or the swarajists, the latter being limited mainly to Bengal. The 'no changers,' in their commitment to agitational politics, became increasingly communal through their involvement in the *tabligh* and *tanzim* movement. Most of the remaining Muslims left the party in reaction to the Nehru Report, which represented the maximum constitutional concessions that the right wing of the Congress, afraid of losing their Hindu support, was willing to make. Dr Ansari attempted to stem the haemorrhaging by forming the All-India Nationalist Muslim Party, but his efforts were undermined by Hindu communalists within the Congress. Eventually, the Nationalist Muslim Party was splintered when the Civil Disobedience Movement triggered off communal riots resulting in the formation of the Ahrars and the Ittihad-i-Millat. The outflow of Muslims, however, was reversed on a smaller scale when Muslim socialists and communists joined the Congress Socialist Party after the Communist Party of India and its affiliates were banned.

On the whole, these developments deprived the Congress of Muslim support in the 1937 provincial elections. The little support it had was mainly among the small urban groups, such as the Ahrars, Ittihad-i-Millat, Shiah Conference, socialists and Congress Muslims such as Azad and Asaf Ali. However, where it had rural support, the North West Frontier

Province was an exception. Here the Khudai Khidmatgars had taken over the local Congress organization and transformed it into a vehicle of Pakhtun ethnicity. Generally, the Congress had been reduced to a Hindu-dominated organization. Overt or covert Hindu communalists acquired considerable power within it, and even its liberal and radical elements could devise no means to win back the waning Muslim support. The decline was acquiring an irreversible character. The Khilafat Movement had marginalized the constitutional wing of the Muslim League, and the few politicians such as Jinnah who remained in all-India politics staged a tentative return over the Simon Commission controversy. Jinnah attempted to revive Hindu-Muslim unity, but his efforts to bridge the widening abyss were unsuccessful. His proposals were spurned by the right wing of the Congress and rejected by the All-India Muslim Conference, around which most Muslims had gathered. The Muslim Conference's primary function was to represent interests, particularly those of the Punjab, at the Round Table Conference. The announcement of the Communal Award paved the way for the Government of India Act of 1935; the organization's main function completed, it became redundant. Fazl-i-Hussain turned his back on all-India politics and returned to the Punjab. Jinnah, who had effectively retired from politics, was urged to return and revive the moribund Muslim League. He again attempted to reach an accommodation with the Congress. The move faced resistance from within the Congress, and Jinnah's proposals were never accepted by the Muslim parties in the provinces. One major obstacle in his path was removed when the Muslim Conference withdrew from the elections, but the regional forces refused to cooperate with Jinnah and the Central Parliamentary Board.

The regional parties were not simply unwilling to come to terms with the Congress. They rejected centralist politics as a whole. This was amply demonstrated by the election results that underlined Jinnah's irrelevance to Muslim politics. The Muslim League's only minor success was among the urban Muslims of the United Provinces and Calcutta. Certainly, they could not have formed the coalition ministry in Bengal if the Congress had played its hand judiciously.

Most rural Muslims backed the non-Congress regional parties. The Unionist Party, the Krishak Proja Party and the Sind United Party were vehicles of regional Muslim interests. They expressed the centrifugal tendencies nurtured by the various constitutional reforms. They varied from region to region in their origin, social composition and extent of support, which explains their varying success at the hustings. The Unionist Party was based on big landlords who had been pampered by colonialism for strategic reasons. Their political cohesion was increased by the role of *biraderis*, which acted as a traditional channel of influence in the rural areas. This strong political base allowed the Punjab to stamp its interests on the constitutional negotiations and to prevent the Muslim League from making any headway in the provincial elections. In contrast, Bengali Muslim regionalism was weak. The cultural chasm between the Urdu speaking urban élites and the Bengali speaking rural population was reflected in the political arena. These political divisions forced them to accept the Punjab's leadership at the all-India level. The failure of Fazlul Huq to get a clear majority was a reflection of these divisions, and created an opportunity for the Muslim League to form a coalition government with him.

In Sind, the demand for separation from the Bombay Presidency was encouraged by the advantages of provincial status seen to have been gained by other provinces. It led to temporary unity between the urban professionals and the landlords, who linked up with all-India politics to acquire provincial status. However, when provincial status was gained, Sindi politics reverted to its local focus, ignoring the all-India stage, and soon lost its fragile unity. Similarly, in the NWFP, the big *khans* became associated with the Muslim Conference to press their claim for provincial status. Despite being unanimously supported by all the parties, the administration initially rejected the demand for responsible government for the province. However, in reaction to the Peshawar disturbance, provincial autonomy was introduced. Its consequence was that the fragile unity of the non-Congress élite collapsed. They became totally absorbed in factional rivalry, to the exclusion of all-India politics, and were unable to oppose effectively the Khudai Khidmatgars in the elections.

The other centrifugal force that was reinforced by the reforms was communitarian politics. It was inextricably linked with urban factionalism, and its politicization exacerbated rivalry between communities. Communalism was a powerful weapon used by unscrupulous politicians to win the support of voters. But the very varied communitarian groups were not all hostile to the Congress. The Ahrars were pro-Congress and moderately successful in promoting a *Sunni* Muslim identification that led them into conflicts with Muslims as well as non-Muslims. However, the openly communalist elements (such as the Calcutta group that had joined the Muslim League) were electorally more successful as a result of the rivalry between Muslims and non-Muslims.

The basic parameters of Muslim politics were established by 1937. Muslims were divided between weak centripetal and strong centrifugal forces. This tension, the natural result of developments since 1919, was crystal clear by that time. The opposition between the two forces formed the framework for the political developments of the 1940s. Redefined in a new context, it remains the basis of politics in Pakistan.

NOTES

1. 'Secretary of State for India, announcement in the House of Commons, 25 August 1917,' cited in *Report on Indian Constitutional Reforms (Montagu-Chelmsford Report)*, (Cmd 9109, 1918), p. 1.

2. R.J. Moore, *Endgames of Empire: Studies of Britain's Indian Problem* (Delhi, 1988), pp. 10-13, 32. John Gallagher, *The Decline, Revival and Fall of the British Empire* (Cambridge, 1982), p. 155.

3. R.J. Moore, ibid., p. 14.

4. David Page, *Prelude to Partition*, pp. 31-35.

5. *Report on Indian Constitutional Reforms (Montagu-Chelmsford Report)*, (Cmd 9109, 1918), pp. 94-95.

6. 'Addresses Presented in India to His Excellency the Viceroy and the Right Honourable The Secretary of State for India,' *Parliamentary Papers, 1918*, Vol. 18 (Cmd 9178), p. 564.

7. *Indian Statutory Commission*, Vol. 1 (Cmd 3568, 1930), pp. 27, 30.

8. *Return Showing the Results of Elections in India* (Cmd 1261, 1921), p. 1.

9. David Page, *Prelude to Partition*, pp. 37-38.

10. *Return Showing the Results of Elections in India*, 1921 (Cmd 1261, 1921), p. 1.

11. Francis Robinson, *Separatism Among Indian Muslims: The Politics of the United Provinces' Muslims, 1860-1923* (Cambridge, 1974), pp. 380-81.

12. Gail Minault, *The Khilafat Movement: Religious Symbolism and Political Mobilization in India* (New York 1982), p. 82.

13. Syed Jamaluddin, 'The Barelvis and the Khilafat Movement' in Mushirul Hasan, ed, *Communal and Pan-Islamic Trends in Colonial India* (New Delhi, 1981), pp. 348-49.

14. Sarah F.D. Ansari, *Sufi Saints and State Power: The Pirs of Sind, 1843-1947* (Cambridge, 1992), p. 85; Francis Robinson, *Separatism Among Indian Muslims*, pp. 266, 419-20.

15. Abdul Bari's Press statement, 20 August 1923, Abdul Bari Papers, cited in Mushirul Hasan, *Nationalism and Communal Politics*, p. 196.

16. Motilal Nehru to M.K. Gandhi, 14 August 1929, in B.N. Pandey, ed, *The Indian Nationalist Movement, 1885-1947: Select Documents* (London, 1979), pp. 63-64; Lajpat Rai's speech at the Agra Provincial Hindu Conference, 27 October 1928; M.R. Jayakar to M.K. Gandhi, 23 August 1929, ibid., pp. 86-88.

17. Shaukat Ali to Dr Ansari, 19 May 1929, in Mushirul Hasan, ed, *Muslims and the Congress: Select Correspondence of Dr M.A. Ansari, 1912-1935* (New Delhi, 1979), pp. 67-71.

18. Moonje Diaries, 22 August 1929; Moonje to Jayakar, 31 July 1929, Jayakar Papers, 437, cited in ibid., p.xxxii.

19. C. Khaliquzzaman, *Pathway to Pakistan* (Lahore, 1961), p. 102.

20. Gyanendra Pandey, *The Ascendancy of the Congress in Uttar Pradesh, 1926-34: A Study in Imperfect Mobilization* (Delhi, 1978), p. 149.

21. NDC, CID, S 358, 'The Ahrar Movement in the Punjab,' pp. 2, 5-7, 47-50.

22. Sir David Petria, *Communism in India, 1924-27* (Calcutta, 1972), pp. 126-29, 132, 254; Sir Horace Williamson, *India and Communism* (Calcutta, 1976), pp. 124, 264, 267.

23. Khizar H. Ansari, *The Emergence of Muslim Socialists in North India, 1917-47* (Lahore, 1990), pp. 159-62. S.S. Zaheer, 'A Note on the Progressive Writers' Association,' in Sudhi

Pradhan, ed, *Marxist Cultural Movement in India: Chronicles and Documents* (Calcutta, 1985), pp. 1-4.

24. David Page, *Prelude to Partition*, pp. 39-40.

25. M.R. Jayakar to M.K. Gandhi, 23 August 1929, in B.N. Pandey, ed, *The Indian Nationalist Movement*, pp. 87-88.

26. Organization of the Conference, n.d., List of Delegates attending the First All-India Muslim Conference, Delhi, 31 December 1928 to 1 January 1929, in K.K. Aziz, ed, *The All-India Muslim Conference, 1928-1935: A Documentary Record* (Karachi, 1972), pp. 24-26, 35-39.

27. Azim Husain, *Fazl-i-Husain: A Political Biography* (Bombay, 1946), pp. 247-48. Fazl-i-Husain to Malcolm Hailey, 20 May 1930, in W. Ahmad, ed, *Letters of Mian Fazl-i-Husain* (Lahore, 1976), p. 75.

28. A. Jalal and A. Seal, 'Alternative to Partition: Muslim Politics Between the Wars,' *Modern Asian Studies*, 15,3(1981), p. 434.

29. IOR, Mss. Eur. E 352 (Fazl-i-Husain Collection), f. 16-17; Fazl-i-Husain to Sikander Hayat, 26 December 1930.

30. W. Ahmad, ed, *Diary and Notes of Mian Fazl-i- Husain* (Lahore, 1976), 22 December 1930, pp. 51-52.

31. Azim Husain, *Fazl-i-Husain*, pp. 254-56.

32. A. Jalal and A. Seal, 'Alternative to Partition: Muslim Politics Between the Wars,' p. 443.

33. Shafaat Ahmad to Fazl-i-Husain, 7 November 1935, in W. Ahmad, ed, *Letters of Mian Fazl-i-Husain*, p. 469.

34. Fazl-i-Husain to Abdullah Khan, 23 September 1935, in ibid., p. 466; Azim Husain, *Fazl-i-Husain*, p. 304.

35. Jinnah's statement to the House, 7 February 1935, *Minutes and Debates of the Legislative Council of India and its Successors, 1935*, i, p. 517.

36. Stanley Wolpert, *Jinnah of Pakistan*, pp. 29-30.

37. P.D. Reeves, 'Landlords and Party Politics in the United Provinces, 1934-37,' in D.A. Low, ed, *Soundings in Modern South Asian History* (London, 1968), pp. 268-74.

38. Stanley Wolpert, *Jinnah of Pakistan*, p. 136.

39. Sarcar to R.M. Chatterji, 18 December 1935, N.N. Sarcar Papers, cited in John Gallagher, *The Decline, Revival and Fall of the British Empire*, p. 197.

40. N.N. Mitra, ed, *Indian Annual Register, Jan.-June 1936*, i (Calcutta, 1936), p. 303.

41. Sikander Hayat to Fazl-i-Husain, 1 May 1936, in W. Ahmad, ed, *Letters of Mian Fazl-i-Husain*, p. 526.

42. Jawaharlal Nehru to Rajendra Prasad, 21 July 1937, in V. Choudhary, ed, *Dr Rajendra Prasad: Correspondence and Select Documents*, i (New Delhi, 1984), p. 63.

43. Maulana Abul Kalam Azad, *India Wins Freedom* (Calcutta, 1959), p. 160.

44. M.S. Leigh, *The Punjab and the War* (Lahore, 1922), p. 44.

45. Imran Ali, 'Malign Growth? Agricultural Colonization and the Roots of Backwardness in the Punjab,' *Past and Present*, 114, February 1987, pp. 119, 124.

46. Craig Baxter, 'The People's Party vs the Punjab "Feudalists",' in J.H. Korson, ed, *Contemporary Problems of Pakistan* (Leiden, 1974), pp. 8-9, 10-11.

47. Fazl-i-Husain, 'Our Political Programme,' Mihr Collection 87, cited in David Page, *Prelude to Partition*, p. 68.

48. A. Jalal and A. Seal, 'Alternative to Partition,' pp. 442-43.

49. Ibid., pp. 443-46.
50. Fazl-i-Husain, 'Punjab Politics,' cited in Azim Husain, *Fazl-i-Husain*, p. 304.
51. Ibid., pp. 310-11.
52. *Return Showing the Results of Elections in India, 1937* (Cmd 5589, 1937), pp. 75-78.
53. Asim Roy, *The Islamic Syncretistic Tradition in Bengal* (Princeton, 1983), pp. 58-71.
54. Rafiuddin Ahmed, *The Bengal Muslims, 1871-1906: A Quest for Identity* (Delhi, 1981), pp. 31, 167.
55. Partha Chatterjee, *Bengal, 1920-47: The Land Question* (Calcutta, 1984), p. 187.
56. Abul Mansur Ahmed, *Fifty Years of Politics As I Saw It* (Dhaka, 1975), pp. 165-68.
57. Bazlur Rahman Khan, *Politics in Bengal, 1927-1936* (Dhaka, 1987), pp. 31-32.
58. John Gallagher, *The Decline, Revival and Fall of the British Empire*, pp. 166-78.
59. *Government of India Act 1935: Indian Financial Enquiry* (Cmd 5163, 1936), p. 20. The issue was revived when the Pakistan government reassumed control of jute revenues nearly a decade later.
60. Mohammad H.R. Talukdar, ed, *Memoirs of Huseyn Shaheed Suhrawardy, with a Brief Account of his Life and Work* (Dhaka, 1987), pp. 15-16.
61. David Cheesman, 'Rural Power and Debt in Sind in the Late 19th Century, 1865-1901' (London Univ. Ph.D. thesis, 1980), pp. 87, 96, 266-67.
62. A.W. Hughes, *A Gazetteer of the Province of Sind* (London, 1874), p. 84.
63. Speech by Harchandrai Vishindas (extract), Chairman, Reception Committee, Annual Session, Indian National Congress at Karachi, 1913, in H. Khuro, ed, *Documents on the Separation of Sind from the Bombay Presidency*, i (Islamabad, 1982), p. 1. The anxiety of Punjabi domination is a constant theme in Sindi politics, which became more significant after partition.
64. 'Addresses Presented in India to His Excellency the Viceroy and the Right Honourable The Secretary of State for India,' *Parliamentary Papers, 1918*, xviii (Cmd 9178), p. 553.
65. Report of the Sub-Committee Appointed by the Fifth Sind Provincial Conference to Consider the Position of Sind in the Montford Reforms 1918, in H. Khuro, ed, *Documents on the Separation of Sind*, i, pp. 15-16.
66. Ibid., p. 20.
67. *Government of India Act, 1935, Government of Burma Act, 1935, Draft* (Cmd 5181, 1936), p. 13.
68. A.K. Jones, 'Muslim Politics and the Growth of the Muslim League in Sind, 1935-41' (Duke University Ph.D. thesis, 1977), pp. 251-53; G.M. Sayed, *Struggle for New Sind: A Brief Narrative of the Working of Provincial Autonomy in Sind* (Karachi, 1949), pp. 3-19.
69. *Census of India, 1931, NWPF, xv, Part I, Report; Part 2, Tables* (Peshawar, 1933), pp. 47-187, 201-2.
70. Akbar S. Ahmed, *Religion and Politics in Muslim Society* (Cambridge, 1983), pp. 29-39.
71. Haji Mirza Ali (Faqir Saheb Ipi) to Nehru, 16 September 1937, in Jawaharlal Nehru, ed, *A Bunch of Old Letters* (London, 1960), pp. 253-54.
72. E. Jansson, *India, Pakistan or Pakhtunistan: The Nationalist Movements in the North West Frontier Province, 1937-47* (Stockholm, 1981), pp. 41-45.
73. Stephen A. Rittenberg, *Ethnicity, Nationalism and the Pakhtuns*, pp. 69-73, 84-89, 120.

74. Ghaffar Khan, PJ7/5612, 1931, No. 917, Letter 299-P.S. 19 January 1932, NWF to Foreign Department cited, in ibid., p. 115.

75. *Indian Round Table Conference*, i (Cmd 3778, 1931), p. 142.

76. *Indian Constitutional Reforms: Government of India's Despatch on the Proposal for Constitutional Reforms* (Cmd 3700, 1930), p. 78.

77. Dipesh Chakrabarty and R. Das Gupta, 'Some Aspects of Labour History of Bengal in the Nineteenth Century: Two Views', *Occasional Paper 40* (Centre for Social Sciences, Calcutta, 1981), p. 7.

78. C.A. Bayly, 'Local Control in Indian Towns: The Case of Allahabad, 1880-1920,' *Modern Asian Studies*, 5, 4 (1971), pp. 291-93,

79. Kenneth Mcpherson, *The Muslim Microcosm: Calcutta, 1918 to 1935* (Wiesbaden, 1974), pp. 55, 72.

80. J.H. Broomfield, *Elite Conflict in a Plural Society: Twentieth Century Bengal* (Berkeley, 1968), p. 274.

81. Mohammad H.R. Talukdar, ed, *Memoirs of Huseyn Shaheed Suhrawardy*, p. 13.

82. NDC, CID, S 358, 'The Ahrar Movement in Punjab,' pp. 25-26, 58-61.

83. NDC, CID, S 358, ibid., pp. 32-35; NDC, CID, Sc 359, 'The Ahmadiyya Sect,' pp. 15-16. The Mubahila group was started by ex-Ahmadiyyas, Abdul Karim and Fazal Karim, who attacked the sect for its heterodox views and its treatment of non-Ahmadiyyas in its stronghold Qadian. NDC, CID, Sc 359, ibid., p. 13.

84. NDC, CID, S 358, 'The Ahrar Movement in Punjab,' pp. 37-46.

85. *Return Showing the Results of Elections in India, 1937* (Cmd 5589, 1937), pp. 75, 87.

2

TOWARDS POLITICAL UNITY:
COMMUNITY CONSCIOUSNESS
VERSUS REGIONAL PULLS, 1937–44

The 1937 provincial elections clearly demonstrated that there was no such thing as a Muslim political monolith. Politically, Muslims were heterogeneous in character, had different interests and aspirations, and most of them were not interested in presenting a unified front at the all-India level. These simple facts, however, raise two questions. Why did the strong centrifugal forces become involved with all-India issues and fall into line with the League centralist strategy? How did religion take over the centre stage? These questions are significant because the advent of the League as an influential organization transformed the Congress–Raj contest during the 1940s into a three-cornered fight that had multiple ramifications.

The strategy that Jinnah eventually developed was neither an instantaneous response nor immediately successful. Only after a period of trial and tribulation did his approach gain coherence and popularity. An important factor responsible for the success of his strategy was the transformation of the political context during the war. The tussle between the Raj and the Congress Party created an opportunity for the Muslim League to grow into an all-India party. Patently, he was in a vulnerable position and the AIML's new centralist strategy a charade. In reality Jinnah had made major concessions to the Muslim majority provinces to gain their support and, in the process, was reduced to becoming their *vakil* at the centre.[1] Jinnah's political survival depended on the success of this gambit — of turning the Muslim League into a credible all-India force. In the face of the Congress' hostility, he hinted in August 1938 to the acting Viceroy, Lord Brabourne, that the League was prepared to collaborate with the British in return for protection from the Congress in the provinces.

With the outbreak of the war, however, it was the Viceroy who cultivated Muslim support. Linlithgow's brusque declaration that brought India into the war against Germany without consulting any Indian politician was tactical indiscretion. The Congress, which governed eight of the eleven provinces, wanted clarifications on Britain's war aims and consultation on India's constitutional future after the war as the price for cooperation. This gave the Muslim League an opportunity to declare support for the war, although it was conditional, to win the government's favour. Linlithgow now saw Jinnah as a useful ally and began to stress the importance of the Muslim League viewpoint, strengthening it as a counterbalance to the Congress, implicitly accepting its claim that it spoke for all Muslims and that the Congress was a Hindu body. Jinnah was gratified by Linlithgow's action that helped hold his party together, and for recognition of the AIML as the representative of the Muslims in the subcontinent. Linlithgow was motivated by the exigencies of the war, and sponsored the Muslim League as a counterweight to the Congress' demand for constitutional advance, and received invaluable aid from Jinnah by his refusal to reach an accommodation with Gandhi during their discussion in November 1939.[2]

Jinnah was granted recognition as an all-India leader, which had previously been beyond his reach. The honour was built into the August Offer of 1940, which gave the League a veto on constitutional advance and allowed Jinnah time to develop his organization. His position was further boosted by the Cripps Mission of 1942 that conceded the principle of Pakistan, although Jinnah rejected the proposals because it only accepted Pakistan by implication. He was taken aback by the extent it went towards accommodating the League's demand that the Muslim provinces would not be compelled to join an Indian Union and should be allowed the option of forming a separate federation.[3] The growth in his stature as a subcontinental leader was the product of the new relationship with the Raj, designed to cut the Congress down to size, and concurrently boosted his attempt to corral Muslims into the League.

The differences between the Congress and Linlithgow played right into Jinnah's hands. The long-awaited statement by the Viceroy on the war aims and the political future of India was an implicit rejection of the Congress' demands that called their bluff, forcing them to resign or eat humble pie. The resignation by the Congress ministries was a major miscalculation. It left the field open for Jinnah. The withdrawal removed the umbrella of patronage and power under which pro-Congress Muslims and their allies were operating. Despite the setbacks, the Congress dug in its heels and refused to accept Jinnah's claim of being the 'sole spokesman' of the Muslims without a challenge. The All-India Azad Muslim Conference, convened in April 1940 by Maulana Abul Kalam Azad, Allah Buksh Soomro, Asaf Ali, Mian Iftikharuddin and other Congress leaders, enhanced the credibility of this opposition and provided an alternative all-India platform for pro-Congress groups. Prominent organizations associated with the Conference were the Jamiat-ul-Ulama-i-Hind, Ahrar Party, All-India Momin Conference, Ittihad-i-Millat, Khudai Khidmatgars, some Shiah groups, the Kashmir National Conference and the Communist Party. The Conference's prestige was enhanced when Fazlul Huq fell out with Jinnah in 1941, over joining the Defence Council, and joined the anti-League rostrum.[4] However, the Quit India campaign in 1942 proved to be an advantage for the Muslim League. With influential Congressmen locked up for the entire duration of the war, the opposition to the League's rhetoric and activities disappeared. Jinnah was able to press home the advantage when Muslim League governments were formed in Bengal, Assam, Sind and the NWFP. The charade of some sort of popular elected government operating in India was important for winning over public opinion for the war in the United States. The Congress' position was further eroded by the support given to the Pakistan slogan by the Communist Party.[5]

Jinnah's new strategy did not emerge immediately after the 1937 elections. At this stage he was still prepared to cooperate with the Congress.[6] Jinnah's main electoral success came from the Muslim minority provinces, and there was an expectation that Muslims in the United Provinces would enter into a coalition with the Congress. Consequently, Jinnah's response to the Congress at the all-India level had to wait for developments in the UP. Muslim loyalties in the UP were divided between the Congress, the Muslim League and the National Agricultural Party. But the province's non-Congress Muslim élites eventually became the staunchest supporters of Jinnah, loyal right to the end. Three factors were responsible: (*a*) the tough stand taken by the Congress in the negotiations, (*b*) the Muslim Mass Contact Campaign, and (*c*) the issue of land reforms; it is probable that without their financial and political resources, Jinnah would not have survived his journey through the political wilderness.

The first consideration which motivated them was that the Congress took a hard line in the negotiations with the Muslim League, insisting that it should merge with the Congress Party. The Congress Party took such a provocative step because the negotiations between Govind Ballabh Pant and Choudhry Khaliquzzaman were creating strains within the party itself. It was opposed by Socialist Congressmen such as Abdul Wali, and Nehru was also concerned about antagonizing the Jamiat-ul-Ulama-i-Hind and those who had left the League, such as Hafiz Mohammad Ibrahim. Nehru feared that favouring the Congress' opponents with ministerial positions could alienate pro-Congress Muslims.[7]

However, the temptation of winding up the United Provinces Muslim League and absorbing it into the Congress was too much for Nehru. The all-India ramification of such an act 'would mean free field for our work without communal troubles'.[8] With these considerations in mind, Nehru, Azad, Pant, Kripalani and Narendra Dev decided to offer strict terms to the United Provinces Muslim League. These had to be accepted *in toto* if Khaliquzzaman and Nawab Ismail Khan were to be co-opted into the cabinet. Khaliquzzaman hesitated, and eventually demanded that the Muslim League members of the assembly should be free to vote on Muslim matters.[9] The Congress rejected the provision and dropped the idea of forming a coalition with the Muslim League. Instead, it nominated Hafiz Mohammad Ibrahim, backed by Maulana Husain Madani and Rafi Ahmad Kidwai, who had the support of the socialist dominated provincial committee. The party thus defused the tension that was building up within the ranks over the issue.

Khaliquzzaman's eventual reluctance to merge with the Congress was dictated by another factor: the Mass Muslim Contact Campaign and its impact on the internal politics of the Muslim League in the United Provinces. Most non-Congress Muslims feared the successful conclusion of the campaign and were determined to resist it.[10] The Nawab of Chhatari, who led the interim government, tried to win them over, but they rejected his overtures out of loyalty to the League and due to their unwillingness to join a cross-communal alliance. Instead, they waited for a lead that could only come from Jinnah, as Khaliquzzaman was busy negotiating with the Congress.[11] Jinnah publicly stated his opposition to any deal made by Khaliquzzaman.[12] It was obvious that he was very disturbed by the developments in the United Provinces, which could have dealt a lethal blow to the All-India Muslim League.

Once Jinnah had made clear his opposition to joining the Congress, he enlisted Shaukat Ali's support in the inevitable showdown with Khaliquzzaman. Jinnah's supporters estimated that if Khaliquzzaman was forced out of the League, he would take with him not more than ten assembly members. However, in the trial of strength that took place in May 1937, Khaliquzzaman was completely defeated and acquiesced to Jinnah's line. The latter's victory was largely due to the considerable alarm over the Congress' Muslim Mass Contact Campaign that many in the League felt was a direct assault on Muslim identity.[13] With the establishment of Jinnah's authority over the United Provinces Muslim

League and the end of vacillation in the League, he launched a communal counter-attack against the Congress, which was spearheaded by the *ulama* and funded by Mohammad Amir Ahmad Khan, the Raja of Mah-mudabad.[14] The Bundelkhand elections were the testing ground for the sectarian strategy which was responsible for the Muslim League's victory. Shaukat Ali led a team of *maulanas*, including Jamal Mian and Mufti Inayatullah of Firangi Mahal, Abdul Hamid Badauni and Karam Ali, and toured the Jhansi constituency. The tactic of using *maulvis* who raised the slogan 'Islam in Danger' resulted in three more by-election victories by the end of that year.

The final factor that made Muslim élites of the province rally around Jinnah was the issue of land reforms. In April 1938, the Pant ministry introduced the Tenancy Bill and the landlords, led by the Nawab of Chhatari, considered delaying it in the upper chamber. Their main concern was about proposals related to ejectment and the realization of rents. The Governor, Haig, urged them to compromise on the reforms fearing that delay would result in peasant radicalization. Pant also wanted to avoid a confrontation, knowing that the left wing of the Congress and the Kisan Sabha would use it to demand the total abolition of the zemindari system.[15] The left's activity constrained the premier's ability to negotiate with the landholders and allowed the Muslim League to take the initiative. The Congress Parliamentary Sub-Committee (composed of Vallabhbhai Patel, Rajendra Prasad and Abul Kalam Azad) offered to arbitrate be-tween the United Provinces government and the landlords. On this ques-tion, the unity of the landholders broke down. The Agra zemindars and some older Awadh *talukdars* were willing to accept arbitration on the Tenancy Bill, but most of the *talukdars* were intransigent. The anti-arbitrationist's resistance was stiffened by the Muslim League, which was implacably hostile to any compromise initiated by the Congress high command.[16] By taking a strong stand against arbitration, the League was able to win over the Muslim landlords.

The League, however, now adopted a restrictive policy on member-ship. No Muslim League worker was allowed to be a member of a landlord party. The Nawab of Chhatari and Sir Mohammad Yusaf were forced to remain in the National Agricultural Party.[17] Despite the restrictions that were imposed on the Muslim zemindars and *talukdars*, many of them (including Chhatari and Yusaf) surreptitiously gave financial support to the League.[18] The zemindars themselves saw the League as another line in the defence of their personal interest and, for this reason, placed their 'money and influence' at the service of Jinnah.[19]

When it became clear to Jinnah that no coalition was going to emerge in the United Provinces, he responded to the call made by Iqbal and others to reorganize the League into a popular body. At the Lucknow session of the Muslim League in October 1937, 'full independence' was declared to be the goal of the party, membership reduced to two *annas*, and an economic, social and educational programme was formulated. All these changes were designed to encourage the Muslim masses to join the organization.[20]

For Jinnah, the problem at this stage was clear: how could a party geared to the objective of Muslim unity under a central leadership meet the expectations of the Muslim political groups whose orientation was local? His two-pronged tactic was to use sectarian propaganda to heighten communal tensions and, on the other hand, to come to some agreement with the provincial groups. He co-opted the community based parties and their leaders, who had previously resisted being associated with the League. Sayed Abdul Aziz of the United Party of Bihar, Sayed Rauf Shah of the Muslim Parliamentary Party of the Central Provinces, Zafar Ali Shah of the Ittihad-i-Millat of the Punjab and Liaquat Ali Khan of the National Agricultural Party of the United Provinces, all of whom had fought the elections on non-League tickets, now joined Jinnah. In the Muslim majority provinces, it was the reaction to the Congress' electoral success that allowed the Muslim League to gain a toe-hold, by exploiting their fear of a Congress dominated centre wherever they lacked a voice. However, their strong sense of independence and the League's weak position made them unwilling to join the League. One *ad hoc* solution to this problem was the Sikander-Jinnah pact in the Punjab. The pact allowed Jinnah to claim that he had support in the province. In fact, the Unionist Party took over the Punjab Provincial League as the price for giving substance to the charade. A similar agreement was reached with Fazlul Huq. The cost to the League here was probably even higher than in the Punjab, and it prevented the Bengal Muslim League from setting up a ministry itself. The arrangement allowed the provincial parties to maintain their organizational identities in return for accepting the AIML as their representative at the subcontinental level.

Jinnah now made a determined effort to consolidate the League's position and pull the remaining urban Muslim organizations into the ambit of Muslim nationalism. The AIML selected points of tension between the Muslim and non-Muslim communities and turned them into an all-India issue. The aim was to widen the gap between the communities, and the process was reinforced by the increasing involvement of many Congressmen in sectarian organizations. Consequently, the League succeeded in making it difficult for pro-Congress Muslim groups to operate, and was effective in winning over the urban élites. The nationalist Muslims, however, retaliated by emphasising the differences among Muslims, and became involved in an agitation that was designed to expose the myth of the Muslim monolith. The League was joined by the Anjuman-i-Khaksaran in this struggle, and they both tried to play down the differences among Muslims. The arrival of the Khaksars gave the League the opportunity of expanding its sphere of influence into mass urban politics, but this was a complicated process that had many variations.

Communal tension was on the increase in the United Provinces and Bihar due to the involvement of many Congressmen in the Hindu Sabha and the Arya Samaj. Their actions, such as the closing down of the slaughter house in Benares, resulted in a steady rise in tension, culminating in communal rioting. From 1937 there was a continual deterioration in the relations between the two communities. This led to fierce clashes in Allahabad and Benares in 1938 in which some Congressmen were involved.[21] Conflict between tenants and zemindars further aggravated the tension, because the Congress agitated for tenants against non-Congress landlords who were mainly Muslims.[22]

For its part, the Muslim League contributed to sectarian tension by launching a virulent campaign against the Congress governments. In the United Provinces, Haig was confident that if the Muslim League joined the Cabinet, the communal issue would die down.[23] The League, however, aggravated tensions by publishing allegations of 'atrocities' and discrimination against Muslims. The Pirpur Report, as well as the ones prepared by Shareef and Fazlul Huq, attacked the Congress across a wide front. The Mass Contact Campaign, the Wardha scheme of education, the use of Hindi in the administration and the singing of *Bande Matram* came in for criticism as attacks on the Muslim identity. There were allegations of discrimination against Muslims in government service amongst other issues. All these charges were vigorously denied by the Congress, and Rajendra Prasad suggested to Jinnah that these should be investigated by Sir Maurice Gwyer, Chief Justice of the Federal Court.[24] Jinnah, realising how flimsy the accusations were, declined the offer of a judicial probe. Linlithgow asked the Governors of Bihar, Central Provinces and the United Provinces to report on Muslim grievances against the Congress Governments. The general conclusion reached by these investigations was that the Muslim League did not have a case.[25] Khaliquzzaman admitted later to Hallett, Governor of the United Provinces, the hollowness of the charges: 'I admit that the charges against Hindu Congress Governments are not proved or not wholly proved,' but the Muslims perceived that they were threatened.[26] It is clear that the various reports were for home consumption, designed to rally Muslims around the League by playing on their fears. The League-Congress controversy polarized Hindu-Muslim relations, making it difficult for Muslim élites to remain outside the League.

The *Madh-i-Sahabah* dispute, however, was a different type of communal issue. Unlike the other issues where the Muslim League intervened, this was an intra-community dispute reactivated by the Ahrar Party and the Jamiat-ul-Ulama-i-Hind. It was a counter-attack by pro-Congress Muslims designed to highlight the divisions among Muslims. The fact that Jinnah, the Nawab of Mahmudabad and other prominent Muslim League leaders were Shiah made the *Madh-i-Sahabah* a potentially divisive issue that could have divided the League along sectarian lines. However, the entry of the Anjuman-i-Khaksaran into the dispute complicated matters, and eventually the original issue was forgotten as the conflict between the authorities and the Khaksars became the central concern. Though the Khaksars backed the League's view of subordinating differences among Muslims, there was rivalry between the two. The League had hoped to expand its influence among the urban poor at the expense of the nationalist Muslims but found that Allama Mashriqi was recruiting more effectively, and was also poaching members from the Muslim National Guards. Mashriqi competed for influence in the same arena as the League and was more successful because he was prepared to resort to extra-parliamentary action.

In the late 1930s, Sunni-Shiah relations sharply deteriorated in the UP, and there were violent clashes between the two communities in several towns. The commonest cause for friction between the two communities was the recital of *tabarra*, a highly provocative practice of denigrating the first three caliphs of Islam for usurping Ali's right as successor to the Prophet and for the murder of Husain at Karbala. The Sunnis had retaliated by reciting *Madh-i-Sahabah* — praise for the companions of the Prophet. The recital first started in 1906, and triggered off serious riots in 1907-8 in Lucknow. The committee of enquiry, chaired by Justice Piggot, concluded that *Madh-i-Sahabah* was a recent innovation and should not be recited during *ashura, chehlum*, and the twenty-first of Ramazan. These recommendations were reluctantly accepted and there was, by 1909, no public recital of *Madh-i-Sahabah*.[27]

Opposition, however, to the restrictions imposed by the Piggot Committee on the recital of *Madh-i-Sahabah* was smouldering in the background. Originally, the issue was used by pro-Congress Muslims as a divisive tactic to demolish the claim of the Muslim League that Muslims were a homogeneous group.[28] The Congress always argued that Muslims 'cannot unite on purely religious issues' and that they were divided between Sunnis, Shiahs, Ahmadiyyas and other groups, which 'continue to...riot'.[29] The Sunnis received direct encouragement from Hafiz Mohammad Ibrahim, a minister in Pant's government. The friction between the two communities resulted in the Tila Mosque riot, which prompted the government of the United Provinces to appoint Justice Allsop to examine the issue. The Allsop Committee upheld the abstract right of Sunnis to recite praises of the first three caliphs in public, but saw the practice as deliberately provocative to Shiahs which could not be condoned or allowed. The publication of the findings of the committee in 1938 angered the Sunnis, and when negotiations with the government were exhausted, Madani launched a civil disobedience campaign in March 1939 that resulted in over 2,000 arrests.[30] Pant appears to have been playing a double game, which eventually backfired. During the Sunni agitation, the Congress and the Shiahs had patched up their differences. But when the government succumbed to pressure and conceded to the Sunnis the right to recite *Madh-i-Sahabah* on *barawafat* day, the Shiahs became violently hostile. The Congress Government's volte-face angered and shocked them and Maulana Nasir Husain, a leading *mujtahid*, led the counter-agitation that resulted in 7,000 arrests, including many women.[31] At this juncture, the Muslim League and the Anjuman-i-Khaksaran intervened only to further complicate the dispute. Both were motivated by the political need to perpetuate the myth of Muslim unity.

Allama Mashriqi, in his inimitably bombastic style, issued several diktats that were ignored, and then personally intervened. When negotiations between the two Muslim communities commenced, he took the credit for the suspension of the Shiah agitation, despite the fact he was not involved in the negotiations.[32] At this stage, Jawaharlal Nehru and Dr Mahmood tried to win over Mashriqi. However, by spring 1939, it became clear that the Khaksar organization was determined to remain independent and the attitude of the Congress to them changed. The Majlis-i-Ahrar led the attack calling the Khaksars the 'gravediggers [*sic*] of Islam'. This was accompanied by a flood of anti-Khaksar *fatwas* and leaflets. The campaign was intensified by the importation of Ahrar reinforcements from the Punjab.[33] Despite this, the Anjuman-i-Khaksaran gained in popularity at the expense of the Ahrar due to their intervention in the *Madh-i-Sahabah* affair. Mashriqi returned to Lahore, securing the release of several Khaksars on the promise that he would not return to Lucknow for a year. The Ahrars taunted him, alleging that the release was secured with an unqualified apology. This was too much for his pride to swallow. He returned to the United Provinces and was promptly arrested. His arrest became the focus of a civil disobedience campaign by the Khaksars. Many of them came from the NWFP and the Punjab. Many of them were ex-soldiers, and they became involved in violent clashes with the police, resulting in 1,000 arrests and six deaths.[34]

At this juncture, the attitude of the Muslim League to the Anjuman-i-Khaksaran changed and they backed them in their conflict with the United Provinces Government.[35] The Muslim press, which had been previously hostile, swung behind Mashriqi and accused Pant's ministry of victimizing the Khaksar organization. The deaths stirred popular feelings in the Punjab and greatly increased sympathy for the organization. Negotiations behind the scenes secured the release of Mashriqi in October that year, and he returned to Lahore without solving the Sunni-Shiah dispute but with his prestige greatly enhanced. The relationship between the League and the Anjuman-i-Khaksaran, however, was a complex one based on their common hostility to the Congress. Once the antagonism with the United Provinces Government ended, the friction between the conflicting ambitions of Mashriqi and Jinnah began to emerge. Allama Mashriqi attempted to sustain his newfound popularity in his typically magniloquent style. Mashriqi's *firman* published in the *Al-Islah* stated that he wanted to recruit twenty-five lakh volunteers by the end of June 1940. However, to the consternation of the League, the Khaksar recruitment drive used deception to enrol Muslim Leaguers by stating 'that the two organisation[s] League and Khaksar are identical'.[36] The Khaksar's action created misgivings within the League, and the lack of clear policy had a detrimental effect on the latter's work. In the United Provinces, the number of National Guards fell by 6,401 from 18,448 and the number of Khaksars increased from 6,738 to 13,855.[37]

Jinnah had been hesitant to take a hard line with Allama Mashriqi for two reasons. First, the prestige of the Khaksar among the Muslims was on the rise and the League gained credibility as an all-India organization by being associated with him. Therefore, the League was willing to sustain the drain of manpower from the National Guards to the Khaksar, particularly in the United Provinces. The other consideration was that Jinnah entertained the hope that at some stage in the future the Khaksar organization would be merged into, or absorbed by, the National Guards. This possibility came close to realization when the Anjuman-i-Khaksaran was banned and Mashriqi locked up.[38] In the Punjab, the Khaksar lost half its membership,[39] and the Muslim League not only began to enrol these members but considered absorbing the entire organization. Abdul Baqi and Bahadur Yar Jung represented the pro-League faction in the Khaksar, and were interested in working in close cooperation with Jinnah.[40] Both organizations were moving closer to each other and Jinnah was anxious that amalgamation should take place. Allama Mashriqi was offered a place on the Working Committee of the All-India Muslim League, and prominent Khaksars were offered executive positions in the provincial Leagues. The sticking point, however, in the negotiations was Mashriqi's insistence that a settlement between the Congress and the Muslim League was a condition for cooperation. When Sir Stafford Cripps visited India, this difference reached new proportions as Mashriqi urged Jinnah that a demand for a united India be put to the British. Jinnah, however, totally rejected the proposal of the Congress for a national government and was adamant in his demand for Pakistan. By now even Mashriqi had become an ardent advocate of Pakistan, but he argued that this could only be achieved if India was independent. Consequently, Mashriqi's repeated attempts to reach an agreement between the Congress and the League only widened the gap between him and Jinnah.[41]

Simultaneously, Mashriqi's popularity suffered a sharp drop when a Khaksar, Rafi Shabbir, attempted to assassinate Jinnah in July 1943. The Anjuman-i-Khaksar incurred considerable opprobrium from the incident, which shifted Muslim opinion away from them and created dissension in their ranks. Some wanted to disband the organization while other rank and file members became critical of Mashriqi's leadership, left the organization and joined the League. Jinnah now clearly distanced himself from Mashriqi and stressed that Muslims could not owe allegiance to two organizations. By mid-1944 the Khaksar's total membership had fallen to 20,000 from 23,000 a year earlier. Even more significantly, leaders such as Dr Nami and Ghulam Mustafa Bhurgiri resigned from the organization.[42] The Muslim League consolidated its position at the expense of the Khaksar organization, established itself as a major influence among the urban masses, and became the exclusive champion of Muslim identification.

As the increase in Jinnah's prestige, popularity and influence coincided with the crumbling of Muslim opposition, he attempted to discipline and contain the various groups that had collected around the League. On paper he instigated the increasing concentration of power in the central organs of the League, particularly the Working Committee and its peripatetic ambassador, the Committee of Action. Originally, the 1938 constitution of the AIML was federal in character, with the Working Committee's powers limited and dependent on the AIML Council for its authority. The 465 members were elected by the provincial Leagues and, to win support of the Punjab and Bengal, Jinnah had to increase their representation. This was counterbalanced by reserving for the President of the League, Jinnah, the right to co-opt representatives to the Working Committee, which allowed him to pack it with loyalists from the Muslim-minority provinces, particularly the United Provinces.[43] However, the rapid rise in Jinnah's prestige due to the August Offer, the Cripps Mission and the increasing popularity of the Pakistan slogan allowed him to amend the constitution. By the mid-1940s, the Working Committee became the principal executive body of the League by assuming new powers that allowed it to 'control, direct and regulate all activities' and to 'suspend, dissolve or disaffiliate any Provincial League' or to take disciplinary action against any member.[44] It became the instrument of domination that was used to discipline independent-minded provincial leaders, such as Sikander Hayat, and to expel Fazlul Huq and G.M. Sayed. Jinnah kept a firm grip on the Working Committee, nominating only those men who were personally loyal to him. He rebuffed attempts by Suhrawardy to increase the

Bengali representation in the Working Committee, and nominated Ispahani and Khwaja Nazimuddin, his supporters — hardly typical members of the Bengal Muslim League.

Jinnah, however, had limited success in establishing a centralized command structure that controlled the provincial Leagues. The central office at first simply issued organizational, political and financial directives to the provincial organizations and urged them to comply, but to little effect. Later, in April 1942, the League formed the Committee for Defence, which consisted of Nawab Mohammad Ismail Khan, Khwaja Nazimuddin, Choudhry Khaliquzzaman and Qazi Mohammad Isa. They toured the provinces ostensibly to organize and rally Muslims for civil defence, but simultaneously used the tours also to restructure provincial Leagues and encourage the dissemination of propaganda in the districts. Great emphasis was placed on recruiting Muslim youth into the National Guards that were supposed to train well-disciplined and highly motivated cadres for the social and economic welfare programmes.[45] By December 1943, the Committee of Defence was superseded by the Committee of Action, which continued famine and civil defence work (previously carried out by its predecessor) and reintensified the propaganda battle by establishing the Committee of Authors, the Constructive Programme, the Economic Committee, the Education Committee, Muslim trade unions and the Women's sub-committee. These were formed to bring together the greatest possible number of Muslims under the Pakistan banner.[46]

The reports of the Committee of Defence and the Committee of Action made sorry reading and showed how uneven, at best, was the centralising process. Not only was the authority of the central leadership over provincial affairs weak, but the influence of the provincial headquarters over the affairs of the district and primary Leagues was also tenuous. In the case of the Punjab Muslim League, until June 1944 and before the expulsion of Khizr Hayat, the district Leagues and the National Guards existed only on paper. There was no methodical record of primary membership (estimated to be about 150,000) and no proper accounts. The Punjab Muslim Students Federation was in an equally disorganized state.[47] The position in the NWFP Provincial League was even worse. In April 1945, the Committee of Action dissolved the Frontier League and, a year later, an Organizing Committee was formed with the responsibility for reorganization and the enrolment of primary and district Leagues.[48] The situation was marginally better in Sind. A rudimentary organization with nearly five hundred and fifty branches had spread to the district and local level, and membership was claimed to have increased to 177,000 by 1944.[49] A confidential report, however, pointed out that the rapid increase in membership was due to competition between some groups in the Sind League, and that many so-called primary branches were fictitious.[50] The organizational arrangements in Bengal were equally inadequate, despite the great progress made by the Bengal Provincial Muslim League in recruiting primary members. Abul Hashim, the General Secretary, estimated that membership was about 550,000 in 1944, but there was no real attempt to form the National Guards or implement a Constructive Programme and famine relief.[51]

Only in the Muslim-minority provinces was the effort to establish the authority of an all-India party and leadership successful. The United Provinces Muslim League was an outstanding example of Muslim political unity under the League. Only five districts and five towns had no League presence, and the total membership was 270,000. The provincial League supervised and kept in constant touch with local branches. Its office was well organized and proper accounts were maintained. AIML directives concerning the National Guards and the popularizing of *Dawn* and *Maushoor* were followed; only the Constructive Programme inspired little activity.[52] However, the United Provinces Muslim League's most important contribution was its conquest of the citadel of learning, Aligarh. While Deoband, Nadwat-ul Ulama and Firangi Mahal were divided over the question of Pakistan, Aligarh University became the mouthpiece which rallied Muslim intellectuals throughout north India. The League used old boys, such as Liaquat Ali Khan, Choudhry Khaliquzzaman and the Nawab of Chhatari to win over their alma mater. The Muslim Students Federation, together with the League, was involved in intensive publicity campaigns, set up fourteen libraries in different hostels, published extensive pro-Pakistan material mainly by Mohammad Noman and Jamiluddin Ahmad, and gained the support of the influential *Aligarh Magazine*. The transformation of Aligarh into a League stronghold was facilitated by the administration and staff, such as the Vice-Chancellor, Ziauddin Ahmad, his deputy, A.B.A. Haleem, the treasurer Obaidur Rahman Khan Sherwani and senior lecturers, such as Jamiluddin Ahmad, M.B. Mirza and Mohammad Afzal Husain Qadri who had become committed supporters of Jinnah. They also provided the intellectual muscle to man the Education Committee and Writers' Committee of the League. Aligarh's support for the Pakistan movement was crucial for winning over the Muslim intelligentsia throughout India and putting them in the forefront of the movement.[53]

The thrust of this argument leads to a paradox. If the supporters of the Muslim League in the greater part of the territory were so disorganized, then how did the party transform itself into a powerful political force with popular roots after the war? The key to understanding how the metamorphosis occurred lay in the realm of ideology. Muslim India, from the 1930s onward, was in a state of intellectual ferment. The Government of India Act was considered by many people to be inadequate in safeguarding

Muslim interests, and this perception gained greater credence after the Congress victories in the 1937 elections. There were several schemes claiming to resolve the problem which influenced Muslims. They varied a great deal in their characteristic strengths and weaknesses. Some were discarded by the Muslim League after examination and others rejected out of hand. The remaining options were never spelled out but, instead, disguised under much rhetoric.

The construction of Pakistan nationalism was far more complex than has often been suggested. The influence of two men was responsible for initiating the process that eventually culminated in the Lahore Resolution. Iqbal's famous presidential address in 1930 to the annual session of the All-India Muslim League, calling for the establishment of a separate Muslim state carved out of the provinces of north-western India, initiated the process. It was complemented by the activities of Choudhary Rahmat Ali who, in 1933, invented the acronym Pakistan, which stood for the four north-western provinces of India. He argued that South Asia was a multinational entity, and Muslims needed to assert their social, cultural, economic and political independence by organizing themselves into a separate federation. He differed from Iqbal by treating the north-western bloc as a federation and not a single unit.[54] During 1937-39, Choudhary Rahmat Ali's influence was responsible for the establishment of various associations and societies, such as the Majlis-i-Kabir-i-Pakistan and the Anjuman-i-Khalida. The Anjuman-i-Khalida had among its sympathizers the Nawab of Mamdot, Abdullah Haroon and Sardar Aurangzeb Khan. The Punjab Muslim Students' Federation had adopted the Pakistan idea and tried to get the Muslim League and Jinnah to accept the scheme.[55] Rahmat's ideas also provoked intellectual responses that resulted in the formulation of alternative strategies, such as Latif's zonal scenario and Sikander's federation model. Both these schemes claimed to overcome the shortcomings of the Pakistan idea. Within the ranks of the Pakistan National Movement, some members (such as Mian Kifayat Ali and Dr Afzal Husain Qadri) were later to produce alternative schemes to Pakistan, which were quite influential within League circles.[56] The Aligarh Scheme proposed by Professor Sayed Zafrul Hasan and Dr Muhammad Afzal Husain Qadri suggested the division of British India into three wholly independent states: north-west India, Bengal and Hindustan, with Muslim urban enclaves where Muslims were in a majority. Hyderabad was to be recognized as an independent state on the same lines as Nepal. The authors' intention was to protect the interests of the Muslims of the minority provinces who were neglected in Iqbal's as well as Rahmat's original schemes.

However, the separatist implications that were emerging were countered by two federalist solutions proposed by Dr Sayed Abdul Latif and Sikander Hayat Khan. Latif's answer, which was favoured by Abdullah Haroon, was the idea of cultural zones. India was divided into four Muslim areas (north-west, north-east, Delhi-Lucknow and the Deccan blocs) and eleven Hindu areas, and the religious homogeneity of the zones would be consolidated by the transfer of population. These culturally autonomous units would then form a federation where the centre would have limited powers and, in this way, would avoid the separatist consequences of Rahmat's scheme.[57] Another federal proposal came from Sikander Hayat in May 1939 when he wanted to reduce the authority of the centre to the minimum. Based on this premise, he produced a seven-unit federation scheme. He deliberately included non-Muslim areas in the north-western bloc so that it would not be associated with the separatist scheme, Pakistan, which he strongly opposed. The centre was weakened in favour of the provinces and left to deal with only foreign affairs, military matters, communications and customs.[58]

In reaction to the federal proposals, a confederal perspective was elucidated in the *Confederacy of India* by A. Punjabi, a pseudonym used by Mian Kifayat Ali. He condemned the Latif and Aligarh plans for suggesting the migration of population and partition, which he felt was an unacceptable price to pay. He castigated Sikander's regional federation on the ground that Punjabi Muslims would not have an overwhelming majority *vis-à-vis* the non-Muslim population in the north-western unit. Kifayat Ali's alternative was an Indian confederacy composed of five federations, and he hoped in this way to avoid partition and the reshaping of provincial boundaries. He also went out of his way to allay the fears of the other constituent elements of the north-western bloc and assure them that they would not be dominated by the Punjab.[59] The scheme was financed by Abdullah Haroon and Mohammad Shah Nawaz Khan, the Nawab of Mamdot, and published with Jinnah's approval. However, the name Pakistan was dropped from the title at his insistence.[60]

The All-India Muslim League formed the Foreign Committee in 1938, which was directed to examine the various schemes. It was made clear that no particular scheme was favoured, and that the whole question was being examined with a view to producing a plan that would optimize Muslim interests. The committee, however, could not arrive at any conclusion, despite being convened several times. By December 1940, the Foreign Committee finally produced a plan, based on the principles outlined by the Lahore Resolution. It recommended the formation of two sovereign Muslim states: one in the north-west consisting of Sind, Baluchistan, the NWFP, the Punjab and Delhi, and the other in the north-east comprising Bengal and Assam and excluding the districts of Bankura and Midnapore, but including the Bihar district of Purnea.[61] The report was sent by the Committee to the AIML, where it lay gathering dust. When Haroon leaked the report, it was immediately repudiated by Jinnah.[62] Later, he also disavowed claims that Latif's plan was being considered by the Foreign Committee, stating only that all the various options were being appraised.[63]

Jinnah had clearly rejected the various schemes for federation,[64] but why did he initially disavow the Haroon report? First, it satisfied the regional demands of the Muslim majority provinces, but the Muslim minority provinces fell outside these independent states, leaving the interests of his staunchest supporters undefended. Secondly, its separatist angle showed Rahmat's influence — either directly or via the Aligarh scheme — which Jinnah was unwilling to admit. Popular perception in the Punjab associated the Lahore Resolution with the Pakistan plan of Rahmat Ali, but Jinnah bitterly resisted acknowledging the term up to 1941, partly due to his antipathy to Rahmat[65] and partly due to pressure from Sikander who was hostile to the Pakistan slogan.[66] Jinnah, however, reluctantly gave way when he realized how it had fired the imagination of Muslims in the Punjab. Perhaps the confederal option suggested by Mian Kifayat Ali was the only viable alternative that could accommodate all the different shades of opinion, and Jinnah's readiness to accept the Cabinet Mission Plan appears to confirm this. For purposes of negotiation, however, he tacitly revived the essence of Haroon's report. From 1941 right down to 1946, Jinnah's and the Muslim League's understanding of the Lahore Resolution was that it called for the establishment of two separate and sovereign Muslim states.

Jinnah's vagueness was reinforced by the different interpretations that became popular in Bengal. Most of them emerged as a reaction to the Lahore Resolution. Fazlul Huq was thinking in terms of an independent state and others, such as Khwaja Nazimuddin, were opposed to any kind of centre. Another view, represented by the East Pakistan Renaissance Society, rejected Muslim nationalism and was the original proponent of Muslim Bengali ethnicity. It was founded by a group of intellectuals led by Mujibur Rahman Khan, and included in its membership associates of the Bengal Muslim League, such as Abul Mansur Ahmed, Abul Kalam Shamsuddin and Khairul Anam Khan.[67] However, with the Jinnah-Gandhi talks in 1944, the protagonists of Purba Pakistan shifted their focus to defining its boundaries. In the Bengal Muslim League, there were two alternative approaches: Greater Bengal and divided Bengal. Raghib Ahsan's scheme, the Confederacy of East Pakistan and Adibistan, envisaged bringing Bangsman (Bengal and Assam) and the tribal areas of Bihar (Chota Nagpore, Santal Parganas, Surguja and the adjoining districts) into a confederation.[68] Shaheed Suhrawardy, Abul Hashim, Hamidul Huq Choudhry and the 'young party' were for Greater Bengal, and were content with a 51 per cent majority provided they got the mineral wealth of Burdwan and Singbhum. It was claimed that this would ease the Hindu opposition as they were demanding the unification of the Bhooms with Bengal.[69] An alternative scheme, supported by Nazimuddin and Akram Khan, visualized a streamlined Purba Pakistan (all of Assam and Bengal, less the Burdwan division and a part of Purnea district in Bihar) that would leave the Muslims with a 58 per cent majority.[70]

Consequently it becomes understandable that Jinnah, in order to maintain apparent harmony between the conflicting perceptions of the Lahore Resolution, preferred not to define it. This ambiguity allowed the co-existence of both the Punjabi and the Bengali interpretations, which were popular rallying calls in their respective provinces. This perhaps explains Jinnah's continuous demand that Pakistan had first to be conceded in principle before it was precisely defined. The League's dominance over Muslim politics was greatly helped by the increasing popularity of the Pakistan demand. The nebulous Pakistan slogan electrified the urban Muslims. In response, they generated a substantial volume of pro-Pakistan literature and propaganda, further strengthening the League's ideological grip. It is difficult to imagine Jinnah achieving such dominance without the ideological hegemony established by the Pakistan slogan. It gave a sense of common purpose and direction to the protagonists of Muslim nationalism, encapsulating their conflicting interests and demands within a nebulous symbol.

At the same time, ideology sowed the seeds of disarray and confusion among nationalist Muslims. The siren call of the Pakistan slogan drew the pro-Congress Muslims closer to the League until there was very little to differentiate them. The former now wavered in their opposition to the Lahore Resolution and qualified their support for the Congress by demanding protection from Hindu domination. In March 1943, the Punjab Majlis-i-Ahrar declared that they had rejected the division of India, and that their conception of Pakistan was 'a form of Government based on the law of the *Shariat*'. The All-India Muslim Majlis took the position that India should be reconstituted into a federation composed of units which would have the right to secession.[71] Madani, who had so vociferously argued against the two-nation theory as divisive and playing into the hands of British imperialism, was, by 1942, modifying his position by proposing an alternative to the strong unitary structure favoured by the Congress. He favoured the establishment of a religious department to protect the religious, economic, cultural and social interests of the Muslims. It would be run along purely religious lines, empowered to legislate to reform the community, and free from federal government interference.[72] Such shifts in position created the perception that there was not much difference between the Muslim federalism of the nationalists and the League's demand for Pakistan.

As Jinnah's all-India status grew, he increasingly turned his attention to the regional parties in the Muslim majority provinces where he had established tenuous links. The convergence of Muslim nationalism and community consciousness placed an array of significant political assets at Jinnah's disposal. The economically powerful élites of the United Provinces, the influential intelligentsia and the extra-parliamentary clout of the urban poor, all unified behind the Pakistan slogan, were arrayed increasingly against the regional parties. However, the multiplicity of identification present in each province meant varying degrees of success for the Muslim League. Regionalism was deeply embedded in the constitutional framework and continued to flourish, despite the increasing pressure brought to bear against it by Muslim consciousness, which was emerging as an overarching nationalism.

The matrix of Muslim politics in Bengal was divided by two currents: the Krishak Proja Party, informed by Bengali sub-nationalism, and the Muslim League, the flagship of community consciousness. Neither element emerged from the 1937 elections with a clear lead, and an alliance was necessary to form a government. Fazlul Huq turned to the Bengal Congress Party for support but, when the AICC hesitated, he accepted the League's offer of a coalition. Evidently, the arrangement was a marriage of convenience. Jinnah urgently needed to demonstrate that the AIML was more than a party of the Muslim minority provinces, and Bengal's support was a feather in his cap. For Huq, the compact allowed him to become premier and gave Bengal a voice at the centre where the Congress was dominant.

Huq had to pay a high price for the coalition with the *proja's* traditional enemies, the zemindars, and the long-term consequence was the rise of the Muslim League at the expense of the Krishak Proja Party. The *quid pro quo* demanded by the Muslim League was the moderation of the Proja Party's election manifesto. The abolition of the zemindari system was replaced by a pledge to hold a committee of inquiry, and the promise of free primary education was made ambiguous. The election promise to release political prisoners was so circumscribed in practice as to make it ineffective. Moreover, the League, represented by Nawab Habibullah, Nawab Musahriff Husain, Khwaja Nazimuddin and Suhrawardy, took four of the six Muslim seats in the cabinet and the Governor, Sir John Anderson, blocked the nomination of Shamsuddin Ahmad, leaving only Huq and Sayed Nausher Ali to represent the Proja Party.

The preponderance of the *ashraf* élite and the shelving of Huq's election promise of *dal-bhat* were to cause a split between the parliamentary wing of the Krishak Proja Party headed by Huq, and the organization led by Shamsuddin Ahmad and Nausher Ali. The Shamsuddin group held an annual conference in Rangpur district, which passed a motion of no-confidence in the Chief Minister. Huq retaliated by convening the assembly party, expelling seventeen members and installing Abul Quasem as secretary. With Nausher Ali's departure, the only Proja member left in the Cabinet was Huq.[73] He was encircled by the Khwaja group and became dependent on them for a majority in the house. The premier, however, was able to improve his position by negotiating the return of Shamsuddin Ahmad and Tamizuddin Khan. Shamsuddin, however, did not remain in the cabinet for long. He resigned when he was unable to keep his promise to his followers: to reduce ministers' salaries, abolish nominations to all local bodies and introduce free primary education. He then teamed up with the Congress and became active in the agrarian unrest, particularly in Chittagong and Burdwan. The 'general intensification of "left-wing" agrarian movements' caused great trepidation among Muslim assembly members and ministers, who feared that the radicalization of the *proja* would undermine their support.[74] Huq and the Muslim League denounced Shamsuddin and whipped up communal passions to counter the radicalization of the Muslim cultivators.[75]

With the decline of the Krishak Proja Party, the Muslim League consolidated its position. The existing Muslim League, a 'dead organization,' was disaffiliated in August 1937; and, at the Lucknow Session of the AIML, Jinnah appointed an Organizing Committee, chaired by Akram Khan, to reorganize the Bengal Provincial Muslim League and to establish a parliamentary party.[76] Great enthusiasm was demonstrated at the AIML session in Calcutta in anticipation of its growth. The Proja Party was seen as the only weapon the League could use against the Mass Muslim Contact Campaign of the Congress, and the League's strength grew at the latter's cost in all the districts.[77] The reorganization of the League, however, was delayed by the rivalry between Akram Khan and Suhrawardy, and Jinnah had to sort out their differences at the Patna Session of the AIML. Most of the organizational work was done by Suhrawardy and, by August 1939, fourteen district branches had been established. The League, however, was still an organization on paper with hardly four thousand members and little support among the peasantry.[78] The limited support for the Bengal League prevented Jinnah from forcing Fazlul Huq to surrender the presidentship of the Krishak Proja Party.[79] Jinnah's unwillingness 'to disturb the hornet's nest' and tolerate the status quo were a clear sign of weakness. However, the kudos for the various watered-down legislations, such as the Bengal Tenancy (Amendment) Act, the Agricultural Debtors' Act and the Moneylenders' Act, went to the League. The Tenancy Act made many *abwabs* of the landlords illegal, reduced the rate of interest on rent arrears by nearly half, and proved to be popular with the cultivators.

Fazlul Huq tried to break his dependence on Jinnah and exploited the wavering in the party. Nazimuddin and Suhrawardy considered Jinnah's intractability harmful to the Muslim cause, and wanted him to state his demands clearly. Herbert had the distinct impression that Huq was ready to break with Jinnah for greater personal independence, and saw supporting the war as an opportunity to legitimize his action. Many in the cabinet (such as Nazimuddin) sympathized with Huq's actions and were disappointed by the AIML's failure to give unconditional support to the War Committees and the Civic Guards.[80] Jinnah, however, was only willing to throw his full weight behind the war effort if Herbert gave an assurance on the Pakistan demand; otherwise, he would adopt a neutral position. Fazlul Huq and Sikander Hayat flouted Jinnah's ban, joined the National Defence Council, and the premier of Bengal aspired to lead a national all-party government pledged to the war effort.[81] Jinnah was warned of the danger of a party split on the issue[82] and was advised not to fight Huq but to keep him in the AIML Working Committee so that he could not oppose Pakistan.[83] However, when Sikander resigned from the National Defence Council, Huq's position became untenable. He resigned from the Council, the Working Committee and the League.

In December 1941, Huq formed the Progressive Coalition Party and started negotiating with Sarat Bose. Originally, the Governor wanted Nazimuddin to form a cabinet,[84] but the plan had to be dropped due to the defection of the Nawab of Dacca and the hostility of the Congress. Subsequently, Fazlul Huq was commissioned to form a government. He was almost immediately handicapped by the arrest of Sarat Bose under the Defence of India Rules. The new ministry, despite nominating Shamsuddin Ahmad, was unable to recover the lost prestige of the Proja Party, which was now only a parliamentary grouping. It was dependent on Huq's personal popularity, which was rapidly declining. Huq's inclusion of Shyama Prasad Mookerjee of the Hindu Mahasabha laid him open to attacks from the League. This vulnerability was exposed by the Dacca riots of 1941, which increased communal tension in Khulna, Bakarganj and Chittagong. Huq was denounced as a traitor to Islam and this, along with the increase in popularity of the Pakistan slogan, began to swing Muslim support away from him.[85] It was ironical that the Pakistan Resolution, proposed by Huq, played an important part in his downfall. Huq was so shaken by the rising strength of the League that, in 1942, he was prepared to retire from Bengal politics if a dignified exit, such as a seat on the Executive Council, was offered to him. Instead, his fall from power was rather undignified and the Governor, concerned that the cabinet was not giving its full support to the war effort, practically forced him to resign from office.[86]

Nazimuddin formed a new ministry with the support of the European bloc in the assembly. Ispahani wanted Jinnah to assist in the selection of the ministers but, realising he had little clout in enforcing any decision, the latter declined. His tactful excuse was that provincial matters should be decided by the parties concerned.[87] However, the League ministry, rather than becoming a credit to Jinnah, was a major embarrassment to the AIML high command due to its inability to deal adequately with the Bengal famine, which resulted in at least two million deaths.[88] Nazimuddin's difficulties were exacerbated by the rivalry between the parliamentary wing and the organization. Suhrawardy's rivalry with the Khwaja group began when he was appointed secretary of the provincial League. He was keen on expanding and organizing the party, but was met by lack of enthusiasm from the Dacca Nawab family. Being leading Muslim zemindars, they wove a complex web of deference and patronage in Muslim Bengal, and did not want the delicate balance of power disturbed. In 1943, Nazimuddin included his brother Shahabuddin in the cabinet; another family member was a parliamentary secretary, and the Dacca District Muslim League was their pocket borough. Ahsan Manzil's clientele included Nurul Amin and Ghayasuddin Pathan of Mymensingh, Yusaf Ali Choudhry of Faridpur, Hamidul Huq Choudhry of Noakhali, Fazlur Rahman of Dacca and others, many of whom were members of the Working Committee. The parliamentary group was accused by Hashim of running a parallel structure consisting of their placemen, and of ignoring the provincial League.

This monopoly, however, was challenged when Suhrawardy was forced to step down as secretary of the party on Jinnah's directive, and Abul Hashim was selected. Unlike his predecessor, whose social base was limited to Calcutta, Abul Hashim went to great lengths to popularize the League in the northern and eastern districts of Bengal and, by 1944, the Bengal Muslim League had penetrated the *mofussil* to become a mass party. Hashim's success was attributed to winning over the *proja* by turning the League into a socialistic and anti-zemindari mass movement.[89] However, the Pakistan slogan he was popularizing differed from Jinnah's interpretation. Hashim rejected the two-nation theory and espoused a multi-nationality concept, in which Bengal was one of the many nations in the subcontinent.[90]

Hashim combined the expansion of the party with its democratization and reorganization, and wanted to assert party control over the ministry. The constitution of the League was amended; every district, irrespective of population, was entitled to twenty-five members in the League Council, and the number of members whom the President could nominate to the Working Committee was reduced.[91] This move undermined the authority of the parliamentary leadership over the council, as the Dacca District League up to then had existed only on paper and the Khwaja group had prevented its organization. Khwaja Shahabuddin, M.R.A. Salim, Fazlur

Rahman and other supporters of Ahsan Manzil who were running for office in the Dacca League suffered a stunning defeat at the hands of Hashim's supporters. With their stranglehold over Dacca city broken, the Khwaja coterie launched a vindictive and slanderous campaign in the press against Hashim accusing him of being a communist,[92] and they lined up parliamentarians against him in a concentrated effort to win control of the Working Committee. Suhrawardy supported the Khwaja group's effort in replacing Abul Hashim with A.M. Malik as secretary, but vociferous opposition from the delegates blocked this move.[93] When this failed, a compromise suggested by Suhrawardy was accepted by the two groups giving them near parity on the Working Committee.[94]

The setbacks for the Khwaja group were also a rebuff for Jinnah. They had followed Jinnah loyally, and he had rewarded them by nominating Nazimuddin to the AIML Working Committee and Khwaja Shahabuddin to the Planning Committee. However, with the rise of Hashim, the conservative leadership was replaced by young radicals who turned the League into a mass party and propagated an egalitarian vision of Bangsman, which differed from Jinnah's Pakistan. Bengali ethnicity was parading in Muslim nationalist clothing, and Jinnah had no control over the only provincial League that had been transformed into a mass organization.

In the elections of 1937, the Punjabi Muslims overwhelmingly voted for the Unionist Party, demonstrating their loyalty to a Punjabi identification rather than one based on community or nationalism. Surprisingly, by October, Sikander Hayat was hobnobbing with Jinnah at the AIML Lucknow Session, and the meeting between the two produced the Jinnah-Sikander pact. Jinnah had to pay a heavy price for the arrangement, whereby the AIML represented the Unionists at the centre. Sikander openly declared that the League would be nothing without the support of the Muslims of the Punjab and Bengal, 'and that both he and the Bengal Premier agreed on using this fact as a lever for insisting' on no interference by Jinnah in provincial matters.[95] Sikander's ambiguous relationship with the Muslim League was determined by the scale of the Congress victory, which had swept aside all the various assumptions concerning the working of the federation. The Unionists feared that a Congress government at the centre would run roughshod over the constitutional provisions designed to protect the minorities and would meddle in provincial affairs, and that it would eventually pressurize the Governor-General to relax his control over the army and increase the share of other provinces in defence at the expense of the Punjab. It was the need for a voice at the centre and the desire that the League-Congress deadlock should continue for a few years which prompted Sikander to throw in his lot with Jinnah.[96]

Sir Khwaja Mohammad Iqbal, Malik Barkat Ali and Ghulam Rasul expressed their concern at the way Sikander was manipulating the pact and devouring the Muslim League. After much delay, a reorganized Punjab Muslim League was formed by Sikander. It included loyal Unionists, and Nawab Shah Nawaz of Mamdot was made president. The 'old' Muslim League supporters were outraged by this development; some resigned, the Montgomery District League asked Jinnah not to affiliate the 'bogus' League, and Barkat Ali warned Jinnah of the detrimental effect on the morale that Sikander's triumph had caused. To the disbelief of Jinnah's supporters in the Punjab, the Committee of Enquiry sent by the AIML, in February 1939, recommended the affiliation of the Punjab Muslim League.[97] The takeover by the Unionists sealed the fate of the Punjab Muslim League and, for the next seven years, it ceased practically all activities. The only notable contribution it made towards the cause of Muslim nationalism was to organize the Lahore session of the AIML in 1940. Not only was it dormant, the limited expansion that had been claimed turned out to be only on paper. The claim of having established thirteen district Leagues and a membership of just under 13,000 was pure fiction. Khalilur Rahman, member of the Punjab Muslim League Working Committee, admitted that the recorded membership figure was only 4,800, and that Sayed Ghulam Mustafa Shah Gilani had toured the province, dissolving the phoney branches and establishing genuine ones.[98] Only limited work was done to popularize the Muslim League, and that was carried out by the Punjab Muslim Students' Federation. The Pakistan Rural Propaganda Committee, established at a Muslim Students' Federation conference chaired by Jinnah in March 1941, toured Sheikhupura district addressing meetings, explaining the programme of the League and opening primary branches. 'In spite of the criminal neglect of rural areas' by the Punjab League, they found an enthusiastic response to the Pakistan slogan.[99]

Sikander, by keeping a tight grip on the Unionist Party, gave little opportunity to his opponents to make any headway in the province. He introduced various pieces of legislation, encouraged by Chhotu Ram, which proved to be popular with the peasants. Agrarian reforms, such as the Six-Year Programme of Rural Reform, the Amendment to the Punjab Land Alienation Act and the Registration of Moneylenders' Act, consolidated the Unionists' hold over their Muslim, Sikh and Hindu supporters.[100] Sikander also carefully guarded his Achilles' heel — communalism — which, if aggravated, would have disrupted the cross-communal alliance. He remonstrated with Jinnah for his highly communal speech at the Calcutta session of the AIML, skilfully defused the Shahidganj issue and restrained the Muslim League into keeping 'Deliverance Day' quiet.[101] When the Pakistan slogan became popular, he planned to bury it because he considered it too provocative.[102]

Sikander, however, could not foresee the war and the impact it would have on Indian Muslim politics. When war clouds darkened the horizon, the Unionists pledged their loyalty, and Sikander complained to Jinnah that he was not making use of his strong position at the centre. He wanted the Muslim League to increase its cooperation with the government to extract greater concessions.[103] Instead, Jinnah banned Muslim League members from joining the war committees and the Civil Guards. Sikander defied Jinnah's ban on joining the war committees and was prepared to resign not only the Working Committee but also his basic membership of the Muslim League. His antipathy to the Pakistan slogan and the need to bolster the morale of his Hindu and Sikh colleagues drove him to break with the Muslim League.[104] Linlithgow, however, intervened and instructed the Governor of Punjab, Henry Craik, to persuade Sikander not to resign. Because of Sikander's successful management of the war effort, Linlithgow did not want his government to be overthrown on the Pakistan issue; not did Linlithgow want to split the League, which he had cultivated so assiduously as a counterbalance to the Congress.[105]

Sikander was now in the unenviable position where his ability to stand up to Jinnah was being undermined by official pressure, despite the deep differences between the two. The terrain was set for Sikander's capitulation over the National Defence Council row. The Viceroy invited Sikander, Huq and Assadullah to serve on the Council, but made the mistake of inviting them not as provincial Chief Ministers but as representatives of the Muslim community. Jinnah was quick to react and assert his claim that only the League represented the Muslims, and ordered the leaders to resign. Sikander's prestige was considerably weakened; many Muslims were 'seriously upset by his abasement at Bombay' and they considered his action damaging to the Punjab's prestige.[106] Jinnah's stock soared in the province and Sikander became powerless to resist the popularisation of the Pakistan slogan.

The Unionist Party unanimously appointed Khizr Hayat Khan Tiwana as premier, in January 1943, to fill the vacancy created by Sikander's sudden death. Jinnah was anxious to assert control over the new Chief Minister, but Khizr used the Jinnah-Sikander pact to thwart him. Although he failed to prevent the establishment of a separate League Party, Khizr remained the head of the Punjab League. When Jinnah insisted that the Unionist Government should be renamed the Muslim League coalition, Khizr did not agree. Glancy encouraged Khizr to resist Jinnah so that the war effort would not be disturbed.[107] His strategy was to ensnare Jinnah by either fighting him on the issue of the war effort or to wait for him to make a false move. He feared that a direct assault on Jinnah would provoke him to play the Islamic card, which Khizr's Muslim supporters would find difficult to resist without any other battle cry to rally around.[108]

Khizr's resolve, however, weakened when Jinnah returned to Lahore in April 1944 and he was ready to surrender. The Unionists existed only in name and had no organization. The Pakistan slogan would be the decisive factor in the next elections, and many of his supporters were ready to desert. He feared that the loyalists would be dumped after the war and that the only two parties which would matter would be the Congress and the Muslim League. He, therefore, did not want to antagonize Jinnah.[109] During the protracted discussions, Jinnah wanted Khizr to change the name of the Unionist ministry, openly adopt Muslim League policies and drop Chhotu Ram from the cabinet.[110] Wavell and Glancy, however, supported Khizr and encouraged him to stand up to Jinnah. Glancy suggested that the dismissal of Shaukat Hayat would serve as a warning to all the other turncoats.[111] Khizr followed this up by forming the Zemindari League to bolster the party, and appointed Jamal Khan Leghari and Nawab Ashiq Hussain to the cabinet in order to reduce the number of desertions from the Unionist ranks from thirty to eighteen.[112]

The talk of forming a Muslim League ministry set off a scramble between the various groups in the League to seize control of the party. There were three groups within the Punjab League: Mamdot supported by Jinnah and the Muslim Students' Federation, Jamal Khan Leghari and his supporters, and Nawabzada Rashid Ali Khan, the President of the Lahore Muslim League, backed by Barkat Ali. Rashid Ali Khan had already challenged Mamdot unsuccessfully earlier in the year by forming the Workers' Board to launch a campaign for mass enrolment and to form a Muslim League Assembly Party. This time he wanted to seize control of the party so that he would be called to form the League ministry.[113] Jamal Khan Leghari had the same intention, but when it became clear that the Unionist government was not going to fall, he accepted Khizr's offer of ministership.

Though the Pakistan slogan was increasing in popularity in the province, the Unionist Party kept a tight grip over the reigns of power. The continued dominance of the Unionists strangled the League and prevented it from becoming a mass party. Punjabi ethnicity was strong. All attempts to undermine regional solidarity by involving communalism were only marginally effective; Jinnah had very little control over developments in the party and was unable to impose a semblance of unity.

In Sarhad, the polls confirmed the political dominance of Pakhtun ethnicity in the province, but the hesitation of the AICC in accepting office gave the Governor, George Cunningham, the opportunity to engineer an anti-Congress coalition. Shaibzada Abdul Qaiyum's minority ministry was short-lived, and Cunningham was forced to accept a Congress government led by Dr Khan that consisted of defectors from the Democratic Party and the Hindu-Sikh Nationalist Party. The cabinet's position was strengthened when, aided by Nehru, Dr Khan settled differences with the 'old school' who had left in 1931, and prepared the way for the reunification of the NWFP Congress.[114]

Dr Khan's ministry followed policies similar to the other Congress governments, but took the lead in dismantling the colonial structure used to support the big *khans*. The measures introduced included the abolition of the posts of honorary magistrate, *zaildar* and most of the zemindari *inams*. Moreover, the practice of recruiting government personnel from the *khani* élite was suspended. The reforms introduced in 1938 (such as the Teri Dues Regulation Repealing Bill and the Agricultural Debtors' Relief) fell below the expectations of the radicals. They desired land redistribution, which was unacceptable as it would have destabilized the *khani* élite as a whole. Instead, Dr Khan selectively exploited *kisan* grievances against the non-Congress *khans*, which led to his increasing friction with them. The Charsadda *khans*, the backbone of the Muslim League, were involved in a bitter dispute with the provincial government and accused ministers of stirring up their tenants. In retaliation they refused to pay their dues, which brought them into collision with the authorities. Ministers accused them of evicting tenants for not supporting the Muslim League. This was, however, a double-edged sword, and the issue came to a head with the agrarian agitations in Mardan. Dr Khan was eventually obliged to use force to restore order at the expense of his popularity.[115]

The all-India decision of the Congress Party to oppose the war was out of tune with the feelings in the provinces, which welcomed military recruitment as it provided scarce resources in economically difficult times. Opposition to the war became another major reason that affected the popularity of the NWFP Congress. Most Congressmen did not welcome the decision of Dr Khan's ministry to resign or the individual *satyagraha*, and there was very little reaction when Azad was arrested.[116] Ghaffar Khan tried to step up the campaign with trained *satyagrahis*. This failed to attract support for the campaign which eventually fizzled out.[117] The lack of enthusiasm allowed Cunningham to resist pressure from the Home Office and the Viceroy to take a hard line against the Congress during the Quit India campaign. He accurately assessed that it was not necessary to ban the party, unlike elsewhere in India, as the agitations were mild in comparison.[118] The Congress-led agitations culminated in *hartals*, picketing of government offices, police stations, courts and liquor shops, but once the leadership was arrested, civil disobedience petered out.[119]

Cunningham, the Governor, deployed *maulvis* in the tribal and settled areas to whip up anti-Congress sentiments with an intensive propaganda campaign.[120] He directed the network operating in the tribal areas until

1941, when it was taken over by military intelligence, which then operated through the District Commissioners and Political Agents. In the 'settled' districts, K.B. Kuli Khan was successful in winning over some elements of the Jamiat-ul-Ulama-i-Sarhad and, together with Cunningham, orchestrated an anti-Congress and pro-war campaign. Dr Khan's daughter's marriage to Flight Lieutenant Jaswant Singh, a Christian, provided ample opportunity for the *ulama* to attack him for being un-Islamic.[121] Significantly, most of the *maulanas* deployed were pro-Muslim League but, more important, the initiative established a network of religious propagandists, which was later to be exploited by the League.

Concurrent with these developments, rifts developed within the ranks of the Congress. Tensions between Dr Khan's ministry and the Provincial Congress Committee emerged over the degree of cooperation with the Raj. Dr Khan ignored the AICC, met the Viceroy and compelled the Peshawar District Board to present an address to him.[122] The Provincial Congress Committee's inability to exercise any influence over the ministry's policies led to a breach between Dr Khan and Ghaffar Khan. Ghaffar Khan accused the ministerial group of ignoring dedicated workers and rewarding toadies and sycophants, which weakened the movement.[123] Differences also emerged within the Provincial Congress Committee. Ghaffar Khan felt that the increasing influence of the Forward Bloc, led by the Khan of Lundkhwar, was inimical to the Khudai Khidmatgars. He separated it from the party, bringing it under his personal control. His resignation from the AICC Working Committee caused unease among some of his supporters, who thought that he had resigned from the Congress.[124] The cumulative impact of failing to form a credible anti-war campaign, the enthusiasm for the war, intra-party differences, the anti-Congress and Islamic propaganda and the personal attacks against the Khan brothers resulted in a fall of the Congress membership by over half to just over 10,000.[125]

Pakhtun ethnicity lost influence by siding with Indian nationalism, but Muslim nationalism was too deeply divided to exploit the situation. The Frontier Muslim League was reorganized in September 1937 when the supporters of Shaibzada Abdul Qaiyum, who had formed the Peshawar District Muslim League, merged with the Provincial League headed by Maulana Mohammad Shuaib. This was a takeover by the Peshawari *khans*. Maulana Shuaib was reduced to titular status, and finally replaced by Sadullah Khan.[126] The Muslim League was a collection of rural élites divided by agnatic and personal rivalries who, in reaction to the anti-*khani* policies of Dr Khan's government and the Khudai Khidmatgars' emphasis on Pakhtun ethnicity, banded together against the Congress. To compensate for that lack of organization and programme, they concentrated on religious appeal and exploited communal tensions. Their tactic of employing *maulvis* to disseminate propaganda was not successful. The Jamiat-ul-Ulama-i-Sarhad remained loyal to the Congress and the *pirs* were indifferent. Capitalising on communal tensions (such as the attempts to revive the Shahidganj issue that led to violence in Mardan, and the Hindu-Muslim riots in Dera Ismail Khan in 1939) provided moderate results.[127]

The Muslim League's chance came in 1943 when Aurangzeb Khan, leader of the parliamentary wing of the party, managed to form a ministry. Aurangzeb's majority was doubtful, and depended on ten of the Congress members of the assembly remaining in jail and on the support of twenty-two independents (including non-Muslims).[128] Lacking organization and ideology, the only factor that held his loose coalition together was the promise of patronage, and this was the root cause of the downfall of the Muslim League ministry. Rampant corruption and partisanship resulted in popular displeasure[129] with the regime, aggravated by the effects of the war, which resulted in shortages and inflation. The ministry used favours (for instance, through its management of war-time rationing) to pay off political debts. The '*Quran-Talaq* ministry'[130] liberally distributed government contracts and permits to assembly members so as to remain in power. The Governor extended the life of Aurangzeb's ministry by postponing the assembly session in the spring of 1944, but Aurangzeb was forced to face the house the following year resulting in his expected downfall. Despite the League gaining office, Muslim identification and Jinnah were irrelevant to the province, and the local concerns of power and Pakhtun ethnicity were the dominant interests.

In Sind, power politics based on agnatic and personal rivalries were the primary concern of the Muslim leadership. Sindi ethnicity only became explicit when external factors, such as the separation of Sind from the Bombay Presidency or the settlement of Punjabis in the canal colonies, were the issues on hand. Otherwise it remained in the background, providing the context for the overwhelming emphasis on provincial affairs. As for Muslim identification, it came into play primarily in the arena of all-India politics, and was brought into the provincial sphere only to shore up advantages in local competition. Consequently, Sindi politics were highly fluid, with groups forming and reforming into political combinations according to the shifting requirements of local power games.

The chaotic situation in the Sind Provincial Assembly that preceded the formation of Ghulam Hussain Hidayatullah's ministry clearly showed that both communal-religious identification and nationalist consciousness were secondary considerations compared to regional power politics. The Sind United Party, the flag-carrier of pro-Congress Muslims, was reduced to a rump by desertions to the ministerial group. Within a short time, however, Hidayatullah was brought down by Allah Buksh Soomro who, with only six Muslim supporters, turned to the Congress and Hindu independents to form a government. Allah Buksh attempted to consolidate his precarious position by negotiating with Jinnah, but the talks eventually collapsed. However, his position improved in 1939 when he won over Hidayatullah with a cabinet post. The latter brought with him a group of *mir* supporters, and reduced the Muslim League overnight to a hollow shell.[131]

The Muslim League was determined to harass Allah Buksh and bring him down. It deliberately selected the Manzilgah issue to expose his dependence on the Hindus. The Manzilgah dispute was over the status of a building in Sukkur that the Muslims claimed was a mosque but was under the control of the Sind Government. The Hindus opposed returning the building to the Muslims as it was located near a *ghat* from which Hindus embarked to visit the sacred shrine of Sadhbelo. The matter had been brought to Hidayatullah's notice but, before he announced his decision, Hidayatullah was forced out of office and replaced by Allah Buksh. The files showed that the deposed premier had decided that no action would be taken but Allah Buksh, within eleven days of assuming office, reopened the case.[132] He intended to use the restoration of the Manzilgah building to the Muslims — his trump-card — as a means to win back the Muslim vote if general elections were forced on him.[132] However, by intervening in the Manzilgah dispute, which culminated in the Sukkur riot of 1939, the Muslim League was to turn the tables on him. The immediate reaction to the government's decision to forcibly take control of the building from the Manzilgah Restoration Committee was two days of rioting in Sukkur, resulting in forty-five deaths. The police also became afflicted with communalism, and they went on a rampage against Hindus. Eventually troops had to be despatched to Shikarpur before the situation was brought under control.[134] The protest was an ideal weapon for the Muslim League to use against Allah Buksh. He had already decided to restore the building to the Muslims but, if he did it under duress, then the League would take credit for it. His refusal, however, would result in a Muslim revolt in his home constituency. The communal dispute also increased strains within his cabinet, dividing it along communal lines and causing it to vacillate. The Chief Minister usurped the function of the Home Minister, Dialmal Daulatram, after he had leaked information to Moonje and Nichaldas Vazirani. The two had exacerbated an already tense situation with several incorrect statements.[135] The ultimate consequence of the Manzilgah agitation was that Allah Buksh's government fell and was replaced by a League coalition, which included independent Hindus.

An additional advantage for the League was the dissension that developed in the influential Jamiat-ul-Ulama-i-Sind, which had remained loyal to Allah Buksh. A number of *maulvis* rejected the pro-Congress line of Mohammad Siddique and Fateh Mohammad on the Manzilgah affair, and resigned from the Jamiat.[136] The continuous use of communal tension by the League made Allah Buksh's attempt to widen his support, by popularizing the Sind branch of the All-India Azad Muslim Conference, difficult. This was directly responsible for delaying the individual *satyagraha* campaign[137] and for the desultory pace of the Quit India Movement.

The Sind Muslim League realized that communal tension was latent in Sukkur district, and they could harass the Chief Minister for refusing to join the Muslim League. The League had wanted to embarrass Allah Buksh, not foment a riot, and Haroon and other League leaders deserted the cause when violence broke out.[138] The violence that overtook the Manzilgah agitation increased the influence of the Sind Muslim League at several levels. When combined with the Pakistan Day celebrations and Jinnah's visits, it extended the boundary of the Sind League and the AIML's influence from the élites to the urban masses. Not only did the popularity of the League spread to the lower middle class, it also politicized women who played a supportive role in the agitation.[139] Finally, it was a breakthrough for Jinnah: he had demonstrated that he could bring down the government and that he was a force which could not be lightly treated. His prestige was further enhanced in the province, when only with his permission could a negotiated settlement be reached.[140] Within limits, the dispute highlighted how the League could win over popular Muslim support and, simultaneously, create communal dissensions. The use of sectarian propaganda against joint electorates in the Shikarpur by-election, and later in the Eidgah Maidan agitation in Karachi, helped rally support on communal issues and prised apart the two communities.

Abdullah Haroon and Sheikh Abdul Majid Sindhi formed the Sind Muslim League in May 1938, and were joined by Ayub Khuro and Ghulam Mohammad Sayed. At the Karachi conference, the number of League assembly members increased to twenty-seven and, despite Jinnah's disapproval, Hidayatullah insisted on being the leader of the League party in the assembly. The optimism of the League, however, was misplaced, and Hidayatullah's tergiversation by joining the Allah Buksh ministry decimated the ranks of the League in the assembly.[141] The next opportunity of getting into the driving seat came with Allah Buksh's dismissal. Ayub Khuro led the Muslim League Assembly Party into an alliance with the Hindu Independents to form the Nationalist Party, and accepted Mir Bandeh Ali as the leader. Khuro defied Jinnah and went ahead to form a coalition.[142] The latter's discomfiture increased when the ministry first passed an Act introducing joint electorates in the local council, and then collapsed, allowing Allah Buksh to return to power.

A full-fledged Muslim League government did not come to power until October 1942, when Hidayatullah became the Premier. The League was anxious to join him, but insisted that he should join the party and accept its programme.[143] The ministry was obliged to work under the 'general supervision and control' of the Muslim League Assembly Party and the Sind Provincial Muslim League Working Committee. It also had to implement a programme of agrarian reform, including the Land Alienation Bill, the Debt Redemption Bill and the Tenancy Bill, and increase the ratio of Muslims in government service. However, when Hidayatullah was installed in office, reforms (such as the Tenancy Bill) were put on ice. He even considered modifying the *jagirdari* legislation that had been passed by Allah Buksh to win the support of the *jagirdars* in the assembly. Much worse for the Sind Muslim League, the various malpractices of the ministry affected the popularity of the party. There were scandals concerning the war-time control of essential goods. Syndicates for cloth, wheat, and so on, were distributed among sycophants and favourites by ministers.[144] Finally the League Government was rocked by a scandal implicating one of its ministers, Khuro, with the murder of Allah Buksh.

Outside the assembly, the Sind Muslim League's message fell on stony ground. Even by 1941, G.M. Sayed admitted there was no credible organization, and that support was limited to the towns and a handful of villages.[145] But, two years later, many rural branches were established and members enrolled, though the impact on the rural masses was limited. Only by incorporating the rural élite was the League able to increase its influence. Motivated by power politics, the major interest of the new members was to control the various local bodies and the assembly through the League organization.[146] The rivalry between the contending groups led to a massive leap in membership and the number of primary branches, but most of the increases were fraudulent. G.M. Sayed attempted to turn the Muslim League into a popular party and became increasingly involved with the Sind Hari Committee, the provincial branch of the All-India Kisan Sabha, whose Muslim members were sympathetic to the Pakistan slogan.[147] This led him to champion the interests of the *haris*, which set him on a course of conflict with the Muslim League ministry. The League was restricted to élite politics, and neither Jinnah nor Pakistan had any significance in the region except for their communal association. The dominant concern was for provincial power, which led to intense rivalry in the assembly and the party.

The success of the Congress in the 1937 elections had deep and manifold ramifications among the Muslims and initiated a major political shift. It shattered the bucolic pastoralism of the Muslim regional parties and caused great unease among the urban groupings. Politicians absorbed in local power games feared that the Congress Party's operation of provincial ministries under the control of a centralized organization, and its rejection of the federal basis of the 1935 Act, would mean that they would be roped into a unitary state. Such fears, paradoxically, forced the Muslim-majority provinces into the arms of the AIML and Jinnah, whose aspirations towards central control were as strong as those of the Indian National Congress. From 1938 onwards, the Congress Party and the British became two major influences in Muslim politics. The Raj encouraged the emergence of Jinnah as an all-India leader, and the Congress contributed by its willingness to go to jail, thus creating the space for the Muslim League to expand into. Under these twin influences, the two mutually opposed tendencies in Muslim politics — the centripetal and centrifugal forces — converged, at least temporarily, and provided the basis for a short-lived unity.

This process, however, implied an uphill struggle. Initially, Jinnah was only able to win over the élites of the Muslim-minority provinces by playing the Islamic card. Among the urban masses, Jinnah was forced to play second fiddle to Mashriqi until the mid-1940s, when the Khaksar star waned. By 1944, the Muslim League was influential among large strata of the urban population throughout India, particularly in the Muslim minority provinces. The League used community consciousness as a battering-ram to break down the resistance of the regional parties. The economic resources of the élites of the Muslim minority provinces funded the pro-Pakistan publicity, which was generated by intellectuals. The hegemony of the Pakistan idea, despite its ambiguities, was thus established. The Pakistan slogan spread from the urban areas into the rural areas of the Muslim majority provinces. The expansion was due to the role of students and *maulvis* in consolidating and spreading the ideological hegemony of Muslim nationalism.

Ideology was the Achilles' heel of the regional parties. The Pakistan slogan, in its different manifestations, was capturing the imagination of intellectuals and polarizing communal relations. Its opponents had no war cry to rally their supporters. Combined with Jinnah's rising all-India status, the Pakistan slogan was able to make Muslim nationalism more influential in the provinces. But Jinnah still had little influence in the running of provincial parties, and his role was mainly negative in that he was only able to break, expel or threaten to expel provincial leaders. The regional parties were strong. Reinforced by the constitutional structure, they were able to resist the advance of the Muslim League. In Bengal, where the League had become a mass organization, this result owed more to the takeover of the party by regionalism rather than to a clear victory for Muslim ethnicity. In the Punjab, the Pakistan slogan was gaining popularity but the continued resistance from Khizr, backed by the British, prevented Muslim nationalism from making deep inroads into the rural areas. However, in Sind and Sarhad, Jinnah and Pakistan had very little influence. In the NWFP, the party was extremely weak and the province was dominated by the Congress; while in Sind the Muslim League was a party restricted to the élites. Consequently, if the entire Muslim population was considered, at this juncture Muslim nationalism had not won even a bare majority over to its side; it was essentially a phenomenon restricted to the urban areas and Muslim minority provinces.

NOTES

1. A. Jalal, *The Sole Spokesman*, pp. 38-41, 46.
2. G. Rizvi, *Linlithgow and India: A Study of British Policy and the Political Impasse in India, 1936-43* (London, 1978), pp. 109-114.
3. R.J. Moore, *Churchill, Cripps and India, 1939-1945* (Oxford, 1979), pp. 67, 85.
4. Linlithgow to Amery, 2 March 1942, in Nicholas Mansergh, ed, *The Transfer of Power, 1942-47*, i (London, 1970), p. 293 (hereafter *TP*), Linlithgow to Amery, 7 March 1942, *TP*, i, pp. 361-62.
5. Sajjad Zaheer perceived Muslim nationalism as the right of self-determination of a minority nationality and conceded the essence of Pakistan by arguing that an independent India would be a union of autonomous states. *Bombay Chronicle*, 14 December 1942, and 1 June 1943.
6. Jinnah on Election Results, 2 March 1937, in P.N. Chopra, ed, *Towards Freedom*, i (New Delhi, 1985), p. 189.
7. Abdul Wali to Nehru, 23 March 1937, ibid., pp. 288-89. Nehru to Prasad, 21 July 1937, in V. Choudhary, ed, *Dr Rajendra Prasad*, i, pp. 63-67.
8. Nehru to Prasad, 21 July 1937, in V. Choudhary, ed, *Dr Rajendra Prasad*, i, p. 66.
9. C. Khaliquzzaman, *Pathway to Pakistan*, p. 162.
10. The mass contact campaign had a degree of success in the urban areas of the United Provinces, Bihar and the Punjab. It eventually, however, foundered on the resistance of the right wing of the Congress, who saw the campaign as a threat to their political dominance. G.B. Pant and J.B. Kriplani created impediments so that Nehru would not have a solid base among the Muslims. The opposition of other Congressmen was based on the awareness that the previous large influx of Muslims at the time of the Khilafat Movement had resulted in influencing Congress policy. Mushirul Hasan, 'The Muslim Mass Contact Campaign: An Attempt at Political Mobilization,' *Occasional Papers, 14* (Nehru Memorial Museum and Library), pp. 25-26, 34-36.
11. IOR, Mss. Eur. F 125/113 (Linlithgow Collection), Haig to Linlithgow, 7 May 1937. Ibid., Haig to Linlithgow, 24 May 1937.
12. *Bombay Chronicle*, 26 April 1937.
13. IOR, Mss. Eur. F 125/113 (Linlithgow Papers), Haig to Linlithgow, 23 April 1937. Ibid., Haig to Linlithgow, 24 May 1937.
14. IOR, Mss. Eur. F 115/2B (Haig Collection), Memo, n.d.
15. IOR, Mss. Eur. F 115/2A (Haig Collection), Haig to Brabourne, 26 September 1938.

16. Ibid.
17. IOR, Mss. Eur. F 125/101 (Linlithgow Collection), Hallett to Brabourne, 26 August 1938.
18. C. Khaliquzzaman, *Pathway to Pakistan*, p. 190.
19. QAA, Shamsul Hasan Collection, United Provinces, vi/24, Nawab Yusaf to Jinnah, 14 January 1946 (henceforth SHC).
20. 25th Session, Lucknow, October 1937, in S.S. Pirzada, ed, *Foundations of Pakistan*, ii (Karachi, 1970), p. 274.
21. In the Dadri riot in Ballia, in 1937, the Hindus were urged on by Baba Raghav Das who was a member of the AICC. His behaviour only reinforced the League's accusation that the Congress was a Hindu party. Chandan Mitra, 'Political Mobilization and the Nationalist Movement in Eastern Uttar Pradesh and Bihar, 1937-42' (Oxford Univ. D.Phil. thesis, 1983), p. 74.
22. IOR, L/P&J/8/686 Coll. 117/EI (Muslim Grievances under Congress Ministries, 1939-1942), Haig to Linlithgow, 10 May 1939.
23. Ibid.
24. Rajendra Prasad, *India Divided* (Bombay, 1947), p. 147.
25. IOR, L/P&J/8/686 Coll. 117 EI (Muslim Grievances under Congress Ministries, 1939-1942), Replies from the Governors of Bihar, Central Provinces and United Provinces to the Governor-General's enquiries on Muslim grievances.
26. IOR, Mss. Eur. F 125/104 (Linlithgow Papers), Hallett to Linlithgow, 29 September 1941.
27. IOR, L/P&J/7/2587 (Sunni-Shiah Controversy in Lucknow), Haig to Linlithgow, 18 April 1939.
28. Ibid.
29. Asaf Ali to Jinnah, in P.N. Chopra, ed, *Towards Freedom*, i, p. 573.
30. IOR, L/P&J/7/2587 (Sunni-Shiah Controversy in Lucknow), Haig to Linlithgow, 18 April 1939. Ibid., Press Communiqué of the UP Government, 30 March 1939.
31. NDC, CID, S 360 (Note on the Khaksars), L.V. Deane, 12 April 1940, p. 28. IOR, L/P&J/7/2587 (Sunni-Shiah controversy in Lucknow), Haig to Linlithgow, 18 April 1939.
32. NDC, CID, S 360 (Note on the Khaksars), L.V. Deane, 12 April 1940, pp. 28-29.
33. NAP, Quaid-i-Azam Papers, F101/47-50, Abdul Aziz to Jinnah, 10 October 1939 (henceforth QAP).
34. NDC, CID, S 360 (Note on the Khaksars) by L.V. Deane, 12 April 1940, pp. 28-29. Shan Muhammad, *Khaksar Movement in India* (Meerut, 1973), p. 38.
35. NAP, QAP, F101/50, Abdul Aziz to Jinnah, 10 October 1939. QAA, AIML 248/10, Press Statement of Abdullah Haroon, 27 September 1939.
36. NAP, QAP, F915/7-9, Syed Imtyaz Karim to Jinnah, 30 December 1939.
37. IOR, L/P&J/8/678 Coll. 117-C-81 (Volunteer Movement in India), Secretary to the Governor-General to Secretary of State, 23 August 1940.
38. Mashriqi republished two pamphlets, *Aksariyat ya Khun* and *Bayt-ul-Maal*, in which he argued for the violent overthrow of the Raj. Sikander Hayat's banning of the Khaksars led to Mashriqi initiating a civil disobedience campaign, which culminated in a bloody confrontation with the police near Unchi Mosque in Lahore. The organization was proscribed in the Punjab, Mashriqi was arrested and Dr Mohammad Ismail Nami took over.

39. NDC, CID, S 360 (Note on the Khaksars) by L.V. Deane, 12 April 1940, pp. 1-9.
40. QAA, SHC, UP iv/25, Nawab of Mahmudabad to Jinnah, 7 December 1940.
41. Shan Muhammad, *Khaksar Movement in India*, pp. 128-32.
42. IOR, L/P&J/8/680 117-C-82 (Khaksar Movement), Extract from Addendum to the Note on Khaksar Movement, 1943-45.
43. A. Jalal, *The Sole Spokesman*, pp. 40-41.
44. QAA, AIML 111, Amendments Proposed in the Constitution and the Rule of the All-India Muslim League, n.d.
45. QAA, SHC Organizational Matters, i/48(1-5), AIML to all Provincial Muslim Leagues, 4 November 1941. QAA, AIML 319/6, Liaquat to t he President of the United Provinces Provincial Muslim League, 13 April 1942. AIML 319/17, Appeal issued by Nawab Ismail Khan to the Muslim youth.
46. QAA, AIML 192/4-7, Proceedings of the First Committee of Action, 2-3 February 1944. AIML 192/12-27, Proceedings of the Second Committee of Action, 25-28 March 1944.
47. QAA, AIML 201/8, Inspection Report 10 on the General Administration of the Punjab Provincial Muslim League and its Central Office, 26 February 1945. QAA, SHC Punjab 1/6, Mumtaz Daultana to Committee of Action, 28 July 1944.
48. QAA, AIML 193/4, Resolution passed by the Committee of Action, 13-15 April 1945. AIML 193/13, Committee of Action, 11-18 April 1946.
49. QAA, AIML 200/37-47, Annual Report of the Sind Provincial Muslim League for the year 1943-44 by G.M. Sayed, President, Sind Provincial Muslim League.
50. QAA, AIML 200/49, Quarterly Report of the Progress of the Muslim League in Sind, n.d.
51. QAA, AIML 201/13, Remarks and Instructions on the BPML by Syed Zakir Ali, 29 March 1945.
52. QAA, AIML 200/24, Inspection Report No. 3 on the working of the UPML by Syed Zakir Ali, 24 July 1944.
53. Mushirul Hasan, 'Nationalist and Separatist Trends in Aligarh, 1920-1946,' in A.K. Gupta, ed, *Myth and Reality: The Struggle for Freedom in India, 1945-1947* (New Delhi, 1987), pp. 18-37.
54. Originally, Choudhary Rahmat Ali considered only north-western India but, by 1944, he had projected ten Muslim nations: Pakistan out of the north-western provinces, Bangistan through the merger of Bengal and Assam, and Osmanistan from the Deccan states. To this were added seven more Muslim countries: Siddiqistan in central India, Faruqistan in Bihar and Orissa, Haidaristan in Hindustan, Munistan in Rajasthan, Maplistan in southern India, Saifistan in western Ceylon, and Nasaristan in eastern Ceylon. These ten nations would then form the Pak Commonwealth of Nations. Choudhary Rahmat Ali, *Pakistan: The Fatherland of the Pak Nation* (Cambridge, 1947), pp. 301-2.
55. K.K. Aziz, *Rahmat Ali: A Biography* (Lahore, 1987), pp. 199-201.
56. K.K. Aziz, *A History of the Idea of Pakistan* (Lahore, 1987), pp. 536, 600.
57. Sayed Abdul Latif, *The Cultural Future of India* (Bombay, 1938), pp. 1, 12-17. Sayed Abdul Latif, *A Federation of Cultural Zones for India* (Hyderabad, 1938), pp. 2,6.
58. The seven units were: Madras Presidency and the southern Indian states; Bombay, Central Provinces and Hyderabad; Bengal; Bihar, Orissa, and the eastern states; the United Provinces and the princely states within its borders; a central unit consisting of

Rajputana and the central Indian states; a north-western unit composed of Sind, Sarhad, Punjab, Kashmir and the Punjab states. IOR, L/P&J/8/689, Coll. 117-7-4A (Alternatives to the 1935 Act), Sikander to Laithwaite, 29 June 1939. Ibid., Extract from a report from CIO, Lahore, 21 March 1939. IOR, Mss. Eur. F125/86 (Linlithgow Collection), Craik to Linlithgow, 5 June 1938.

59. The confederacy consisted of five federations: the Industan Federation, Hindustan Federation, Rajasthan Federation, the Deccan States' Federation and the Bengal Federation. 'A. Punjabi,' *A Confederacy of India* (Lahore, 1939), pp. 6-17, 195-200.

60. K.K. Aziz, *A History of the Idea of Pakistan*, pp. 533-36.

61. NAP, QAP, F274/141, Abdullah Haroon, Chairman, Foreign Committee, AIML, to Jinnah, 23 December 1940.

62. K.K. Aziz, *A History of the Idea of Pakistan*, p. 651.

63. NAP, QAP, F370/65, Jinnah to Latif, 15 March 1941.

64. Sikander's plan was disavowed by the separatist implication of the Lahore Resolution.

65. Jinnah had labelled him an 'irresponsible person' and his plan as crazy. In turn, Rahmat ridiculed Jinnah as the '*Boozna* of Bombay' and pilloried the AIML as a crowd of careerists and opportunists. The dispute continued for six years and ended with the Lahore Resolution of 1940. But relations remained cool and the Muslim League refused to acknowledge the fact that it had adopted many of Rahmat's ideas and attributed the honour for inventing the Pakistan scheme to Jamaluddin Afghani and Iqbal. Khan A. Ahmad, *The Founder of Pakistan: Through Trial to Triumph* (1942), pp. 19-20. Finally, when Rahmat Ali visited Pakistan in 1947, he was threatened by Liaquat Ali, the Prime Minister, that, if he did not leave, he would be declared *persona non grata*. K.K. Aziz, *Rahmat Ali*, pp. 303-4.

66. There was disagreement between Sikander and Jinnah over the phrase Pakistan. Sikander wanted Jinnah to drop it but was the only one against the term on the Working Committee. Their differences led Sikander to consider the political implications that, if he resigned from the party, an open split would cost him only six or seven urban seats. IOR, L/P&J/8/690 Coll. 117-E-4-B (Pakistan), Craik to Linlithgow, 4 March 1941.

67. Abul Mansur Ahmed, *Fifty Years of Politics as I Saw It*, pp. 242-43.

68. NAP, QAP, F204/324-329, Confederacy of East Pakistan and Adibistan, 1944.

69. NAP, QAP, F204/320, Raghib Ahsan to Jinnah, 14 August 1944.

70. IOR, L/P&J/5/151, Casey to Wavell, cited in H. Rashid, *The Foreshadowing of Bangladesh* (Dhaka, 1987), p. 183.

71. Presidential Address by Nawabzada Mahmood Ali to the Punjab Majlis-i-Ahrar Conference, 31 March 1943, in A.M. Zaidi, ed, *Evolution of Muslim Political Thought in India*, vi (Delhi, 1979), p. 582.

72. Presidential Address by Maulana Madani to the Jamiat-ul-Ulama-i-Hind, 20 March 1940. Ibid., p. 598.

73. H. Rashid, *The Foreshadowing of Bangladesh*, pp. 88-96.

74. IOR, Mss. Eur. F 125/39 (Linlithgow Collection), Brabourne to Linlithgow, 17 February 1939. Ibid., Reid to Linlithgow, 5 May 1939.

75. Ibid., Reid to Linlithgow, 22 May 1939.

76. NAP, QAP, F305/30, Hassan Ispahani to Jinnah, 19 January 1939.

77. IOR, Mss. Eur. F 125/37 (Linlithgow Collection), Brabourne to Linlithgow, 5 May 1938.

78. This figure was calculated on the basis that the BPML submitted Rs 50 to the AIML

as 10 per cent of its membership fees of two annas per member. QAA, AIML 39/12, Fazlul Huq to the Secretary of the AIML, 9 August 1939.

79. NAP, QAP, F305/35, Hassan Ispahani to Jinnah, 11 April 1939.
80. IOR, Mss. Eur. F 125/40 (Linlithgow Collection), Herbert to Linlithgow, 22 June 1940.
81. Ibid., Herbert to Linlithgow, 10 July 1940.
82. NAP, QAP, F 392/45-48, Nazimuddin to Jinnah, 10 June 1941.
83. NAP, QAP, F 364/25-27, Khaliquzzaman to Jinnah, 24 June 1941.
84. IOR, Mss. Eur. F 125/41 (Linlithgow Collection), Herbert to Linlithgow, 5 December 1942.
85. IOR, Mss. Eur. F 125/42 (Linlithgow Collection), Secretary of the Governor of Bengal to the Secretary to the Viceroy, 4 August 1942.
86. Ibid., Herbert to Linlithgow, 23 April 1942. Mss. Eur. F 125/43 (Linlithgow Collection), Secretary of the Governor of Bengal to the Secretary of the Viceroy, 29 March 1943.
87. Jinnah to Hasan Ispahani, 15 April 1943, in Z.H. Zaidi, ed, *M.A. Jinnah: Ispahani Correspondence, 1936-48* (Karachi, 1976), p. 357.
88. Several factors were responsible for this major catastrophe: the loss of rice imports from Burma due to the Japanese advance, the Denial Policy which caused the collapse of the distribution system, the League's failure to deal with refugees and food distribution and Downing Street's preparedness to see Indians starve. P. Moon, ed, *Wavell: The Viceroy's Journal* (London, 1973), pp. 68, 122.
89. QAA, SHC, Bengal iv/18, Raghib Ahsan to Jinnah, 15 November 1944.
90. Abul Hashim, *In Retrospection* (Dacca, 1974), p. 23.
91. Ibid., pp. 62, 66.
92. QAA, SHC, Bengal iv/18, Raghib Ahsan to Jinnah, 15 November 1944.
93. QAA, SHC, Bengal iv/19, Raghib Ahsan to Jinnah, 17 November 1944.
94. QAA, SHC, Bengal iv/21, Raghib Ahsan to Jinnah, 19 November 1944.
95. IOR, Mss. Eur. F 125/88 (Linlithgow Collection), Craik to Linlithgow, 17 May 1939.
96. Ibid., Craik to Linlithgow, 19 May 1939.
97. Ian Talbot, *Punjab and the Raj*, pp. 126-30.
98. NDC, CID, S 410 (Punjab Police Abstract of Intelligence), no. 8 by Deane, 21 February 1942, p. 89.
99. QAA, AIML 230/10, Muhammad Ashraf to Jinnah, 28 June 1941.
100. Ian Talbot, *Punjab and the Raj*, pp. 117-19.
101. IOR, Mss. Eur. F 125/86 (Linlithgow Collection), Craik to Linlithgow, 25 April 1938. Ibid., Emerson to Linlithgow, 5 April 1938. Mss. Eur. F 125/88 (Linlithgow Collection), Craik to Linlithgow, 28 December 1939 (hereafter Mss. Eur. F 125/88).
102. Mss. Eur. F 125/91, Glancy to Linlithgow, 10 July 1942.
103. Mss. Eur. F 125/88, Craik to Linlithgow 26 February 1939.
104. Mss. Eur. F 125/90, Craik to Linlithgow, 4 March 1941.
105. A.I. Singh, *The Origins of the Partition of India, 1936-47* (Delhi, 1987), pp. 65-66.
106. Mss. Eur. F 125/91, George Abell to Gilbert Laithwaite, 11 January 1942.
107. A.I. Singh, *The Origins of the Partition of India*, p. 100.
108. Mss. Eur. F 125/92, Brander to Laithwaite, 21 July 1943.
109. Glancy to Wavell, 14 April 1944, *TP*, iv, p. 880.
110. NDC, CID, S 412 (Punjab Police Abstract of Intelligence), No. 14 by Rich, 1 April 1944, p. 191.

111. Wavell to Glancy, 15 April 1944, *TP*, iv, p. 882. Glancy to Wavell, 24 April 1944, *TP*, iv, pp. 922-25.

112. Wavell to Amery, 16 May 1944, *TP*, iv, p. 969.

113. NDC, CID, S 411 (Punjab Police Abstract of Intelligence), No. 26 by Deane, 26 June 1943, p. 359.

114. NDC, CID, S. 393 (NWFP Political General), No. 42, 18 October 1937, p. 30.

115. S.A. Rittenberg, *Ethnicity, Nationalism and the Pakhtuns*, pp. 143-48. IOR, Mss. Eur. F 125/72 (Linlithgow Collection), Cunningham to Linlithgow, 26 May 1938.

116. NCD, CID, S 401 (NWFP Police Secret Abstract), No. 1 by Hodder, 7 January 1941, p. 1.

117. Ibid., No. 7 by A. St. John Wood, 18 February 1941, p. 22.

118. Rittenberg, *Ethnicity, Nationalism and the Pakhtuns*, p. 168.

119. NDC, CID, S 402 (NWFP Police Secret Abstract), No. 37 by Hodder, 15 September 1942, p. 104. Ibid., No. 44 by Hodder, 3 November 1942, p. 124.

120. Cunningham to Linlithgow, 28 September 1942, *TP*, iii, p. 56.

121. Cunningham to Linlithgow, 8 August, 1942, *TP*, ii, p. 5. The political nature of these attacks become all the more apparent as the pro-Muslim League *ulama* ignored the religious transgression by Jinnah's daughter of marrying a Parsi, in March 1940. NDC, CID, S 400 (NWFP Police Secret Abstract), No. 13 by Wagstaffe, 26 March 1940, p. 92.

122. NDC, CID, S 393 (NWFP Political General), Report by Attaullah, 25 April 1938, p. 131.

123. NDC, CID, S 393 (CID Peshawar), diary No. 45, 2 January 1946, p. 42.

124. NDC, CID, S 394 (CID NWFP), Report, 24 July 1939, pp. 88-93. Ibid., (Weekly Confidential Diary, Peshawar), 3 March 1939, p. 29. The Khudai Khidmatgars were estimated to be between forty and sixty thousand strong in 1938, mainly concentrated in the Peshawar-Mardan area and organized into 280 village committees. They were well drilled and uniformed, but Ghaffar Khan was genuinely non-violent. IOR, Mss. Eur. F 125/72 (Linlithgow Collection), Cunningham to Linlithgow, 9 June 1938.

125. Rittenberg, *Ethnicity, Nationalism and the Pakhtuns*, pp. 174-75. The figures do not include the Khudai Khidmatgar membership, but a similar decrease also occurred there.

126. QAA, SHC, NWFP i/74, Sadullah Khan to Jinnah, 7 March 1944.

127. Rittenberg, *Ethnicity, Nationalism and the Pakhtuns*, pp. 150, 160-62.

128. The Akalis had joined Aurangzeb's cabinet on the strict understanding that the question of Pakistan would not be raised, and because Dr Khan refused to guarantee seats for the Sikhs in a future government. The Mahasabha were also prepared to enter into an alliance, but negotiations broke down when Aurangzeb refused to concede the speakership of the House to Mehr Chand Khanna. A.I. Singh, *The Origins of the Partition of India*, p. 92.

129. QAA, SHC, NWFP, i/74, Sadullah Khan to Jinnah, 7 November 1944.

130. The expression literally means taking an oath on the Koran and reneging on it. The ministry acquired this name owing to its readiness to make promises which were unlikely to be fulfilled. QAA, SHC, NWFP i/60, Sadullah Khan to the Committee of Action, 8 August 1945.

131. *Report of Court of Inquiry Appointed under Section 3 of the Sind Public Inquiries Act to Enquire into the Riots which Occurred at Sukkor in 1939* (Karachi, 1940), p. 48

(hereafter *Report on Sukkor Riots*). QAA, AIML 248/15, Political Situation in Sind by Muhammad H. Rashidi, n.d.

132. *Report on Sukkor Riots*, p. 48.
133. IOR, L/P&J/7/2892 (Manzilgah Occupation), Note by R.M. Maxwell, August 1940.
134. IOR, L/P&J/7/2892 (Manzilgah Occupation), Summary of Events, n.d.
135. IOR, L/P&J/7/2892 (Manzilgah Occupation), Synopsis, n.d.
136. NDC, CID, S 428 (Sind Police Secret Abstract), No. 2 by Eates, 13 January 1940, p. 19.
137. NDC, CID, S 428 (Sind Police Secret Abstract), No. 47 by Eates, 30 November 1940, p. 19.
138. IOR, Mss. Eur. F 125/88 (Linlithgow Collection), Craik to Linlithgow, 28 December 1939.
139. NAP, QAP, F 460/1-3, G.M. Sayed to Jinnah, 1 November 1939.
140. *Report on the Sukkor Riots*, p. 61.
141. QAA, AIML 248/15, Political Situation in Sind by Muhammad H. Rashidi, n.d.
142. IOR, Mss. Eur. E 372 (Dow Collection), Dow to Linlithgow, 22 October 1942.
143. NAP, QAP, F 854/33-42, A Note by G.M. Sayed, n.d.
144. QAA, SHC, Sind ii/38, Note by S.F. Kachhi, n.d.
145. NAP, QAP, F 460/27, G.M. Sayed to Abdullah Haroon, 17 January 1941.
146. QAA, AIML 200/37-47, Annual Report of the Sind Provincial Muslim League, 1943-44, by G.M. Sayed.
147. QAA, AIML 200/49, Quarterly Report on the Progress of the Muslim League in Sind, n.d.

3

A BRIEF MOMENT OF POLITICAL UNITY: MASS NATIONALISM AND COMMUNAL RIOTS, 1945–47

Throughout the early 1940s, Jinnah tried to mobilize Muslim opinion around a central focus — the League. The regional parties, however, proved to be powerful centrifugal forces defying the attempts of the AIML to make inroads into the rural areas. Despite the increasing authority of the Muslim League at the centre, it could not win over the provincial parties. The constitutional arrangements gave them many powers. As long as the India Act of 1935 remained the bedrock of Indian politics, the regional parties flourished. They had a personal interest in avoiding the control of any centralizing political authority. However, when the war ended in May 1945, the edifice that sustained the regional groupings — the basic assumptions of Indian politics — was questioned in the parleys concerning the future of India. It was in this context that Muslim nationalism was able to achieve political unity.

The tortuous constitutional negotiations also tested Jinnah's centralizing strategy. The key to understanding his approach lies in his emphasis on treating parity and sovereignty as synonymous and, therefore, interchangeable. The elusive goal that either demand could achieve via different paths was that of equal status with the Congress. What is striking is that Jinnah's search for equality with the Congress led him to make several dramatic revisions of his understanding of Pakistan. Before discussions with the Cabinet Mission, the AIML declared that Pakistan would have to be a sovereign independent state. Jinnah, however, settled for the confederal arrangement outlined in the Cabinet Mission Plan, with parity in the constitution-making body. When the Mission Plan fell through, he returned, to his position of demanding a sovereign state, but still backed Bengal's attempt to become independent and only after its failure did he ultimately accept a 'moth-eaten Pakistan'.[1] To complicate matters, his negotiating posture also had to cope with internal opposition. He was forced to follow a narrow path that would not aggravate dissensions in the ranks or surrender his ambition of equality with the Congress on constitutional level. Jinnah's difficulty was that he had to square the different interpretations of Pakistan held by his adherents with what was being offered by the Raj and the Congress. He tried to draw the various centrifugal forces into a tighter orbit, but his hold remained tenuous right down to partition. Pressures from the ranks of the League forced Jinnah to perform a delicate minuet, whereby he attempted to harmonize the conflicting aspirations of his supporters with the imperatives of his negotiations at the centre.

In June 1945, Lord Wavell announced the convening of a new Executive Council that was more representative of the political parties than its predecessors had been, and which was equally divided between caste Hindus and Muslims.[2] Gandhi and Azad challenged Wavell on the principle of parity but he remained resolute, only conceding that the Congress could nominate Muslims and Scheduled Castes. The Governor of the Punjab, Glancy, and Khizr were also against the Congress-League parity as it forced the Unionists to seek representation on the Council through the Muslim League. Khizr, knowing that his ministry could only survive if it was represented at the centre, wanted a non-Muslim League representative on the reconstituted Executive Council.[3] When the conference was convened, the principle of parity was accepted by all sides, but the question as to who would nominate the Muslims remained unsettled. Wavell made it clear that the provinces, particularly the Punjab, would be represented and the Congress demanded the right to nominate two Muslims to the Council. All these demands undermined Jinnah's claim to be the 'sole spokesman' of the Muslims and proved to be the main stumbling block to an agreement. Jinnah countered by proposing the idea of a Muslim veto. When this was rejected out of hand by the Viceroy, Jinnah then claimed the right to nominate all Muslims to the Executive Council. The conference broke down on Jinnah's obdurate insistence that the League represented all Muslims and his demand of parity with all the other parties combined.[4]

Wavell wondered why Jinnah had bothered to come to Simla at all. The latter's dilemma was that he was under pressure from his supporters who wanted the conference to succeed. Nazimuddin and Assadullah were dependent on the support of the Congress, and Liaquat was keen to participate in the interim government.[5] But if Jinnah had accepted the terms outlined by Wavell, the Muslim League would have drowned in the babel of tongues claiming to represent the Muslims. In such a scenario, the League would have found itself outflanked by Congress Muslims such as Azad and Ghaffar Khan, on one side, and Khizr Hayat, representing the Unionists, on the other. This would have encouraged Jinnah's nominal supporters in Bengal and Sind to go their own way. Jinnah first tried to wriggle out of this quandary by approaching the Jamiat-ul-Ulama-i-Hind and other nationalist Muslim organizations, hoping to persuade them to join him. In return Jinnah was willing to nominate a nationalist Muslim to the interim government, provided he selected him.[6] On the failure of this behind-the-scene manoeuvre, Jinnah raised the stakes by demanding all or nothing. Wavell hesitated to call Jinnah's bluff, and finally agreed with Glancy and Casey that it would be unwise to go ahead with the plans for an interim government without the League.[7]

Jinnah's derailment of the Simla Conference had multiple ramifications among the Muslims. His ability to resist British pressure and not modify his demands was seen as a sign of strength. As a result, his personal standing soared, but this success masked the mixed reaction within the League. The inherent contradictions between the vested interests of different groups subsumed within the League were aggravated by the failure of the conference. The Muslim majority provinces were disappointed, particularly Sind and the Punjab, by the collapse of the conference.[8] In sharp contrast, Khaliquzzaman eulogized Jinnah for the tactics he had adopted at Simla, claiming that his 'grim determination and overpowering sagacity alone saved the situation'.[9] The various responses highlighted Jinnah's difficulty in maintaining a strategy acceptable to most of his supporters.

Wavell's inability to force Jinnah to give up his demand to be the 'sole spokesman' of the Muslims meant that India's future was either with the League or the Congress, and that the loyalist parties were effectively excluded from playing a role in future developments. The deadlock in the negotiations had destabilized the centrifugal forces and made them susceptible to Muslim nationalism. The bitter recrimination between the League and the Congress, after the collapse of the Simla Conference, aggravated communal sentiment and made the position of the Unionists as champions of the cross-communal alliance increasingly untenable. The call for fresh elections, designed to test the conflicting claims of the various parties, acted as a signal to many opponents of the League that the time had come for a change in loyalties. It confirmed the worst fears of Glancy and Khizr about the Simla Conference, that without a Unionist on the Executive Council, the Unionist Government would not last.[10] There were some spectacular defections to the League just before the elections, especially in the Punjab. Firoz Khan Noon, Sayed Amjad Ali and Khizr's own brother forsook old loyalties; and in the Frontier, Khan Abdul Qaiyum Khan turned his back on the Khudai Khidmatgars and pledged allegiance to Jinnah.[11]

Jinnah claimed that a positive election result would be considered by the League as a mandate for Pakistan. His audacity, combined with the dithering of his adversaries to grasp the nettle on the Pakistan issue, contributed to the rising tide of Muslim public opinion in his favour. The British failed to expose the implications of partition for the Punjab and Bengal, and the Congress failed to budge from its stance on a unitary centre. Mass Muslim nationalism assisted the League and resulted in the party winning nearly 87 per cent of the Muslim vote in the Central Legislature elections and 75 per cent of the vote in the provincial elections.[12]

In preparation for negotiations with the Cabinet Mission, Jinnah convened, in April 1946, the Legislators Convention. Suhrawardy moved the main resolution, 'that the zones comprising Bengal and Assam in the north-east and the Punjab, North West Frontier Province, Sind and Baluchistan in the north-west of India, namely Pakistan zones, ...be constituted into a sovereign independent State'.[13] Its novelty lay in the fact that it dropped all reference to two independent Muslim states, which the League and Jinnah had persistently advocated since the Lahore Resolution of 1940. It was designed to pull together his provincial supporters, particularly those from Bengal, who were strong advocates of two sovereign states. Hashim's protests were a mere irritant to Jinnah. His authority had reached a new zenith, making Hashim and Suhrawardy reluctant to clash with him when unity, or more importantly cosmetic unanimity, was crucial.[14] The Convention provided an explicit definition of Pakistan, and demanded its implementation without delay by the creation of a Pakistan Constituent Assembly. This was Jinnah's opening gambit in the negotiations with the Cabinet Mission. His inability, however, to sustain his claim to represent all Muslims weakened his hand in the negotiations that followed. Even the facade of a consensus in the League was quickly demolished when the Cabinet Mission interviewed the chief ministers, and it became apparent that the League's foundation was based on the shifting sands of regional interests. Suhrawardy demolished the two-nation theory by arguing that religion was not the only determining factor, and attached great importance to linguistic ties.[15] Hidayatullah's only interest was that the centre should be kept out of Sindi affairs. Mamdot said that he wanted the whole of the Punjab. He was prepared to come to terms with the Sikhs but had no idea what Sikhistan meant.[16] The point was driven home even harder when non-League Muslim opinion was contacted. Dr Khan declared that Sarhad only wanted autonomy and restricted powers for the centre, and refused to concede that there were any political differences between Hindus and Muslims,[17] while Khizr foresaw differences, between Sindis, Pakhtuns, Baluchis and Punjabis emerging once they were brought together into one state.[18]

The Cabinet Mission offered a truncated Pakistan — an independent sovereign state consisting of only the Muslim-majority areas. This was rejected by Jinnah as it was totally unacceptable to his supporters in the Muslim-majority provinces. He was more interested in the confederal alternative, Plan A, consisting of two groups — Pakistan and Hindustan — with a weak centre. The Congress, however, was unwilling to go beyond offering a federal arrangement where the residuary powers were vested in autonomous provinces. Cripps prepared a compromise solution which was a three-tier structure: an all-India Union composed of two sub-federations of Pakistan and Hindustan based on the existing provinces. The arrangement appealed to Jinnah, although it replaced a sovereign Pakistan with federating groups, because it allowed for a sub-federation legislature that gave the League a structure to impose control over the Muslim majority provinces and parity in the interim government. The proposed grouping was unacceptable to the Congress as it wanted a unitary structure. The proposals were watered down during the negotiations, and what finally emerged was again a three-tier edifice with the centre exercising power over defence, foreign affairs, communications and revenue. There was no parity between the Congress and the Muslim League; the two Muslim groupings were not binding on the constituent provinces; residuary powers and not sovereign rights were invested in the provinces; and there was no right of secession. Even worse for Jinnah was the fact that the preamble to the plan explicitly rejected Pakistan, which angered many Muslim Leaguers.[19]

Yet, despite this rejection, Jinnah approved the Mission Plan. Acceptance produced an almost audible sigh of relief from the Muslim-majority provinces[20] and the Muslims from the minority provinces also endorsed it.[21] Jinnah was himself in favour of accepting,[22] and had received assurances from Wavell that there would be parity in the interim government between the League and the Congress.[23] He was, however, nervous of facing his Working Committee as the preamble's explicit rejection of a sovereign Pakistan had incensed his supporters.[24] In June 1946, Jinnah persuaded the AIML to reject the preamble and to accept the body of the statement as consistent with the principle of Pakistan. He argued that the plan conceded the essence of Pakistan and the decennial review of the constitution would allow them to leave the Union if they wanted to. This nimble footwork was needed to prevent a split in the League between the politicians and the religious leaders but, still, thirteen Leaguers, such as

Hasrat Mohani and Abdus Sattar Niazi, hardline separatists, voted against Jinnah.[25]

However, Nehru's press statement[26] was interpreted as evidence of the Congress' *mala fide*, and induced Jinnah to redefine Pakistan. The Muslim League retaliated by instigating a non-violent civil disobedience campaign in August. But the constitutional negotiations at the centre, the communal rift created by the election campaign and the Direct Action campaign produced a volatile cocktail. All the pent-up communal hatred exploded in the great Calcutta killing, which sent shock waves throughout India. As the carnage spread to Bihar and the United Provinces, the League supporters there were won over to the idea of partition and were now prepared to migrate.[27]

Jinnah returned to his previous position of demanding a sovereign and independent state comprising six full provinces, and made this clear to Attlee and later to Mountbatten. The League had, by now, developed a phobia to the Mission Plan, but partition of the provinces[28] was still unacceptable to the Punjab and Bengal, despite the build-up of pressure in Bihar. Consequently, Jinnah had to seriously consider any plan which would keep these provinces undivided, even if it meant modifying his interpretation of Pakistan again. Suhrawardy told Mountbatten that he preferred the Cabinet Plan option, but if that was not possible, he was ready to have a united independent Bengal outside Pakistan.[29] Mountbatten, despite being sympathetic to the idea, could not wait long, and gave him only two months to pull it off. Jinnah was delighted by the proposition of a united independent Bengal, even though it would be outside Pakistan,[30] and responded positively to Suhrawardy's plea that if the discussion on 'sovereign Bengal' was to have any chance, Jinnah must fight off the demand for partition.[31] Jinnah obliged by robustly rejecting partition and argued for the entire provinces of the Punjab and Bengal to be included in Pakistan. To give Suhrawardy the necessary breathing space, he argued that the issue of partition of the two provinces had to be settled by a plebiscite and upped the stakes by raising the demand for a corridor.[32]

By supporting Suhrawardy's initiative, Jinnah also raised the possibility of an undivided Punjab joining Pakistan. Jinnah, however, had no control over events in the province that was burning. The Punjab League was anxious to overthrow Khizr's ministry and to form a government. However, instead of negotiating with the Sikhs and Hindus, the leadership remained adamant that the Muslims were entitled to rule the province on their own, and urged their supporters to maintain the agitation.[33] The complacency of the Muslim League was eventually exposed by the Sikhs becoming committed to partition. However, when partition of the province was announced by Delhi, it came as a great shock, and the Punjab League had to put in considerable effort in keeping up morale.[34] Failure of the plan for a Pakistan that included the whole of Bengal and the Punjab had its silver lining for Jinnah. His relationship with Suhrawardy was, at best, strained; he had little control over the affairs of the Bengal League and the partition of the province led to his supporters, the Khwaja group, taking over. This made it easier to keep east Bengal within the orbit of the League's centralizing strategy. However, if the troublesome Suhrawardy had succeeded with his plan, Jinnah felt secure in the knowledge that it was a poisoned chalice for Nehru and Patel. It would have been a major blow to their attempt to establish a centralized state creating great problems for them in extending control over their non-Muslim supporters. Once the proposal for a sovereign united Bengal proved to be still-born, due to the insistence of the Congress on partition, the focus shifted to the fate of Sind and the NWFP. The referendum in Sarhad and the election triumph in Sind gave the League the victories needed to bring these provinces into Pakistan. Jinnah, in order to consolidate his hold over 'moth-eaten Pakistan' and to make sure that the deal was honoured, insisted on becoming the Governor-General of Pakistan; otherwise, he would be unable to control the centrifugal currents that were operating in the country.[35]

The central thrust of Muslim nationalism, asserting a monolithic Muslim identity, created irrevocable problems at the central and provincial levels. To win seats sectarian propaganda was successfully used, which heightened communal tensions, making it difficult for pro-Congress Muslims to maintain cooperation with non-Muslims. However, to avoid partition of the two provinces the League needed non-Muslim cooperation, which was now not forthcoming. Consequently, the short-term success rebounded in the longer term, forcing the League to accept the division of the Punjab and Bengal.

The transformation of Muslim nationalism into a mass movement was crucial to Jinnah's strategy. Without a popular following, both the British and the Congress would have ignored him and come to a mutually satisfactory arrangement. Economic nationalism was in the background during the early 1940s but became increasingly significant during and after the elections. Its effect was to draw in the masses, previously untouched by Muslim nationalism, and unite them with the élites in a common cause. The intellectuals provided the publicity and ideas that were disseminated during the run-up to the elections. The campaign was funded by the mercantile communities, and the *pirs* provided the means to reach the rural population. Pakistan was successfully projected as an Islamic panacea, which would solve all the problems of the Muslims. At a later stage government officials and military personnel supported the League and placed their expertise at the service of Muslim nationalism.[36]

To urban professionals, Pakistan was a land of opportunity free from

Hindu and Sikh competition for education and jobs. The League, in December 1943, established a Committee for Education to review and foster all forms of instruction and training. Its purpose was not simply to insist on separate Muslim institutions, a demand that at the time coincided with the defence of the Urdu language, a key issue in the competition for jobs with non-Muslims. In the long term, the Muslim League claimed that Pakistan promised to activate a vast number of schemes for social, economic, industrial and educational development. These plans required a substantial number of educated personnel, and the Committee for Education had to consider the provision of trained professionals.[37] The significance of economic nationalism among the urban middle class partly explains the strong association of students and the intelligentsia with Muslim nationalism. Jinnah said 'Aligarh is the arsenal of Pakistan'[38] and this was no idle boast. Its students provided dedicated peripatetic bands touring the remote corners of Muslim India, and the staff joined the Committee of Writers, led by Jamiluddin Ahmad, which produced the literature used by the students.

Equally, expectations among the Muslim trading communities — the Memons, Bohras, Khojas and Chiniotis — had increased due to the activities of the League. They perceived Pakistan to be free from non-Muslim competition, presenting greater opportunity for them and, consequently, threw their weight behind the League. The Haroons and Ispahanis occupied important positions in the party hierarchy both at the provincial and all-India level, and provided financial support. The generosity of the Ispahanis along with the Raja of Mahmudabad made the launching of *Dawn* possible.[39] The Adamjees rallied the Calcutta Memons to support the movement and the Habibs, Shaikhs and Wazir Alis contributed financially to Jinnah's war chest[40] which, by 1945, had amassed nineteen lakh rupees.[41]

Jinnah, through Hassan Ispahani's efforts, was able to bring the various magnates together into a single body to represent Muslim entrepreneurs. The Federation of Muslim Chambers of Commerce and Industry was formed in 1943 out of the merger of the various regional chambers of commerce and the All-India Muslim Chamber of Commerce and Industry, Bombay.[42] Jinnah also encouraged entry into industry and finance but the response was slow. The first Muslim bank was established only in the 1940s by the Habib family, and they later invested in shipping, insurance and industry. These efforts were consistent with the views of the AIML Planning Committee convened with the remit to evolve a development plan, particularly in the Pakistan areas, for post-war reconstruction.[43] The mercantile community was considered the economic nucleus around which this project could take shape. The reconstruction programme assumed that the League would hold the portfolios of finance, or planning and development, plus agriculture in the interim government.[44] However, the ideological ambiguity as to whether Pakistan was to be separatist in character or a unit within some all-India framework was to cause serious friction within the Planning Committee.[45]

Later, when the League joined the interim government, Muslim bureaucrats began to openly support it. Chaudhri Mohammad Ali, Financial Adviser to the Military Finance Department, at this crucial juncture threw his weight behind Jinnah and strongly advised him to take the finance portfolio in the interim government that was being offered by the Congress. When Liaquat became Finance Minister, he became his unofficial adviser.[46] Similarly, the Muslim officers of the armed forces, most of whom were abroad fighting the war, backed the Muslim League at the last moment. One indication that the League had some support among the Muslim officers came when the entire Muslim staff of the Dehra Dun Academy declared their support for Jinnah.[47] A concrete endorsement came from Mohammad Musa, who advised Nawab Ismail Khan, the League representative on the Nationalization Committee of the Indian Armed Forces.[48]

Economic nationalism was also a potent force among some of the rural population of the Muslim-majority provinces. Pakistan was presented as a Muslim utopia that would banish the harsh drudgeries of life. The *maulanas* and *pirs* were used extensively to spread the word, particularly in the run-up to the provincial elections of 1945-46. The Chisti *sajjada nashins* of the Punjab,[49] the Pir of Manki Sharif of Hazara, Hafiz Moinniuddin, the Pir of Chittagong and Mohammad Ali Rashdi of Sind threw in their lot with the League on the promise that the *sharia* would be applied in Pakistan. Consequently, they emphasized the new millennium that would be ushered in by the establishment of the *sharia*. This line of propaganda proved very influential in winning grass-roots support for the League in the rural areas.

Simultaneously, the League's manifestos in the Punjab and Bengal were injected with socialist rhetoric. Credibility was enhanced by the various radical elements joining the party. Quite often the two different ideologies were so intertwined that it was difficult to differentiate between them. The conflation of the secular and the spiritual was epitomized by Abul Hashim, secretary of the Bengal Muslim League. He denied that he was a communist or a capitalist but called himself a *rabani* — a Muslim who believed in an egalitarian Islamic state. Hashim's radical blend of Islam transformed the Bengal Muslim League into what Raghib Ahsan proudly described to Jinnah as a revolutionary mass movement, committed to the abolition of the zemindari system and the Permanent Settlement.[50] His radical interpretation allowed him to accept the offer from the General Secretary of the Communist Party of India, P.C. Joshi, to help organize the Bengal Muslim League as a democratic and progressive organization.[51] In the Punjab, Mumtaz Daultana, the secretary, an ex-card carrying member of the Communist Party, brought in top communists into the party, such as Abdullah Malik, Danial Latifi and Jahanian.[52] They were mainly involved in organizational work and Danial Latifi wrote the party manifesto, which had a socialistic bias. It promised the nationalization of key industries and banks, land reforms, relief from the Hindu *bania* and the rent collector and offered various alternatives for the demobbed soldiers who were returning home.[53] The utopian rhetoric had a seductive lure for the rural population of Bengal which had been the victim of famine, and to the peasantry of the Punjab chafing under war-time restrictions. Thus, for the rural poor, whatever way they looked at Pakistan, either in its spiritual or temporal aspect, they saw it as a millennial resolution to their privation.

The League's advance was made easier by the declining influence of the Congress over Muslims. The Congress was not keen on fighting the elections based on a restricted franchise, and their reluctance was aggravated by the restrictions on the party and its members that continued to be enforced.[54] Once these impediments were removed, the nationalists were forced to turn their attention to the question of winning back Muslim support. Maulana Azad had reached the conclusion that a definite policy on what he called the Muslim question was required. However, first, the pro-Congress Muslims needed to organize themselves, agree on the future constitution and then persuade the Congress to accept it. He appealed to Gandhi with the plea that the Muslims should be allowed to reach a consensus. He suggested a federal structure composed of autonomous units with the right to secession, combined with joint electorates and reserved seats, parity in the central executive and the central legislature, and the provision that the head of the federation should alternately be a Muslim and a Hindu; this would make Muslims drop the idea of partition.[55] Gandhi was unenthusiastic, and Jamshed Mehta urged the All-India Congress Committee to resist granting self- determination to the provinces.[56] Despite this response, the principle of autonomy was adopted by the nationalist Muslims. It did not, however, have the desired result and only heightened the confusion, with many Muslims unable to differentiate between their position and that of the Muslim League.

In preparation for the elections, the pro-Congress Muslims were invited by Maulana Madani to New Delhi to confer. The Jamiat-ul-Ulama-i-Hind, the All-India Momin Conference, the Muslim Majlis, the Khudai Khidmatgars and the Krishak Proja Party agreed to form a central parliamentary board; they would have a common manifesto demanding immediate freedom and disputing the League's claim to be the 'sole spokesman' of the Muslims. Despite this, the Congress and its allies did poorly in the Central Legislature elections and received only about 10 per cent of the vote.[57] Their biggest handicap was that the League had made great advances during the war and the Congress had insufficient time to recover ground after being released from jail. Kazmi said that in the United Provinces there was hardly three weeks, and in some areas only two weeks of canvassing before the elections. Many sympathizers suffered from defeatism due to the long absence of the nationalists from the field but, at the hustings, the people began to respond. Madani's contribution was particularly important, as his devastating critique of the notion of Pakistan as a British ploy to delay departure began to have an effect.[58] The Khudai Khidmatgars' support was also important and contingents were sent to join the campaign in the United Provinces and Bihar.[59] The Nationalist Muslims and the Congress, however, fared as badly in the provincial elections as in the central elections securing only 11 per cent of the Muslim vote.[60] However, despite the success of mass Muslim nationalism, the elections were not an unqualified victory for the League. Its success was restricted to the urban areas of India and to major parts of rural Punjab and Bengal. In large parts of rural Sind, NWFP and Kashmir, Jinnah and the League were of little significance. The Muslim League faced resistance in varying degrees in all the Muslim majority provinces, and when the Congress failed to win Muslim votes, it turned to forming ministries. In Sarhad, the Khudai Khidmatgars won handsomely and formed the government. In Sind, the nationalists, allied with G.M. Sayed, produced a deadlock, with both the League and the Congress having equal support in the house. Significantly, for the first time in Punjab, a Congress coalition came to power when the Congress-Akali-Unionist alliance was formed.

By forming ministries, it was possible for the Congress to sustain its claim through the tortuous negotiations with the League that it also represented Muslims. On this basis, they refused to accept Jinnah's demand for parity in the Cabinet Mission Plan and in the interim government. Finally, on 10 July 1946, Nehru openly repudiated the Mission Plan on the basis that Sindis and Pakhtuns were against grouping and being dominated by Punjabis. There was no intention of allowing Assam to be subordinated to Bengal by being aggregated in the same group. The centre would liberally interpret the common subjects, use the control over finance, taxation and foreign trade to settle inter-provincial disputes and intervene in emergencies due to administrative and economic crises.[61] The Congress intended to deploy the centre to limit the provinces' room for manoeuvre.

Only after Nehru entered the interim government did the Congress try to bring the AIML back to the negotiating table. On 6 August, the Congress Working Committee, as a gesture, announced that it was willing to accept the Cabinet Mission Plan but held that each province had the right 'to form or join a group or not'. The sovereign character of the constituent assembly was emphasized, as was its right to function and promulgate a constitution without interference from any external authority.[62] The Congress Working Committee believed that the Damocles sword of partition would pull the Muslim majority provinces back into the fold. Azad believed that if partition was announced, it was highly likely that there would be a revolt in the League, with Muslim Bengal seceding from the party, and that there was also a slim chance of this happening in the Punjab.[63] Patel argued that if Pakistan was to consist only of Muslim Punjab and Sind, 'there was a real chance that either Mr Jinnah would be forced to come to my terms, or be overthrown by the League'.[64]

Jinnah, however, turned the tables on the Congress by supporting Suhrawardy's attempt for a united independent Bengal. Gandhi supported the plan but Nehru was dead set against it, unless an independent Bengal was loosely linked to India.[65] Instead, the Congress demanded the partition of Bengal and the Punjab and the transfer of power to two independent states. By making the Congress accept the onus for partition, Jinnah halted desertion from the League camp and undermined the position of pro-Congress supporters. The success of this manoeuvre left the Frontier Congress and G.M. Sayed rudderless and sealed their political fate. The Khudai Khidmatgars wanted the alternative of becoming independent, but this was refused by all parties. Neither the League nor the Congress countenanced that possibility due to the impact it would have had on the other provinces. In the Sind elections, G.M. Sayed's support melted away. His supporters knew which way the wind was blowing and deserted him for the League. The price that the Congress was willing to pay for a centralized state was to sacrifice their Muslim supporters. The only alternative that would induce the Muslim League to remain in a united India was a weak centre, but the Congress would have had problems in controlling their non-Muslim supporters under such an arrangement.

Focusing exclusively on the politics at the centre, the inconsistencies of mass Muslim nationalism are often overlooked. By shifting the analysis to an examination of the political developments in the Muslim-majority provinces, it becomes clear that the rise of mass Muslim nationalism was not a unilinear triumph but a complex process marked by deep inner contradictions. There was no uniformity in the way the Muslim League was transformed into a mass party in the Muslim-majority provinces. The provinces witnessed a complex and difficult struggle involving regionally oriented forces, local interests, ethnicity and community-consciousness. Its nature and emphasis varied from province to province, being determined, over a period of time, by shifting local circumstances. The elements of consistency which emerge are that the centrifugal elements in the Muslim majority provinces resisted the centripetal impulses of the League high command, and the local pulls were present in varying strength depending on the province, despite the upsurge in Muslim nationalism.

In Bengal, a mass movement had emerged which asserted a Bengali-Muslim identification. It was loyal only to the leadership of the provincial Muslim League and not to the high-command. The party leaders took over the Bengal parliamentary group, displaced the pro-Jinnah cohort from positions of power and conducted an election campaign that swept the combined opposition aside. However, it left Jinnah in the uncomfortable situation where he had to accommodate the strong regionalist current in Bengal with his two-nation theory at the centre. Consequently, when he claimed the election results were a mandate for Pakistan, in reality the situation was more complex.

Feuding between the Bengal Muslim League and its parliamentary wing erupted again when elections were announced for the first quarter of 1946. The Khwaja group wanted to stem the rot and resist the increasing authority of Hashim and his supporters. Nazimuddin attempted to capture the nine-man Parliamentary Board and distribute election tickets to his supporters. The rules favoured the Khwaja group, as the President of the provincial League and the Leader of the parliamentary party would be *ex officio* members, and one each from the Lower and Upper House of the Bengal Assembly would be elected. Suhrawardy, who up to now had sided with the Khwaja group, had expected to be elected from the Lower House, but Nazimuddin nominated Fazlur Rahman and Nurul Amin.[66] Suhrawardy now joined Abul Hashim in preventing Nazimuddin from winning two more seats, in order to have clear majority. Nazimuddin was warned that his supporters were misleading him and that he should compromise, but he was so confident of victory that he ignored all advice. The Hashim-Suhrawardy group won all five seats[67] and Nazimuddin was so unnerved by the defeat that he seriously considered withdrawing from politics. Neither he nor Shahabuddin stood in the elections. Nazimuddin toyed with the idea of seeking employment with the princely state of Hyderabad but was advised by Casey and Liaquat to drop the idea.[68]

Suhrawardy's successful bid for leadership of the party was extremely important. It meant that the Hashim-Suhrawardy group would be distributing tickets for the provincial elections to their supporters; it marked the subordination of the parliamentary group to the organization and was a defeat for Jinnah. Suhrawardy was too independent for Jinnah's liking and his distrust became crystallized into a cold hostility between the League high command and the Hashim-Suhrawardy group. The tension between the two was most apparent when the issues of financing the election campaign and establishing a weekly party journal were raised. Hassan Ispahani, Jinnah's most loyal supporter, resigned from the Working Committee in protest and warned him that the present constitution of the Working Committee would prevent the Muslim magnates of Calcutta from funding the forthcoming elections.[69] Jinnah was perplexed by the development and at first was uncertain how to respond. He clearly distrusted Suhrawardy and rejected his application for Rs 50,000 from the Central Fund.[70] The Bengal League launched a major fund-raising campaign, the entire provincial machinery was thrown into action and the district committees were given targets of between Rs 250 to Rs 500 to be raised for the Provincial Election Fund. A substantial number of students, League workers and supporters were employed in the fund-raising campaign.[71] Just before the elections, however, Jinnah had to concede that the provincial League had inadequate funds for the campaign and contributed two lakh rupees. The money was not transferred to the provincial League but to a special Committee of Control, consisting of Jinnah loyalists, to administer the fund for the AIML.[72]

The friction between the AIML and the Bengal League re-emerged when Abul Hashim tried to establish a weekly party journal reflecting his views. The need for it had become far more urgent as the *Azad* was acting as the mouthpiece of the Khwaja group. Thus Hashim arranged for the publication of the Bengali weekly, *Millat*. When he approached Jinnah for his approval, he was advised not to publish in the name of the Muslim League but only in his personal capacity. Hashim went ahead anyway and, on 16 November 1945, published it as the Bengal League's official organ. At its peak the circulation reached 35,000 copies a week.[73]

The AIML also actively helped the Khwaja group to remain an influential force in Bengal politics. Direct intervention by Jinnah, along the lines of Sind, was out of the question. The Hashim-Suhrawardy group had mass support and organizational backing which rendered any such attempt futile. Consequently, when Akram Khan requested Jinnah to intervene on his behalf, he was rebuffed.[74] An opportunity, however, arose over the appeals made to the Central Parliamentary Board regarding the distribution of tickets. Complaints were made that Suhrawardy was ignoring pro-Khwaja supporters and nominating former Proja Party assembly members (such as Shamsuddin Ahmed) as candidates.[75] The Board accepted twenty-two appeals. Nearly all were Nazimuddin's supporters, such as Sayed Abdus Salim, Khwaja Nooruddin and Abul Kalam Shamsudin.[76] When Jinnah visited Bengal he stressed the need for unity, and Khwaja Nazimuddin and Shahabuddin were forced to linger on the sidelines waiting for the moment to strike back once the polling was over.

The campaign had little input from the central leadership and was essentially a provincial affair. It was initiated with great gusto, with a meeting of half a million persons in Calcutta.[77] League parties led by Abul Hashim, Suhrawardy and Nazimuddin toured the *mofussils* and were received with great enthusiasm. Jinnah addressed meetings only in Calcutta and his message was simple: they were fighting for Pakistan, and the Muslim League stood for the poor. Liaquat Ali Khan also visited the province briefly, presiding over a League conference in Gaffargon where they faced stiff opposition from Maulana Shamsul Huda, a local divine. Students belonging to the Bengal Muslim Students League played a prominent role, and it was claimed by the League that 20,000 persons were involved in the campaign.[78] Abul Mansur Ahmed collected 300 persons, and targeted them against Fazlul Huq and Nausher Ali who were contesting the elections in Barisal and Bagerhat. Abul Hashim and his radical supporters won over the rural vote by successfully harnessing Islamic and socialistic propaganda and, in this enterprise, they were aided by the Communist Party.[79] The Khwaja group exclusively deployed *pirs* and *maulvis*, whom they inducted into the service of the League. At the request of the party, Maulana Abdul Hai Siddiqui of Furfura convened a conference of the Jamiat-ul-Ulama-i-Islam to neutralize the influence of the pro-Congress *ulama*. Maulana Shabbir Usmani endorsed the party by stating that it was the Islamic duty of Muslims to ensure the victory of the League.[80]

The nationalist Muslims were brushed aside by the wave of support for the Bengal League. This was despite the particular attention that the Congress paid to the province so as to invalidate Jinnah's claim that only he represented the Muslims. The Congress sponsored the Bengal Muslim Parliamentary Board, consisting of the Krishak Proja Party, the Jamiat-ul-Ulama-i-Hind and nationalist Muslims. However, the result of the Central Assembly elections shook the pro-Congress forces. The Muslim League swept the polls in all six Muslim constituencies and the nationalists suffered a humiliating defeat. Defection from the nationalist parliamentary board took place, Shamsuddin Ahmed joined the League in December 1945 and others followed suit.[81]

Fazlul Huq had detected that, since 1943, major changes in Muslim politics had taken place, which was why he denied being against Pakistan.[82] He tried to return to the Muslim League but Jinnah was not willing to have him at any price. Huq's transformation was based on the realization that most Bengali Muslims wanted Pakistan, and considered the League to be better placed to look after their interest than any regional party. Unable to return to the fold, he fought the elections on the issue of agrarian reform. His powerful oratorical skills and political stature prevented him from being consigned to the dustbin of history. The Jamiat-ul-Ulama-i-Hind held a conference that Maulana Husain Madani attended, along with other *ulama* and a number of Ahrar and Khaksar volunteers from north India. Despite the generous supply of money and men by the Congress, they were unable to make much headway.[83] The Bengal Muslim League won 113 seats, and the Krishak Proja Party and the independents together secured only 9 seats.[84]

The widening gap between Hindus and Muslims was an important reason for the failure of the Muslim nationalists. Their position was made impossible by the Bengal Congress. It had shed its left wing and adopted a Hindu populist programme indistinguishable from the Mahasabha's agenda, though the nationalist rhetoric was not abandoned.[85] By 1944 communal relations had become highly polarized, and Calcutta officials recognized that the situation was ready to explode at the slightest provocation. The League's election campaign made the situation worse, and it became uncontrollable with the launching of the League's Direct Action programme on 16 August. The latter consisted of a complete *hartal*, a mass rally, public meetings and congregations in mosques, mobilization of the Muslim student population and parading of the National Guards — men and women — in different parts of the city. The action was intended to demonstrate popular support for the League, but it exploded into a homicidal orgy of violence.[86] Suhrawardy's intemperate behaviour inflamed passions further and the stage was set for the resulting carnage.[87]

When Muslim League supporters tried to enforce the *hartal* on Hindu shops in north Calcutta, Congress and Mahasabha supporters began to interfere with the Muslim processions. This triggered off a vicious cycle of violent reprisal that left at least 4,000 dead and 10,000 injured. The violence consisted of large crowds battling it out on the streets, and attacks by small hit-squads on isolated families and individuals belonging to the 'enemy' community. Calcutta, however, was not a Bengali city but a cosmopolitan one; therefore, the violence was to send tremors not only throughout Bengal but all across north India up to Khyber Pass. The fact that the crowds consisted of migrant workers from Bihar, the United Provinces, the Punjab and the Frontier meant that once the news of the butchery reached their home villages, talk of revenge was on everyone's lips. Immediately the rioting spread to Noakhali, an area that previously had no record of communal rioting; it was an extension of the Great Calcutta Killing though the action was initiated by a single person, Ghulam Sarwar.[88]

The riots brought partition inexorably closer, and both the Hindu Mahasabha and the Congress called for the division of India. However, a faint glimmer of hope existed and alternatives to partition were discussed between Sarat Bose and Kiran Shankar Roy of the Congress, and Suhrawardy and Hashim.[89] The consultations followed a twin-track approach of negotiating for an immediate coalition government, on the one hand, and simultaneously thrashing out a compromise on the constitutional future of a united Bengal.[90] The following agreement was reached: the Free State of Bengal was to decide its relationship with the rest of India, and elections to the legislature were to be based on joint electorates with reserved seats. Once the proposals for the Free State of Bengal were accepted, Bengal would not be partitioned and a new coalition ministry would be formed. Excluding the Chief Minister, the cabinet would consist of equal numbers of Muslims and Hindus, and both communities were to have an equal share of the services.[91] The whole scheme, however, collapsed in the face of Congress opposition. Nehru and Patel vetoed the scheme on 27 May by announcing the formal rejection of the united Bengal scheme.[92]

There was considerable opposition to the united Bengal plan within the League, and it became another issue in the rivalry between Suhrawardy and Nazimuddin. Nazimuddin made a political comeback; he was elected to the Central Assembly in a by-election caused by the death of Hasan Suhrawardy and was installed by Jinnah as Liaquat's deputy in the Assembly. He tried to dislodge Suhrawardy's grip on the party by encouraging Fazlul Huq, who had accepted Jinnah's amnesty and returned to the party, to bid for the presidentship of the Provincial League.[93] Although Akram Khan withdrew his resignation, the manoeuvre widened the differences between Suhrawardy and Hashim.[94] The former had aligned himself with Hashim for pragmatic reasons and was not interested in the radical ideas espoused by him. The *Millat* became increasingly critical of Suhrawardy's ministry for failing to carry out any of the election pledges, and the tussle between the party and the parliamentary group reappeared.[95]

The Hashim-Suhrawardy group's support for a united independent Bengal was based on their understanding of the Pakistan slogan that partition would be a disaster, reducing east Bengal to a stagnant backwater. Their interpretation was derived directly from the Lahore Resolution of 1940 and they were opposed to a single Pakistan state. Hashim warned that *akhand* Pakistan would lead to domination by western Pakistan and the Urdu language, which would result in the imposition of an alien bureaucracy over Bengali Muslims.[96] However, some of their supporters, such as Shamsuddin, the Labour Minister, were all too pleased to get rid of that white elephant, Calcutta.[97] An important factor influencing the political calculations was the geographic location of the politicians' social base. Suhrawardy and Hashim's enthusiasm for unity was based on the realization that partition would result in the loss of Calcutta and Burdwan, their old stamping ground, leaving them politically vulnerable.

The Khwaja group, mainly based in east Bengal, understood this permutation quite well and realized that partition would rid them of their major rival. Nurul Amin, who aspired to the premiership, calculated that the probability of success would be in his favour only if Bengal was divided. He won over Hamidul Huq Choudhry, a committed Greater Bengal supporter, with the offer of ministership in an east Bengal government, which he hoped to form.[98] However, the Khwaja coterie had become confused by Jinnah's support for the united Bengal plan. Nazimuddin vacillated, sometimes supporting separation and at other times stating that it would be a disaster.[99] It is possible that he approached Kiran Roy with identical constitutional proposals for a united Bengal on the condition that he talked to them and excluded Suhrawardy.[100] Akram Khan, solidly behind the idea of an *akhand* Pakistan, argued that an independent Bengal meant surrendering the principle of the two-nation theory[101] and was hostile to the idea of the Free State of Bengal. When power was transferred, Suhrawardy and Hashim entered the political wilderness; they were expelled from the party along with at least 50,000 of their supporters.[102] Nazimuddin became the Chief Minister of the East Bengal government and the portfolios were distributed among his supporters.

Squaring Bengali regional interests with Jinnah's all-India strategy became an intractable problem for the leader of the Bengal Muslim League. They had pursued the vision of an independent and sovereign Bengal and bent Jinnah's will to accommodate it, only to find that it was torpedoed by the Mahasabha and Congress. Partition resulted in the downfall of the Hashim-Suhrawardy group, the very people who had turned the Bengal Muslim League into a mass organization, and allowed the pro-Jinnah group to take over the party's leadership. Nazimuddin's legitimacy, however, came from the AIML leadership at the centre, not from the mass base located in east Bengal — a fact that acted as a major constraint on his leadership. He was more responsive to the mood of the high command than to the grass-roots of the party.

In the Punjab, only when the regionalists were expelled from the party did organizational work and propaganda activity get started. However, on its own the success of the League would have been limited, and events outside the province were to have an important influence. The turning point came after the failure of the Simla Conference, which resulted in mass desertion from the Unionist Party. The other vital factor was the *pirs* joining the League after Jinnah had reached an understanding with them. These two groups were to pull in local networks of *biraderi* and *pir-muridi* relations that turned the Muslim League into a mass organization. The League, however, was to discover that winning the Muslim vote was not going to put them into office, and this brought Punjabi regional interest into conflict with Jinnah's all-India strategy.

The expulsion of Khizr Hayat from the Muslim League was followed up with the reconstruction of the party organization and the expansion of the Muslim League Parliamentary Party through defections from the

Unionists. Though this work began to be taken seriously during the second half of 1944, it was only in the following year that the League could claim to be the party of the masses. The initial difficulty was that most of the district Leagues existed only on paper and were dominated by Khizr's supporters. Shaukat Hayat toured the districts organizing 'the preliminary scaffolding'. This process was helped by the Communist Party that had been supporting the Muslim League's attempt to overthrow the Unionists, and when Mumtaz Daultana became the League's secretary, they encouraged their members to join. Danial Latifi and Abdullah Malik resigned from the Communist Party and joined the League where they put their organizational skills to good use.[103]

By July 1945, the basic infrastructure was in place. Shaukat Hayat, Mumtaz Daultana, Raja Ghazanfar Ali Khan and Sayed Mustafa Shah Gilani undertook agitational tours in Ambala division, Multan district, Rawalpindi and Sargoda.[104] The membership figures, however, were poor and the AIML Inspection Committee estimated that there were only 150,000 members.[105] The hold of the Unionists over the countryside remained strong, and they continued to win by-elections in Hoshiarpur, Kanara and Jhajjar.

The Unionist government had become synonymous with inflation and wartime regulations, and was accused by the League of favouring non-Muslims. These negative factors, however, were insufficient to ensure the success of the League at the polls. To widen its appeal, a socialist manifesto was drawn up by the former Communist Party member, Danial Latifi. The manifesto's proposals for structural reforms gave an economic underpinning to community consciousness by presenting Pakistan as an Islamic utopia where the peasantry's position would be transformed. The juxtaposition of the spiritual and temporal character of Pakistan helped to legitimize and consolidate the position of the landlord leadership of the Muslim League.

However, victory in the elections was dependent on successfully wooing the rural élite. This was not achieved until after the collapse of the Simla Conference. Large scale defections took place as the Noons, Daultanas, Hayats, Pirachas and Dastis bolted from the Unionist stable, realizing that the days of inter-community collaboration had ended and that the future was with the Muslim League. Khizr's clansmen, Malik Sardar Noon, Mohammad Mumtaz Khan Tiwana and his parliamentary private secretary, Sayed Amjad Ali, joined the League. Cynically, Firoz Khan Noon openly admitted to Glancy 'that he did not believe in Pakistan' and wished 'that the term had never had been invented'.[106] Despite their motives, they used their *biraderi* network, influence over their tenants and wealth to win over voters for the League. Furthermore, Congress leaders such as Mian Iftikharuddin joined the Muslim League, bringing with them many nationalist Muslims.

Jinnah was warned by Afzal Husain Qadri that *maulvis* and *maulanas* alone were not adequate for a successful outcome in the elections. The *pirs* had to be won over, and their support was crucial for success in the rural areas. To win in the urban areas, he suggested that the students had to be better organized.[107] Only some *pirs* (such as the Gilanis of Multan and the Sayed of Shergarh) were members of the League. Most *pirs*, however, issued *fatwas* during the election campaign and the League's propaganda began to show a marked increase in religious symbolism. The slogan 'Islam in danger' and the notion that the Pakistan campaign was a *jihad* were evoked with greater frequency.[108] Pir Fazal Shah of Jalalpur threatened his audience that if they did not vote for the League they would become *kafirs* and would not be allowed funeral prayers.[109] The League was also supported by 5,000 student activists from Islamia College, Lahore, backed by contingents sent from Aligarh.[110] The combination of *pirs*, students, zemindars and political workers aroused an unexpected wave of support and drew in a varied cross-section of society. In Shergarh the organizer, Pir Sayed Ashaq Hussain, was responsible for a gathering consisting mainly of zemindars. While at Okara and Arifwala the notable feature was the large presence of communists and Congressmen, the meeting in Chichawanti drew mainly canal colonists.[111]

The Unionists did not surrender; they simply deployed the same tactics of using Islamic rhetoric to influence the voters. However, they were restrained by the knowledge that a ministry could only be formed with the cooperation of non-Muslims. Khizr introduced Islamic idioms in his speeches, formed an alliance with the Ahrar Party and enlisted *maulvis* from the Jamiat-ul-Ulama-i-Hind to bolster his campaign.[112] To counter the influence of the reformist *ulama*, the pro-League Jamiat-ul-Ulama-i-Islam held a conference in January 1946 in Lahore. Many Deobandi, Brelvi and Ahl-i-Hadith *ulama* attended, but Jinnah failed to win them over. The *khatib* of Badsahi Mosque, Maulana Ghulam Murshid, and the chief organizer of the pro-League *ulama* admitted that the most influential *ulama* were still loyal to the Jamiat-ul-Ulama-i-Hind. Consequently, Jinnah's emphasis on gaining the support of the *sajjada nashins* was a decisive counter to the reformist *ulama*, particularly in the rural areas where their influence was weak.[113] Only the *pirs* could influence the combination of *biraderi* and *sufi* networks in the countryside, and the Unionists only had some *pirs* (such as the Quershi *sajjada nashins*, the Pir of Makhad, the *sajjada nashin* of Pakpattan and the Gaddi Nashin of Sultan Bahu) on their side.[114]

The problems of the Unionists were compounded by the lack of any organization, and their dependence on the network of power and patronage in the countryside which was slipping through their fingers. Their biggest weakness was the lack of a rallying cry to counter the Pakistan slogan, which put them on the defensive. The Unionist Party's manifesto stressed economic achievement, provincial autonomy, complete independence and free education. In the face of the magnetic Pakistan slogan, which was offering something for everyone, the resistance of the Unionists collapsed. The elections resulted in a landslide victory for the Muslim League, which won all the urban seats and left only twenty rural seats to the Unionist Party.[115]

The formation of a ministry, however, eluded the Muslim League as their electoral campaign, particularly the Pakistan slogan, exacerbated communal tension, making it difficult to include non-Muslims in the cabinet. The statements of Firoz Khan Noon, Qaiyum Khan and Ghulam Mustafa Shah Gilani that Muslims should arm themselves and be prepared to fight a civil war to achieve Pakistan[116] killed the possibility of an agreement with the Akalis. Khizr was called to form a coalition, which infuriated the League, and their anger boiled over when the National Guards were banned in early 1947. The League launched a civil disobedience movement, confined mainly to the urban areas, particularly Lahore, to overthrow Khizr. The processions and rallies defying the government ban were spearheaded by students, party workers and women, which forced Khizr to throw in the towel.

The immediate reaction to Khizr's resignation was communal strife. The uncompromising position adopted by the League that Muslims had a right to form a government on their own pitchforked Hindus and Sikhs into launching a 'war against Pakistan'.[117] When Firoz Khan Noon did offer them five portfolios it was too late, and the Sikhs were unwilling to respond to these overtures. Their silence and the partition statement of the Congress ended all discussion at the provincial level.[118] No Muslim Leaguer favoured partition of the province, and the east Punjab members of the League protested to Jinnah over the division of the province.[119] However, Tara Singh had set his heart on Khalistan and argued that supporting partition was a bargaining counter to be used against the Muslim League. Jinnah had already conceded a Sikh homeland in Pakistan but, if pressure was sustained, he would grant Khalistan where Muslims in east and central Punjab would be held hostage for the welfare of Sikhs in west Punjab.[120] Later they realized that by demanding Khalistan they had brought forward the reality of partition and undermined Sikh solidarity.[121] For the Sikh plan to succeed, confidence between the communities had to be restored. Instead, what was already an electrifying situation became even more explosive when shock waves from the Calcutta and Bihar riots hit the province. The communal situation became volatile when Sikh refugees from Hazara, victims of revenge attacks by

Black Mountain tribals, arrived in Rawalpindi.[119] The Sikhs began to prepare for civil war. Tara Singh's war fund target of fifty lakhs rupees was oversubscribed;[122] he received substantial amounts from Calcutta Marwaris[123] and military support from the Faridkot and Patiala states.[125] The whole province became a disturbed area with the Rashtriya Swayam Sewak Sangh, the National Guards and the Akali Fauj becoming involved in a spiralling cycle of terrorist activity[126] complemented by attacks from trans-border Pakhtuns and Dogra incursions from Jammu and Kashmir state. The orgy of violence triggered off total panic in the entire province forcing the mass migration of communities.

The ultimate contradiction of Muslim nationalism in the Punjab was that by exclusively mobilizing Muslims they could not form a government. It brought home the clash between regional interests influencing the Punjab League's leadership and the needs of the AIML at the centre. The single-minded determination to overthrow Khizr was the product of provincial ambitions. By ignoring the widening communal breach and the increasing hostility of the Sikhs, it precipitated the violence that made partition — the very thing they were against — inevitable.

The NWFP Muslim League was hopelessly divided and organizationally inactive. Its ability to form a ministry depended on the Congress members of the assembly remaining in jail and, once in power, it discredited itself with abuses of office. The League was unable to fulfil the basic functions of a political party, and its over dependence on aristocratic élites condemned it to defeat in the elections. In contradistinction, the Sarhad Congress was well-established and well-organized at the popular levels and Dr Khan's ministry had a better reputation for public welfare and administrative integrity. The AIML was forced to intervene, revamp the party and widen its popular base by excluding many of the old leadership and injecting fresh blood. However, even these drastic measures on their own could not assure an endorsement for Pakistan in the referendum.

The intra-party disputes within the League only added to Aurangzeb's difficulties and, like other provincial Leagues, it took the form of a struggle for power between the provincial party and the ministerial group. However, the personal enmity between Aurangzeb and Sadullah Khan, former President of the NWFP Muslim League, created organizational havoc and retarded the possibility of expanding the organization. Attempts by Sadullah to convene a session of the AIML in Peshawar, and to expose the damage that the provincial ministry had caused to the progress of the League, provoked a sharp riposte from the Chief Minister, and he deployed the police to harass him.[127] The confrontation between the ministry and the party organization reached a climax, in March 1945, when Sadullah with four supporters voted with the no-confidence motion that led to the downfall of Aurangzeb's ministry.[128] The AIML eventually responded to the rising number of complaints against the League ministry by despatching the Committee of Action to tour the province. It concluded that no party structure existed. In April 1945, Qazi Mohammad Isa dissolved the League; a year later he formed an Organizing Committee to restructure it, enrolled a large number of primary members and toured the districts.[129] However, Isa's co-opting of the ministerial group to the central advisory board intensified faction fighting. These groups struggled first for supremacy of the Organizing Committee that was running the League so that they would be well placed to capture the parliamentary board and influence the selection of candidates before the impending provincial elections. The ministerial group dominated the Selection Board and made partisan selections, nominating the rich and powerful in preference to dedicated party workers.[130] The candidates represented the wealthiest and the most aristocratic families in the province and could not compensate for the lack of organization. The problem was compounded by the dissipation of their meagre resources in fighting all the thirty-eight Muslim seats in the province. The League fought the elections on the single issue of Pakistan. To Aurangzeb, its essence meant the 'safeguarding of Muslims' interests at the centre' but he was exasperated by the party youth who believed the slogan to mean separation. More importantly, the slogan was unintelligible to most of the rural population who were unimpressed by the threat of Hindu domination.[131]

The League, however, was strengthened by elements that up to then had been outside the party. The defections of Qaiyum Khan, deputy leader of the Congress assembly group, and Samin Jan Khan brought organizational skills, which were now put to work for the League. The Sarhad Students' Federation was revived, a training camp at Charssada was established and reinforcements from Aligarh fortified their activities.[132] The students were complemented with *maulanas* belonging to the Jamiat-ul-Ulama-i-Islam who were invigorated by Maulana Thanvi's visit to Peshawar. However, the credit for popularizing the League goes to the Pir of Manki Sharif. He joined only after Jinnah had assured him that the *sharia* would be established in Pakistan.[133] He was responsible for winning over other *sajjada nashins*, such as the Pir of Zakori, the Pir of Wana, and the Pir of Ama Khel who exploited their *pir-muridi* network in favour of the League during the elections. The Pir of Manki Sharif was also responsible for taking the fight into the Peshawar area, the bastion of Ghaffar Khan, where he had a large number of followers. He also popularized Muslim nationalism in the tribal areas, where neither the League nor the Congress politicians were allowed to intervene.[134]

With the fall of Aurangzeb's ministry and the release of Congress assembly members, Dr Khan's return to office became irresistible. His tenure marked a sharp departure from the dubious practices of his predecessor. The formation of syndicates for the distribution of essential commodities won him support. The more positive image of the Congress ministry, combined with careful selection of only winnable seats and the support of the Ahrar's or the Jamiat-ul-Ulama-i-Sarhad's candidates where they stood a better chance, went in their favour. Once the differences with Ghaffar Khan were patched up, the Khudai Khidmatgars and the Congress toured the districts emphasizing their Pakhtun identity and anti-*khani* position and promised economic reforms. All this was well received.[135] Dr Khan led the Congress Party to a clear victory, winning thirty of the fifty seats in the assembly. However, a closer examination of the Muslim vote shows that the League was slightly ahead.[136] This was the base that the revitalized League used to launch Direct Action against Dr Khan. A forty-man Organizing Committee sent by the AIML superseded Qazi Isa's *ad hoc* committee and weeded out old party members, or else demoted them. Mian Ziauddin was sacked, and Aurangzeb Khan and Bakht Jamal Khan demoted and replaced by new leaders emerging from the party's rank; these were people such as Jalaluddin, ex-Congressmen such as Qaiyum Khan and a new generation of young men from the *khani* hierarchy, represented by Mohammad Ali Khan. The irony was that the tactics developed by the Congress were effectively used by the League in the civil disobedience movement with some new variations.[137]

After a couple of false starts, the Muslim League's Direct Action took off and became inextricably linked with communal violence. A council of war, consisting of Mian Mohammad Shah, Mian Abdul Shah, and Sher Bahadur Khan of Badrashi went underground and was assisted by the Pir of Manki Sharif and Major Khurshid Anwar, the head of the AIML National Guards. In the initial stages, the renunciation of titles, processions, meetings and *hartals*, accompanied by a membership drive, were quite effective and peaceful. Novel elements that were successfully used included Radio Azad Pakistan broadcasting in the vicinity of Peshawar, which transmitted the time and location of meetings and demonstrations. Also, women protestors, mainly from the Punjab, played a significant role by making it difficult for the ministry to resort to violent police action, and their restrained response encouraged other women to protest.[138] However, when communal reverberations detonated by the Great Calcutta Killing struck the region, extra-parliamentary action deteriorated into savagery. Medical missions returning from Bihar showed at meetings 'skulls and bloodstained pages of the *Quran*,' which stoked the fires of hatred. The deteriorating law and order situation was further exacerbated by the civil war conditions in the Punjab.[139] Communal violence was sporadic in the Peshawar and Hazara area but, in April 1947, Dera Ghazi Khan was sacked by rioters. The flow of non-Muslims out of the province triggered off retaliatory attacks. Dogra strikes against Muslims in Poonch and Sikh action in the Punjab polarized the Sarhad, resulting in further counter raids.[140]

A referendum was proposed by Lord Mountbatten and accepted by Nehru to the dismay of the Frontier Congress. The referendum undermined the position of the Frontier Congress and left it with no alternative strategy to resist Pakistan. Ghaffar Khan's response was that they should have the option to become independent, but this was rejected by all concerned. The Viceroy was against Pakhtunistan because it was not economically viable, and the League and the Congress were not prepared to set a precedent which the other provinces might follow. In reality, the Pakhtunistan slogan was raised to regroup support and as a negotiating posture vis-à-vis the League. As a rallying cry it made little headway in the face of the angst gripping the province. Communal violence had effectively depressed the significance of Pakhtun ethnicity, and Muslim consciousness had become more important. Ghaffar Khan also tried to extract concessions from the Muslim League. He was prepared to join the League and to accept the constitution of Pakistan if three conditions were met: the *sharia* would be introduced, no British officers would remain after independence, and Punjabis and Shiahs would not be allowed to dominate Pakhtuns. When this failed he told his supporters to wait for six months, anticipating that the Pir of Manki Sharif would leave the League when he realized that the *sharia* was not going to be implemented.[141]

The sudden collapse in the support for the NWFP Congress and the concomitant rise in the popularity of the League were due to events taking place outside the province. The communal violence sweeping across north India polarized the Sarhad, where previously communal issues had been subordinate to regional concerns. This fed into the League's civil disobedience campaign and led Mountbatten to believe that the province was becoming ungovernable, and that to pacify the area it had to be allowed to decide its future in a referendum.[142] However, the Congress' fear that India was becoming ungovernable led them to accept the principle of partition which was the death-knell for their supporters, particularly in Sarhad. The Red Shirts were rudderless. They raised the Pakhtunistan issue as a bargaining chip, but it could not prevent the eclipse of Pakhtun ethnicity by Muslim nationalism.

The Sind Muslim League was in worse shape than the party in the NWFP. Like its Sarhad counterpart, regional perspectives dominated the League. Its main concern was the politics of 'ins' and 'outs' that were grounded in agnatic and personal rivalries. These issues underpinned the friction between the party organization and the parliamentary wing, with the former attempting to bring League assembly members under its control. Jinnah tried several times to settle the differences but was eventually forced, just before the elections, to expel G.M. Sayed from the party. The act simply externalized the intra-party dispute, and Sayed opposed Hidayatullah in the elections with the blessing of the Congress.

Sayed's ambition was to win over the *haris* and turn the League into a mass organization and, for this end, was keen on agrarian and social welfare reforms. Reforms, however, were an anathema to Hidayatullah's government, which was dependent on the *mir* bloc in the assembly. Therefore, Sayed accused the assembly party of damaging the Muslim cause, which prompted a counter-accusation from Hidayatullah that he was trying to establish a Sayed Raj.[143] In April 1944, Sayed called on the ministers to resign after first taking control of the League Council and the Working Committee. The resolution was designed to test the assertion that parliamentary activities were subject to party control. The competition between the parliamentary group, led by Hidayatullah, Khuro and Yusaf Haroon, and the party organization, led by Sayed and Mohammad Hashim Gazdar, was underpinned by rivalry between the *mirs* and *sayeds*. The AIML Working Committee tried to put their heads together and effect a compromise to maintain the status quo.[144] However, the bitter dispute continued, and Hidayatullah again complained to Jinnah that Sayed was trying to dominate. Sayed had removed Yusuf Haroon from the secretaryship of the Muslim League and was now insisting that Sayed Mohammad Ali Shah should be made a minister. Hidayatullah was emphatic that he was not prepared 'to leave the selection of the candidates to the Assembly to Sayed's sweet will'.[145] Yusuf Haroon, Managing Director of the *Alwahid*, retaliated by using the paper to initiate personal attacks against Sayed and Gazdar and formed a parallel League. Sayed's opportunity to counter these moves came with the Shikarpur by-election, when he was able to reject Hidayatullah's son's candidature in favour of his nominee Ghulam Nabi Pathan. He was able to get the AIML to back his decision, and the League lost the seat to Moula Buksh, the brother of the murdered Allah Buksh.[146] The altercation continued, and this time Sayed colluded with Moula Buksh, Abdul Majid and Nichaldas to overthrow Hidayatullah's government. However, the premier, with the help of the Governor, was able to turn the tables against his adversaries and brought Moula Buksh into the government.[147] This led to a severe reprimand from Jinnah for contravening the principles of the League and a warning that if Moula Buksh did not join the party he would be dropped.[148] Ghulam Husain Hidayatullah was prepared to defy Jinnah and resign from the League, but he was related to the Haroons by marriage and they applied pressure on him through his wife and made him comply. Moula Buksh was unable to form a coalition, and Hidayatullah was recalled.[149]

The quarrels between the *sayeds* and the *mirs* increased as the elections approached. In August 1945, Jinnah was forced to go to Karachi and patch up the differences. The Muslim League's difficulties were temporarily sorted out and Jinnah handed out tickets, not based on loyalty but to candidates most likely to win.[150] However, when he departed, the Sind Parliamentary Board collapsed due to internecine quarrels and G.M. Sayed, by October, was openly defiant of the League high-command.[151] Jinnah threw his weight behind Hidayatullah, and Sayed was forced to resign from the Working Committee and the League.[152] His departure did not bring harmony. Khuro was also working against Hidayatullah, and the Talpurs enlisted the Khaksars to enhance their strength in the assembly. This state of affairs continued right down to the elections.[153] Furthermore, in Sind the League was not a mass phenomenon, and the crucial factor for success was the support of the rural élites and important *pirs*, such as the Pirs of Hala and Jhando. Winning over these bloc votes by any means was crucial. Candidates entertained rural notables lavishly, and it was notorious that their declared expenditure was a fraction of the actual cost.[154] The Governor, Dow, estimated that between fifty and one hundred lakh rupees were spent on the elections.[155]

The Congress was anxious to do well in the province, and planned to win most of the Hindu seats and reach a compromise with the Muslims. It was prepared to offer four portfolios (including the premiership) and four parliamentary secretaryships to Muslim members so as to establish a Congress-dominated coalition government.[156] G.M. Sayed, backed by the Congress and nationalist Muslims, claimed, at the time of the elections, that he supported Jinnah's Pakistan but opposed the Muslim League on local issues. The coalition won twenty-nine seats against the Muslim League's twenty-eight: the balance was fine but the League had won most of the Muslim votes.[157] The Governor, however, had made it clear to the Viceroy that he was not prepared to see a coalition government led by Sayed. He was convinced that it would lead to instability, and was worried that the loyalty of the predominantly Muslim police and services would become suspect if a Congress-led coalition was installed.[158] Instead, Hidayatullah, who managed to win the support of the European assembly-members, was tipped to form the ministry. The coalition, however, was not workable and elections were called.

The League was reorganized. In February 1946, Liaquat formed an Organizing Committee headed by Yusuf Haroon and Gazdar (who had deserted Sayed) that enrolled new members and scrutinized the election of office-bearers. Many from the opposition deserted. These included Nabi Buksh Bhutto, Pir Ali Shah and Rahim Buksh, the son of Allah Buksh Soomro. They were joined by students from Aligarh and the Punjab and the Gilani *pirs* of Multan in the election campaign.[159] The communal shock waves from Bombay and eastern India coincided with the election campaign, and the Muslim League's rhetoric shifted from being anti-Congress to unashamedly communal. A series of Bihar Day *hartals* in Karachi, Sukkur and Nawabshah and speeches emphasizing the Bihar atrocities resulted in deteriorating communal relations.[160] The non-Muslim population was on the verge of panic during the conflict in the Punjab, and two-way migration began with Biharis arriving and some Hindus leaving. With the convergence of all these factors, the Sayed-Congress coalition was routed in the elections. The Sind Progressive Muslim League (led by G.M. Sayed and Sheikh Abdul Majid Sindhi) fell back increasingly on Sindi ethnicity and anti-Punjabi and anti-Bihari rhetoric. They wanted Sind for Sindis, were against migration from Bihar, and were unwilling to be grouped with the Punjab unless the provinces were sovereign and had the right to secede.[161]

The League failed to become a mass organization in Sind. The fate of the elections was decided by the support of the landed, tribal and spiritual leaders who were able to deploy their traditional influence in favour of candidates. This explains how Sayed, with the backing of the Congress, was able to deny the League victory in the provincial elections. The stalemate, however, in the assembly led to another election in December 1946. This time the Congress' acceptance of partition and the deterioration in communal relations sealed the fate of their supporters in the province, and Sind joined Pakistan. Sayed, struggling to maintain a politically viable alternative, raised the issue of Sindi ethnicity as a rallying cry, but to little effect.

The political equilibrium was destabilized by the constitutional deadlock at the centre which followed the Simla Conference. The realization that the future was with Indian and Muslim nationalism made regionalism vulnerable to the onslaught of parties advocating alternative foci of central control. Muslim nationalism capitalized on the political uncertainties and won over many adherents from the provincial parties. An important factor that widened the League's arena of influence was the increased significance of economic nationalism. It opened channels of communication between the élites and the masses, drew in groups previously unaffected by Muslim nationalism and gathered them around the banner of Pakistan. Combined with the weakness of the Congress among the Muslims, partly due to the fact that many Congressmen had been incarcerated during the war, it gave the League too great a head start for them to catch up. All these factors combined to induce a widespread shift in Muslim support from regional parties and nationalist organization to the Muslim League.

For a brief moment Jinnah was able to achieve political unity, and he used this as the basis to extract the maximum constitutional concessions from the British and the Congress. However, the centralization process was weak and its frailty was at the root of ideological confusion. Jinnah's understanding of Pakistan changed because of pressures from within the party, and he had to accommodate these different interpretations so as to avoid a revolt against his leadership. The problem was compounded by the League's lack of strong party-structure to control and enforce discipline over the regional supporters. Jinnah's personal authority was of limited value in the periphery. The exceptions where the organization or Jinnah intervened successfully were in the NWFP and the expulsion of Khizr and Sayed. But the constructive ability of the AIML was non-existent, and once the opposition had been removed it was up to the provincial leaders to repair the damage and advance the cause of the party.

Moreover, the various sections of the orchestra that Jinnah conducted marched to their separate rhythms. In Bengal and the Punjab, strong regional interests paraded in the garb of Muslim nationalism. In Sarhad and Sind, the matter was complicated by the emergence of ethnicity as a counter to Pakistan. However, mass nationalism, constitutional negotiations and the Civil Disobedience Movement mounted by the League coalesced to create conditions for the communal fury that engulfed northern India. The angst drove the Muslim majority provinces into the arms of the League and the Congress demanded partition both for the country as a whole and in two Muslim majority provinces.

Consequently, Pakistan was defined by circumstances and not by design, and this fact was behind the many problems that the country faced after partition. There was no single interpretation of Pakistan held either by Jinnah or the Muslim majority provinces, the League had no significant party structure, and there were strong regional and ethnic forces located in the provinces. All these were to become the source of major problems after independence.

NOTES

1. Jinnah's address to the AIML Council Meeting, Lahore, 30 July 1944, in Pirzada, ed, *Foundation of Pakistan*, ii, p. 495.

2. Except for the Viceroy and the Commander-in-Chief of the army, it was intended to be an entirely Indian Council, with the important portfolios of the interior, finance and foreign affairs in Indian hands. P. Moon, ed, *Wavell: The Viceroy's Journal*, p. 120.

3. Khizr felt that the Punjab, which had remained steadfastly loyal, was being betrayed and passed over in favour of the Congress and the League. 'He said I was handing power over to the enemy, that my veto was "dead mutton", and prophesied chaos and disaster all round.' Ibid., p. 144.

4. Ibid., pp. 120, 141-50.

5. Wavell to Amery, 1 July 1946, *TP*, v, p. 1182.

6. NDC, CID, S 426 (Secret Punjab Fortnightly Report), second half of July 1945, p. 63.

7. Wavell to all Provincial Governors, 30 June 1945, *TP*, v, p. 1175. Casey to Wavell, 2 July 1945, *TP*, v, pp. 1177-80. Glancy to Wavell, 3 July 1945, *TP*, v, pp. 1195-96.

8. A.I. Singh, *The Origins of the Partition of India*, p. 125, fn. 134.
9. SHC, UP, iv, Khaliquzzaman to Jinnah, 23 July 1945. Cited in A. Jalal, *The Sole Spokesman*, p. 36, fn. 46. Some more extreme views even criticized Jinnah for being too soft, and felt that he should have boycotted the conference. QAA, SHC, Bengal iv/42, Raghib Ahsan to Jinnah, 29 June 1945.
10. P. Moon, ed, *Wavell: The Viceroy's Journal*, p. 144.
11. NDC, CID, S 413 (Punjab Police Secret Abstract of Intelligence), No. 32, Rich, 1 September 1945, p. 291. Ibid., No. 47, Bridgeman, 15 December 1945, p. 447. In true Punjabi tradition, many Unionist families had a foot in both camps. Ibid., No. 43, Dean, 17 November 1945, p. 401.
12. *Return Showing the Results of Elections to the Central Legislative Assembly and the Provincial Legislatures in 1945-46* (New Delhi, 1948), pp. 8, 55.
13. QAA, AIML 280/56, Resolution placed before the AIML Legislators' convention, 9 April 1946.
14. The only opposition came in the Subjects' Committee from Abul Hashim who protested that the Convention could not modify the Lahore Resolution. Jinnah's initial defence was that the reference to state was a typographical error, but when Hashim proved this to be incorrect by referring to the original minutes, Jinnah said, 'I do not want one Pakistan state but I want one Constituent Assembly for the Muslims of India.' When the resolution was presented to the Convention, Hashim absented himself, so avoiding the humiliation of being forced to propose the resolution in the open session. Abul Hashim, *In Retrospection*, pp. 109-10.
15. Note of Meeting between the Cabinet Delegation, Wavell and Suhrawardy, 8 April 1946, *TP*, vii, p. 163.
16. Note of Meeting between the Cabinet Delegation, Wavell and Hidayatullah, 4 April 1946, *TP*, vii, p. 126.
17. Note of Meeting between the Cabinet Delegation, Wavell and Dr Khan Sahib, 1 April 1946, *TP*, vii, p. 75.
18. Note of Meeting between the Cabinet Delegation, Wavell and Khizr Hyat (*sic*), 5 April 1946, *TP*, vii, p. 147.
19. A. Jalal, *The Sole Spokesman*, pp. 186-202.
20. The Muslim League ministers were not keen 'Pakistanis,' and were relieved that Bengal was not going to be partitioned. Record of Cabinet Delegation, Wavell and Burrows, 24 May 1946, *TP*, vii, p. 675. There was general relief with the Muslim League statement in the NWFP and Sind as well. Ibid., pp. 852, 872.
21. NAP, QAP, F 469/40, Nawab Yusaf to Jinnah, 7 May 1946.
22. A. Jalal, *The Sole Spokesman*, p. 202, fn. 81.
23. Jinnah to Wavell, 8 June 1946, *TP*, vii, p. 841.
24. Note by Major Watt, *TP*, vii, p. 684.
25. A. Jalal, *The Sole Spokesman*, p. 202, fn. 84.
26. The first thing is we have agreed to go into the Constituent Assembly and we have agreed to nothing else. What we do there, we are entirely and absolutely free to determine. We have committed ourselves to no single matter to anybody.

    'In regards [*sic*] to minorities, it is our problem and we shall no doubt, succeed in solving it. We accept no outside interference in it — and therefore, these two limiting factors [arrangement for minorities and an Anglo-Indian treaty] to the sovereignty of the Constituent Assembly are not accepted by us.'

'The big probability is from any approach to the question, there will be no grouping. Obviously Section A will decide against grouping. Speaking in betting language there was four to one chance of the North-West Frontier Province deciding against grouping. Then Group B will collapse. It is highly likely that Assam will decide against grouping with Bengal. I can say with every assurance and conviction that there is going to be finally no grouping there because Assam will not tolerate it under any circumstances whatever.' (Nehru's Press Statement, Bombay, 10 July 1946), in *Indian Annual Register*, 1946, xi, p. 146.

27. NAP, QAP, F 565/101, Mazhar Inam, Chairman of the Provisional Migration Committee to Jinnah, 12 November 1946. The decision to leave their ancestral homes and migrate was not an easy one. Even the most ardent Leaguers found sentimental and emotional reasons to be very influential in determining whether they would depart for Pakistan or not. Many luminaries of the League (such as the Nawab of Mahmudabad and Hasrat Mohani) stayed behind. The ultimate irony was that the staunchest and most committed members of Muslim nationalism found that Pakistan was a bitter-sweet pill which, in the end, could not protect their interests.

28. Liaquat said that if the Cabinet Mission Plan was renamed the Mountbatten Plan, 'psychologically he was sure that on both sides it would stand an incomparably better chance of being accepted than anything with the name "Cabinet Mission" attached to it.' Record of Interview between Mountbatten and Liaquat, 10 April 1947, *TP*, x, pp. 331-32.

29. Record of Interview between Mountbatten and Suhrawardy, 26 April 1947, *TP*, x, p. 448.

30. Minutes by Ismay and Mountbatten, 26 April 1947, *TP*, x, p. 450.

31. NAP, QAP F 458/75-79, Suhrawardy to Liaquat, 21 May 1947.

32. Statement made by Jinnah, 11 May 1947, *TP*, x, p. 777. India and Burma Committee, 26th meeting, 21 May 1947, *TP*, x, p. 921.

33. When he toured the Attock district, Daultana 'told the people in at least one village that if they could stick it out for a fortnight or three weeks, all proceedings against them would be withdrawn and the officials who have suppressed the disturbances would be given a hot time.' Jenkins to Mountbatten, 30 April 1947, *TP*, x, p. 506.

34. NDC, CID, S 415 (Punjab Police Secret Abstract of Intelligence), No. 24, Sutton, 14 June 1947, p. 307.

35. A. Jalal, 'Inheriting the Raj: Jinnah and the Governor-Generalship Issue,' *Modern Asian Studies*, 19, 1 (1985), pp. 43-49.

36. Chaudhri Mohammad Ali, *The Emergence of Pakistan* (New York, 1967), p. 84. General Mohammad Musa, *Jawan to General: Recollections of a Pakistani Soldier* (Karachi, 1984), pp. 65-68.

37. QAA, SHC, UP v/94, Mohammad Afzal Husain Qadri presenting draft Terms of Reference of the Education Committee of the AIML to Jinnah, 5 December 1943. Nawabzada Liaquat Ali Khan, *Muslim Educational Problems* (1st 1945, 2 ed., Lahore, 1952), pp. 25, 31-32.

38. Jinnah to Zahid Hussain, 5 December 1945, SHC, cited in M. Hasan, 'Nationalist and Separatist Trends in Aligarh,' p. 131, n. 97.

39. Jinnah to Ispahani, 3 October 1942, in Z.H. Zaidi, ed, *M.A. Jinnah*, pp. 305-6.

40. S.A. Kochanek, *Interest Groups and Development: Business and Politics in Pakistan* (Delhi, 1983), p. 21.

41. NAP, QAP F/56, AIML Fund, Statement for the period 27 May 1942 to 30 November 1945.
42. Hassan Ispahani to Jinnah, 3 September 1943, Z.H. Zaidi, ed, *M.A. Jinnah*, p. 369.
43. QAA, SHC, AIML 66, Haleem to Jinnah, 3 August 1944.
44. QAA, SHC, AIML 110, Haleem to Jinnah, 8 June 1945.
45. NAP, QAP, F1092/310-314, Haleem to Jinnah, 28 August 1945.
46. Chaudhri Mohammad Ali, *The Emergence of Pakistan*, p. 84.
47. QAA, SHC, UP, ii, The Muslim Staff, Indian Military Academy, Dehra Dun to Jinnah, 29 October 1946.
48. General Mohammad Musa, *Jawan to General*, pp. 65- 68.
49. The *pirs* of Taunsa in Dera Ghazi Khan district, Sial Sharif in Shahpur district, Jalapur in Jhelum district and Golra in Rawalpindi backed the League. David Gilmartin, 'Religious Leadership and the Pakistan Movement in the Punjab,' *Modern Asian Studies*, 13, 3 (1979), p. 512.
50. QAA, SHC, Bengal iv/18, Raghib Ahsan to Jinnah, 15 November 1944.
51. Abul Hashim, *In Retrospection*, pp. 39-40.
52. NAUS, RG 59, Box 4144, 790D.00/9-1250, Candreva to the Department of State, 12 September 1950.
53. Punjab Muslim League Manifesto, *Pakistan Times*, 8 August 1947.
54. Colvile to Wavell, 25 August 1945, *TP*, vi, pp. 94-95.
55. Jenkins to Mr Abell, 28 August 1945, *TP*, vi, pp. 155-57.
56. *Bombay Chronicle*, 12 September 1945.
57. *Return Showing the Results of Elections to the Central Legislative Assembly and the Provincial Legislatures in 1945-46* (New Delhi, 1948), p. 8.
58. *Bombay Chronicle*, 11 December 1945.
59. NDC, CID, S 395 (CID NWFP Peshawar), Report from Special Branch Lucknow, 28 February 1946, p. 30.
60. *Return Showing the Results of Elections to the Central Legislative Assembly and the Provincial Legislatures in 1945-46* (New Delhi, 1948), p. 55.
61. Nehru's press conference, Bombay, 10 July 1946, N.N. Mitra, ed, *Indian Annual Register, July-December 1946*, ii (Calcutta, 1946), pp. 145-47.
62. Congress Working Committee Resolution, 10 August 1946, *TP*, vii, pp. 217-18.
63. Record of Interview between Mountbatten and Sardar Patel, 12 April 1947, *TP*, x, p. 213.
64. Record of Interview between Mountbatten and Maulana Azad, 12 April 1947, *TP*, x, p. 215.
65. Nehru believed 'that partition now would anyhow bring East Bengal into Hindustan in a few years.' Mountbatten to Burrows, 16 May 1947, *TP*, x, pp. 849-50.
66. Abul Hashim, *In Retrospection*, pp. 89-90.
67. QAA, SHC, Bengal iii/95, Hassan Ispahani to Jinnah, 1 October 1945.
68. H. Rashid, *The Foreshadowing of Bangladesh*, pp. 199-204.
69. QAA, SHC, Bengal iii/95, Hassan Ispahani to Jinnah, 1 October 1945.
70. QAA, SHC, Bengal iii/14, Jinnah to Suhrawardy, 30 October 1945.
71. *Star of India*, 5 November 1945, cited in H. Rashid, *The Foreshadowing of Bangladesh*, p. 224.
72. NAP, QAP, F 52, Jinnah to BPML, 9 March 1946.
73. Abul Hashim, *In Retrospection*, p. 99.

74. QAA, SHC, Bengal iv/6, Jinnah to Akram Khan, 27 August 1945.
75. QAA, SHC, Bengal ii/6, Hafiz Moniruddin to Jinnah, 7 February 1946. SHC, Bengal ii/7, M.A. Bari to Jinnah, 7 February 1946.
76. H. Rashid, *The Foreshadowing of Bangladesh*, p. 206.
77. QAA, SHC, Bengal iii/15, Suhrawardy to Jinnah, 29 December 1945.
78. *Star of India*, 8 January 1946, cited in H. Rashid, *The Foreshadowing of Bangladesh*, p. 226.
79. Abul Hashim, *In Retrospection*, pp. 101-2.
80. H. Rashid, *The Foreshadowing of Bangladesh*, p. 227.
81. Ibid., pp. 213-14.
82. Huq envisaged Bengal being autonomous but not separate from India. *Bombay Chronicle*, 4 February 1943.
83. H. Rashid, *The Foreshadowing of Bangladesh*, pp. 228-29.
84. N.N. Mitra, ed, *Indian Annual Register, January-June 1946*, i (Calcutta, 1946), pp. 231-32.
85. A notional 'Hindu identity' was constructed and politicized, which promoted the assertion of Hindu superiority and the rejection of Muslim majority rule, Joya Chatterji, 'Communal Politics and the Partition of Bengal' (Cambridge Univ. Ph.D., 1990), p. 257.
86. Suranjan Das, *Communal Riots in Bengal, 1905-1947* (Delhi, 1991), pp. 160-66.
87. Interview with Hamidul Huq Choudhry, 9 September 1988.
88. Suranjan Das, *Communal Riots*, pp. 170-75, 192-95.
89. During the discussions for a united and independent Bengal, Mountbatten raised the objection to Suhrawardy that if Bengal was to become a socialist republic then that fate would debar its entry into the Commonwealth. Instead, he suggested that the description the Free State of Bengal would be adequate for the moment and later, when the constitution was formed, they could call themselves what they liked. Mountbatten to Burrows, 16 May 1947, *TP*, x, pp. 849-50. Burrows to Mountbatten, 19 May 1947, *TP*, x, pp. 903-4.
90. Burrows to Mountbatten, 28 May 1947, *TP*, x, pp. 1023-24.
91. Of the legislature's thirty members, sixteen were to be Muslims and fourteen to be non-Muslim. Burrows to Mountbatten, 19 May 1947, *TP*, x, pp. 905-6.
92. Gandhi to Sarat Bose, 8 June 1947, H.H. Rahman, ed, *History of the Bangladesh War of Independence*, i (Dhaka, 1982), p. 34. Sarat Bose was dropped by the Congress in 1947, alienated from his supporters, out of touch with his community, and was a leader without any following. Joya Chatterji, 'Communal Politics and the Partition of Bengal' (Cambridge Univ. Ph. D., 1990), p. 300.
93. NAP, QAP F 458/54-56, Suhrawardy to Jinnah, 20 February 1947.
94. Hashim was also a candidate for the office but Suhrawardy, along with Nazimuddin, threw his weight behind a Council Resolution asking Akram Khan not to resign.
95. H. Rashid, *The Foreshadowing of Bangladesh*, p. 270.
96. Ibid., pp. 299-300.
97. NAP, QAP F10/24-32, Memo from Calcutta District Muslim League, The Indian National Maritime Union, The Asansol Subdivision Muslim League to Jinnah, 31 May 1947.
98. Ibid.
99. Ibid.

100. Burrow to Mountbatten, 28 May 1947, *TP*, x, p. 1023.
101. NAP, QAP F 458/75-79, Suhrawardy to Liaquat Ali Khan, 21 May 1947.
102. The Bengal League's membership in 1944 was estimated at 550,000, and by 1947 the figure should have increased substantially. However, by 1949, membership had dropped to 500,000. The large fall, probably greater than 50,000, was due to attempts by the leadership to keep Suhrawardy and his supporters out of the party. NAUS, Microfilm on the Internal Affairs of Pakistan, Roll 1, 845F.00/3-549, Inaugural session of the Pakistan Muslim League, 19 February 1949.
103. NDC, CID, S 412 (Punjab Police Abstract of Intelligence), No. 12 Rich, 18 March 1944, p. 164. CID, S 412, No. 22 Rich, 1 July 1944, p. 359.
104. In Sheikhupura, the Nawab of Mamdot and others presided over a meeting of eight thousand persons, and in Multan fifteen thousand persons attended a League meeting. QAA, SHC, Punjab i/6, Report by Daultana on the activities of the Punjab Provincial Muslim League to the AIML Committee of Action, 28 July 1944.
105. QAA, AIML 201/8, Inspection Report No. 10 on the general administration of the PPML by Zakir Ali to the AIML Committee of Action, 26 February 1945.
106. I.A. Talbot, *Punjab and the Raj, 1849-1947*, pp. 200, 237, fn. 61.
107. QAA, SHC, UP v/100, Qadri to Jinnah, 9 August 1945.
108. NDC, CID, S 414 (Punjab Police Abstract of Intelligence), No. 4 Dean, 26 January 1946, p. 42.
109. NDC, CID, S 414 (Punjab Police Abstract of Intelligence), No. 5 Dean, 2 February 1946, p. 54.
110. Jinnah gave fifty thousand rupees to the students for their expenses. Ibid. NDC, CID, S 414 (Punjab Police Abstract of Intelligence), No. 7 Dean, 16 February 1946, p. 84.
111. QAA, SHC, Punjab i/30, The League Speakers' Partys [*sic*] Tour of Montgomery District, 10 January 1945.
112. NDC, CID, S 414 (Punjab Police Abstract of Intelligence), No. 5 Dean, 2 February 1946, p. 55.
113. D. Gilmartin, *Empire and Islam*, p. 215.
114. NDC, CID, S 414 (Punjab Police Abstract of Intelligence), No. 6 Dean, 9 February 1946, p. 68.
115. N.N. Mitra, ed, *Indian Annual Register, January-June 1946*, i (Calcutta, 1946), pp. 231-32.
116. NDC, CID S 414 (Punjab Police Abstract of Intelligence), No. 18 Dean, 4 May 1946, p. 220.
117. NDC, CID, S 415 (Punjab Police Abstract of Inteliıgence), No. 10 Dean, 8 March 1947, p. 105.
118. NDC, CID S 415 (Punjab Police Abstract of Intelligence), No. 11 Dean, 15 March 1947, p. 116. Firoz's offer was part of an intrigue to depose Mamdot from the presidentship of the party. Mamdot had failed to get elected from his estate in Ferozepur district, and if the Sikhs had accepted Firoz's offer, then the parliamentary leadership would have been snatched from Mamdot as he was not an assembly member. CID, S 415 (Punjab Police Abstract of Intelligence), No. 17 Sutton, 28 April 1947, p. 202.
119. NDC, CID, S 415 (Punjab Police Abstract of Intelligence), No. 24 Sutton, 14 June 1947, p. 310.
120. NDC, CID, S 415 (Punjab Police Abstract of Intelligence), No. 15 Sutton, 12 April 1947, p. 172.

121. NDC, CID, S 415 (Punjab Police Abstract of Intelligence), No. 26 Sutton, 28 June 1947, p. 337.
122. NDC, CID, S 414 (Punjab Police Abstract of Intelligence), No. 45 Dean, 23 November 1946, p. 542.
123. NDC, CID, S 415 (Punjab Police Abstract of Intelligence), No.21 Sutton, 24 May 1947, p. 261.
124. NDC, CID, S 415 (Punjab Police Abstract of Intelligence), No.14 Sutton, 5 April 1947, p. 155.
125. NDC, CID S 415 (Punjab Police Abstract of Intelligence), No. 33 Sutton, 16 August 1947, p. 413. Proceedings of the meeting of the Partition Council held on 10 July 1947, M.M. Sadullah, ed, *The Partition of the Punjab, 1947*, i (Lahore, 1983), p. 152.
126. NDC, CID, S 415 (Punjab Police Abstract of Intelligence), No. 23 Sutton, 7 June 1947, p. 290. CID, S 415 (Punjab Police Abstract of Intelligence), No. 33 Sutton, 16 August 1947, p. 413.
127. QAA, SHC, NWFP i/90, Asadul to Jinnah, 20 December 1945.
128. QAA, SHC, NWFP i/60, Sadullah Khan to the Committee of Action, 8 August 1945.
129. QAA, AIML 193/13, Proceedings of the Meeting of the Committee of Action, 11 April 1946.
130. QAA, SHC, NWFP i/90, Asadul to Jinnah, 20 December 1945.
131. Cunningham to Wavell, 27 February 1946, *TP*, vi, pp. 1085-86.
132. NDC, CID, S 406 (NWFP Police Abstract of Intelligence), No. 1 Mc Crea, 1 January 1946, p. 1.
133. Actually, Jinnah was ambiguous in his assurance to the Pir of Manki Sharif: he simply assured him that an overwhelmingly Muslim country could not formulate a constitution other than one which was based on 'Islamic ideals.' Jinnah to Pir Manki Sharif, 18 November 1945, in Sayed Wiqar Ali Shah Kaka Khel, 'Muslim League in the NWFP, 1936-1947' (Peshawar Univ. M.Phil. thesis, 1986), appendix 7.
134. NDC, CID, S 406 (NWFP Police Abstract of Intelligence), No. 47 Mc Crea, 19 November 1946, pp. 148-49.
135. Cunningham to Wavell, 27 February 1946, *TP*, vi, p. 1085. NDC, CID, S 395 (CID Peshawar), No. 45, 2 January 1946, p. 42. S. Rittenberg, Ethnicity, Nationalism and the Pakhtuns, pp. 195-96.
136. Cabinet Delegation to India, 13 March 1946, Election returns for Punjab, Sind, Assam and NWFP, *TP*, vi, pp. 1192-95. Ian Talbot, *Provincial Politics and the Pakistan Movement: The Growth of the Muslim League in the North West and North East India, 1937-47* (Karachi, 1988), p. 20.
137. S. Rittenberg, *Ethnicity, Nationalism and the Pakhtuns*, p. 176.
138. Ibid., p. 365, NDC, CID, S 407 (NWFP Police Abstract), No. 20 Mc Crea, 20 May 1947, p. 75.
139. NDC, CID, S 406 (NWFP Police Abstracts of Intelligence), No. 45 Mohammad Alam Khan, 5 November 1946, p. 140. CID, S 406 (NWFP Police Abstracts of Intelligence), No. 52 Mc Crea, 31 December 1946, p. 164.
140. NDC, CID, S 407 (NWFP Police Abstract of Intelligence), No. 1 Mc Crea, 7 January 1947, p. 1. CID, S 407, No. 16 Mc Crea, 22 April 1947, p. 57. CID, S 407, No. 36 Mc Crea, 9 September 1947, p. 36. The tribal areas were vocal advocates of Pakistan, and once the rioting began they became involved in raids against Hindus and Sikhs. The politicization of the tribes was the link between the partition riots and the Kashmir war.

The arrival of refugees from Poonch, combined with encouragement from the League leadership, led to the raid into the Kashmir valley which was treated as an extension of the fighting surrounding partition. CID, S 406 (NWFP Police Abstract of Intelligence), No. 42 Aslam Khan, 15 October 1946, p. 129. CID, S 407 (NWFP Police Abstract of Intelligence), No. 39, 15 October 1947, p. 133.

141. NDC, CID, S 396 (CID Peshawar), 26 June 1947, p. 9. CID, S 396 (CID Peshawar), 25 August 1947, p. 51.

142. Members of the administration were involved with the League, and the Governor, Olaf Caroe, turned a blind eye to their activities because he wanted Sarhad to join Pakistan. Hence the hostile reception Nehru received while visiting the province. This was mainly due to the activities of Iskander Mirza and the Pir of Manki Sharif who were rallying the tribesmen against the Congress while the Political Agents conveniently looked the other way. Wali Khan, *Facts are Facts: The Untold Story of India's Partition* (New Delhi, 1988), pp. 116-21.

143. QAA, SHC, Sind ii/38, Note by S.F. Kachhi, n.d. QAA, SHC, Sind ii/32, Hidayatullah to Jinnah, 24 October 1944.

144. QAA, SHC, Sind iii/67, Jinnah to Gazdar, 12 December 1944.

145. QAA, SHC, Sind ii/45, Hidayatullah to Jinnah, 1 November 1944.

146. QAA, SHC, Sind iv/4, Hidayatullah to Jinnah, 20 December 1944. SHC, Sind iv/10, G.M. Sayed to the Central Parliamentary Board, December 1944. SHC, Sind iv/27, Hidayatullah to Jinnah, 29 December 1944.

147. QAA, SHC, Sind v/27, Report in Brief, 28 February 1945. The Governor warned Moula Buksh that he would only call Hidayatullah to form a ministry. If he failed no one else would be asked and section 93 would be applied. Ibid.

148. QAA, SHC, Sind v/35, Jinnah to Hidayatullah, 3 March 1945.

149. IOR, Mss. Eur. E 372, Box 2 (Dow Collection), Dow to Wavell, 17 March 1945.

150. Ibid., Dow to Wavell, 20 September 1945.

151. Ibid., Dow to Wavell, 18 October 1945.

152. QAA, SHC, Sind vii/28, Abdul [*sic*] Rashid Arshad Makhdum to Jinnah, 26 December 1945.

153. QAA, SHC, Sind vii/36, Abdur Rashid Arshad Makhdum to Jinnah, 14 January 1946. SHC, Sind vii/68 letter to Jinnah, 14 August 1946.

154. IOR, Mss. Eur. E 372, Box 2 (Dow Collection), Dow to Wavell, 4 September 1945.

155. Ibid., Dow to Wavell, 5 October 1945.

156. Ibid., Dow to Wavell, 18 October 1945.

157. Cabinet Delegation to India, 13 March 1946, Election Returns for Punjab, Sind, Assam and NWFP, *TP*, vi, pp. 1192-95.

158. Minutes by Turnbull and Monceath, 7 September 1946, *TP*, viii, pp. 445-47.

159. Ian Talbot, *Provincial Politics and the Pakistan Movement*, p. 54.

160. NDC, CID, S 434 (Sind Police Secret Abstract), No. 37 Ghulam Kadir, 14 November 1946, p. 340. CID, S 434, No. 46 K.R. Eates, 16 November 1946, p. 431.

161. NDC, CID, S 434 (Sind Police Secret Abstract), No. 21 K.R. Eates, 25 May 1946, p. 193. CID, S 434, No. 51 Ghulam Kadir, 28 December 1946, p. 428.

4

PAKISTAN, 1947–53:
OPPOSITION TO CENTRALISM

Pakistan was defined territorially by the pulls and pressures of subcontinental politics during the last days of the Raj. It was in no sense a product of long-term historical developments. Consequently, there were difficulties, many of them unforeseen, confronting the Muslim League's efforts to establish its authority in the new state. There were many thorny problems that had to be solved if Pakistan was to emerge as a viable sovereign nation. The League now had to settle old unsolved questions that it had successfully evaded so far. It had to resolve the ideological confusion inherent in the very concept of Pakistan and harmonize the strong centrifugal currents in the provinces with the aims of the leadership. Simultaneously, it had to physically transport its organization to Karachi, set up a new government centre and stabilize the social, economic and political situation. The solution arrived at, partly through contingent circumstances and partly by design, was to adopt a centralized state structure.

There were several factors invigorating the efforts to centralize. One important determinant was the influence of partition on the nascent Pakistani state. Jinnah's assumption of the governor-generalship was to ensure that the sovereignty of Pakistan did not go by default. The tortuous negotiations over the division of assets and the conflict over Kashmir confirmed the correctness, at least in his eyes, of this decision. There were disputes over the division of the Government of India's cash balances, debts and immovable assets like the communication network, railways, defence and industrial installations. Unable to settle the differences,

Pakistan entered into several standstill agreements on customs and tariffs, import controls and inland trade, which remained intact until March 1948. The continuing economic integration with India undermined Pakistan's claim to sovereignty. Reinforcing the estrangement was the dispute over the division of the army. Pakistan received 36 per cent of the Indian army but was denied an equitable share of the equipment. The question of having a viable armed forces acquired new significance as the dispute over the princely states, particularly Kashmir, unfolded and Afghanistan refused to recognize the Durand Line. The dispute over assets and territory reinforced the perception that the establishment of a strong centre was crucial to Pakistan's survival as an independent state.[1]

The administrative chaos caused by the lack of infrastructure and basic equipment needed even to house the government in Karachi and enable it to function only served to reinforce the push for a strong centre.[2] This was another reason for Jinnah to assume the governor-generalship because he provided, in his person, a nucleus around which a central authority could be built to control the provinces and act as a focus for Muslim nationalism.

The anxiety over centralization, however, preceded partition. It reflected the weakness of the political leadership, especially in the areas encompassed by the new state. The establishment of a strong centre was their life-line for survival. The ramifications of partition did not generate, but merely enhanced, this concern. The Pakistan movement was a congeries of forces galvanized by the League's rivalry with the Congress. Their built-in contradictions and incompatibility inevitably resurfaced with a vengeance after partition. The problem was compounded by the fact that most of the leaders were Muhajirs, and had little electoral support in the country. Liaquat, himself, fell into this category: he was from the United Provinces but was nominated to represent a constituency from East Bengal in the Constituent Assembly. The All-India Muslim League, acutely aware of these handicaps, abandoned its position on a loose centre declared in the Lahore Resolution and pushed for the formation of a unitary structure before independence. In July 1947, Liaquat, at Jinnah's behest, prepared the blueprint for the establishment of a highly integrated state along the recommendations of the Rowlands Report on the Bengal Administration. The proposals followed the pattern of Whitehall and rejected the federal features formally adopted by the Indian government.[3]

Liaquat argued that the best way to unify the civil service was through the appointment of the Secretary General as the head of the Pakistan Administrative Service. He would oversee all the government departments, be responsible to the Prime Minister and advise him on senior appointments. In this way, cabinet policy could be implemented quickly and efficiently by a cohesive administration.[4] This suggestion, when carried out, transformed the hitherto segmented civil service by unifying it under the Secretary General, and made it independent of ministers. Chaudhri Mohammed Ali was nominated Secretary General, and given independent and direct access to the departmental files. He consolidated his authority by setting up, under his chairmanship, the Planning Committee, composed of secretaries from all the ministries. In reality the Committee was a parallel cabinet composed of and headed by bureaucrats. All important decisions were first reached there and then presented to the Cabinet for token approval.[5]

The other component of the state that the Jinnah group wanted to strengthen was the army. The immediate task was the reconstruction and re-equipment of the armed forces. However, with the conflict over Kashmir, these tasks were accompanied by the expansion of the army, resulting in the allocation of up to 70 per cent of the national budget on defence in the years 1947-50.[6] Jinnah envisaged that Pakistan required an army of 100,000 troops, complemented by an air force and navy of equivalent strength, to defend the country's territory.[7] But, more importantly, it would be the ultimate lever for enforcing the authority of the central government.

The centralizing process, however, suffered a major setback at this early stage when Jinnah died in September 1948. The one person who could have guided the Muslim League through the political mine-field and consolidated the leadership's position was gone. Undoubtedly, the chances of even Jinnah succeeding in establishing a unitary structure were slim. An important reason why the centralizing process met with so much resistance was the ethnic composition of the military-bureaucratic oligarchy. It did not reflect proportionately the ethnic diversities of Pakistan, and the process of centralization alienated those not represented adequately in its ranks. The two dominant groups were the Punjabis and Muhajirs, who were also the dominant element in Liaquat's cabinet. The top layer of the bureaucracy at the time of partition consisted of 133 Muslim Indian Civil Service/Indian Political Service officials who opted for Pakistan. Of these, only one was from Bengal[8] and the rest were mainly Muhajirs and Punjabis. Moreover, most of the powerful bureaucrats, such as the Secretary General, Chaudhri Mohammad Ali, and the Chief Secretary to the East Bengal Government, Aziz Ahmad, were Punjabis. The Secretary for Defence, Iskander Mirza, was the one exception. Similarly, the army was mainly recruited from the Punjab and the NWFP, with hardly any recruitment from Bengal, Sind and Baluchistan. The British recruiting policy was so narrow that 75 per cent of the Pakistan army came from three districts of the Punjab (Rawalpindi, Jhelum and Campbellpur) and from two districts of Sarhad (Mardan and Kohat).[9]

For the ruling group centralization became an urgent necessity, as challengers to the Muslim League had mushroomed at the all-Pakistan level. They threatened to steal the mantle of legitimacy by propagating populist alternatives. The knee-jerk response was to reject political plurality and drift towards a one-party state. The first manifestation of this process came with Jinnah's declaration of March 1948: 'Every Mussalman should come under the banner of the Muslim League, which is the custodian of Pakistan, and build it up and make it a great state before we think of parties amongst ourselves which may be formed on sound and healthy lines.'[10]

The movement away from political plurality was initially in reaction to the emergence of the language movement in East Bengal. However, the first target of Jinnah's wrath was the People's Organization which, within three months of its formation, had been summarily dealt with. It seems paradoxical that the state felt so threatened by the fledgling party and was constrained to react with such vehemence. However, Ghaffar Khan and Dr Khan commanded a substantial popular following in the NWFP. In recognition of this fact, the carrot and stick were used, unsuccessfully, to win them over. Both were asked privately and publicly to join the Muslim League by the League high command, and Mohammad Ali Jinnah even offered Dr Khan the governorship of the province if he joined.[11]

Instead, on 6 March 1948, Ghaffar Khan formed the All-Pakistan People's Party, later renamed the People's Organization. It was dominated by prominent pre-partition opponents of the League, and included G.M. Sayed and Abdul Majid Sindhi from Sind, Abdul Samad Khan Achakzai from Baluchistan and Sheikh Husamuddin of the Ahrars from the Punjab. Significantly, it was attended by five Congress members of the Constituent Assembly from East Bengal at its first convention in May. Clearly, the party had the potential of becoming a national opposition to the ruling party, with a presence in the assembly and enough cadres to make an impact on the streets as well. However, the People's Organizations' support for provincial autonomy, linguistic and cultural freedom, better relations with India and a mildly socialistic programme were too much for the League to stomach.[12]

Many in power were inclined to equate loyal political opposition with anti-Pakistani activity. *Dawn*, the semi-official paper of the government, contemptuously described the People's Organization as an attempt to reactivate the 'Indian Congress' fifth column',[13] and the Frontier government arrested Ghaffar Khan on charges of sedition. It was claimed that he, with the assistance of the Faqir of Ipi, intended to synchronize the destabilization of Sarhad province with the expected advance of the Indian army towards the region. This view was rejected by Z.A. Bokhari, Controller of Broadcasting, who said that there was no convincing evidence to indict Ghaffar Khan on treason charges, and that 'many small men' in the cabinet had acted for political and not security reasons.[14] The government was aware that the 'home front was cracking' and the emergence of an all-Pakistan opposition would only accelerate this process. Hence they selectively targeted the Red Shirts, the backbone of the fledgling party.[15]

The military-bureaucratic oligarchy's over-sensitivity to any opposition led them to react fiercely, even to the small left opposition. There was great trepidation in government circles that the newly formed Socialist Party and Communist Party of Pakistan[16] would link up with the anti-centre opposition.[17] Consequently, in the spring of 1948, when police action was taken against the agrarian agitation in the Frontier province, the socialists and communists were rounded up along with the Khudai Khidmatgars. However, what brought down the full wrath of the government on the Communist Party was the establishment of numerous front organizations that attracted prominent intellectuals. The CPP became so buoyed up by its success that it tried to convert its popularity into electoral success. However, not only did it fail to win a single seat in the Punjab provincial elections but, six months later, its star was on the wane due to its complicity in the Rawalpindi Conspiracy Case. The Communist leadership had been approached by Major General Akbar Khan, but they had postponed taking any action.[18] Their complicity gave Liaquat the pretext to initiate a witch hunt and pre-empt the emergence of a Communist-led opposition. The Communist network was smashed, and the entire Central Committee and the leadership of the Pakistan Trade Union Federation, Progressive Writers' Association, Hari Committee and Kisan Sabha were rounded up and arrested.[19]

In East Pakistan, the Communist Party was run from Calcutta and dominated by Hindus. It was mainly influential among the tribals on the Assam borders, the scheduled castes of Khulna and among organized labour and students in Dacca and Chittagong. Greater success, however, only came when they decided to cooperate with the Awami Muslim League on the language issue. This manoeuvre was responsible for the proliferation of front organizations, such as the Democratic Youth League, the Progressive Writers' Association, the East Pakistan Students' Federation and the Peace Committee. Of these organizations, the Youth League, led by Mahmud Ali and Oli Ahad, was most active among the students and academics of Dacca University who were in the vanguard of the language and anti-BPC movement.[20] Later, in 1952, another organization, the Ganatantri Dal, led by Mohammed Danesh and Mahmud Ali, was formed which allowed the non-Muslim cadre to participate directly in the anti-centre movement.

The League leadership's most serious challenge came from Shaheed Suhrawardy, who attempted to weld dissident Muslim Leaguers into an all-Pakistan opposition. It was patent that Liaquat and the Khwajas of Dacca recognized Suhrawardy's political acumen and sagacity and considered him a serious threat. On 3 June 1948, the Premier of East Bengal, Khwaja Nazimuddin, barred Suhrawardy's entry into the province. Next, in March 1949, his membership of the Constituent Assembly was cancelled, and in May he was expelled from the Muslim League. Suhrawardy was forced to settle in Karachi, and almost immediately began to work for the formation of an All-Pakistan opposition. The Civil Liberties Union and the Pakistan Democratic Party, both established in 1949, were dummy organizations floated to test the political waters.[21] The first serious political opportunity that came Suhrawardy's way was the intra-party dispute in the NWFP Muslim League, which led to the formation of the Awami League. The party was led by the Pir of Manki Sharif and the Khan of Lundkhwar, and was later joined by Pir Ilahi Buksh, the ex-premier of Sind. Suhrawardy's political association with the Awami League began when he joined in their press attacks against the Frontier Revenue Minister, Mian Jaffar Shah. However, Suhrawardy did not join the organization; instead he called his old Muslim League workers and colleagues in East Bengal to form the East Pakistan Awami Muslim League, under the leadership of Maulana Bhashani. To coordinate the provincial opposition, Suhrawardy formed the Pakistan Awami Muslim League in March 1950. Liaquat Ali Khan recognized the gravity of the situation and 'declared war' in October on the Awami League, derided the idea of a multi-party democracy and sought to legitimize his stance by claiming that Jinnah's statement of March 1948 was still pertinent.[22] The declaration was a tacit admission that the monopoly of the Muslim League was breaking up and the strongarm methods used to suppress the opposition were counterproductive.

Suhrawardy made the Punjab his stamping ground, where he was joined by Abdul Sattar Niazi, a member of the Punjab assembly, and Mahmuda Begum; the latter headed the women's section along with the wife of Pir Ilahi Buksh of Sind. The greatest support came from the refugee population of northern Punjab and Montgomery district, areas which Suhrawardy extensively toured. Despite his thorough and methodical organizational work, observers were sceptical about his chances of making any serious headway in Punjab politics.[23] Suhrawardy's ambitions, however, were given a boost when, in November 1950, the Nawab of Mamdot announced his resignation from the Muslim League and established the Jinnah Muslim League. The two parties merged on 25 January 1951 to form the Jinnah Awami Muslim League, and its organizing committee consisted of Suhrawardy, the Convenor, the Nawab of Mamdot, Abdul Bari, the Pir of Manki Sharif and Pir Ilahi Buksh. With this cobbled-together coalition, the JAML prepared for the provincial elections. It won thirty-two seats in the Punjab, but the success went mostly to Mamdot's supporters. In the NWFP, in the same year, the JAML won only four seats.[24]

Suhrawardy then concentrated on East Bengal and toured the province with the Pir of Manki Sharif and the Khan of Lundkhwar. Nurul Amin attempted to disrupt the tour with Muslim League demonstrations and, through the implementation of Section 144, tried to curb the right of assembly. These attempts to thwart the opposition were accompanied by a barrage of propaganda led by Nazimuddin, Ghulam Mohammed and Fatima Jinnah emphasizing unity through Islam and the menace of 'provincialism'.[25] None of these attempts succeeded in dampening Suhrawardy's popularity and, in March 1952, three independent members of the East Bengal Legislative Assembly formed the parliamentary wing of the Jinnah Awami Muslim League. In December that year, the East Pakistan Awami Muslim League affiliated with the JAML to become its most important section. The influence of East Bengal in the JAML increased with the departure of Mamdot in 1953, leaving the party with support in only the NWFP and Sind in West Pakistan. With the announcement of provincial elections for the following year, Suhrawardy increasingly became preoccupied with the politics of East Bengal.

The construction of a new centre in Karachi was inhibited by the lack of finance and a basic infrastructure, and foreign policy was seen as the way of providing the solution. It was hoped that by aligning Pakistan with the western alliance it would provide the investment needed to establish a strong centre. However, Pakistan's difficulties in developing a credible foreign policy became an impediment. From the outset, Jinnah was keen on establishing strong ties with the United States of America. However, his appeal for a $2,000,000,000 loan package to the United States was turned down.[26] The Truman administration was not prepared to assume direct responsibility for security in the subcontinent, and wanted to work through collaborators. It saw the Commonwealth as a suitable vehicle for furthering the USA's interests, and encouraged Britain to maintain an active presence in the region.[27] The Kashmir issue, however, bedevilled Pakistan's relations with Britain. The Pakistani establishment had been antagonized by the unwillingness of the C-in-C, General Gracey, to execute Jinnah's orders and send troops into Kashmir. Gracey finally agreed to take limited action when Indian troops advanced beyond Baramula, but ordered all British officers out of the combat zone and informed his opposite number, General Bucher, of the counter-move.[28] The result was that many in the army, particularly among the junior ranks, began to question the reliability of British officers, and argued that they could do without them.[29]

Consequently, Clement Attlee's repeated offers of an alliance were rejected because they did not include Kashmir. By 1951, Pakistan's opposition had softened slightly and Liaquat was willing to discuss defence without Kashmir on the agenda. However, he refused to commit any troops towards a regional alliance as long as the Kashmir problem was outstanding.[30] These obstacles to closer relations were compounded by Britain's refusal to sell weapons to Pakistan out of fear that such sales would jeopardize much larger defence contracts with India. There was also some irritation over the question of Pakistan's membership to the Commonwealth. It was prepared to leave the Commonwealth when constitutional adjustments were made allowing India to remain a member, despite it becoming a republic. The only thing that held her back was the realization that such a step would give India a free hand in influencing Britain.[31] The coolness in Anglo-Pakistan relations made Britain reluctant to include Pakistan in the Middle East Defence Organization, despite the eagerness of the USA. Pakistan could not see the value of an alliance if it did not enhance its security, especially *vis-à-vis* India. Britain's dilemma was that it could not simultaneously accommodate the conflicting interests and priorities of both India and Pakistan. The Commonwealth Relations Office correctly perceived that Karachi's hesitation concerning the pact was a negotiating ploy. If membership of the MEDO included military re-equipment, it would have changed Liaquat's tune, but at the unacceptable price of alienating New Delhi.[32]

In reaction to being orphaned by the West, Liaquat turned to a neutral, pan-Islamic and anti-colonial foreign policy, hoping to gain the support of the Arab states for Kashmir.[33] Despite the Foreign Minister, Zafrullah Khan's insistence that alignment with Muslim countries was the cornerstone of Pakistan's policy,[34] Liaquat made no genuine attempt to establish Pakistan's credentials as a neutral power. The pan-Islamic posturing was nothing more than a ruse to mollify internal opposition and lead Pakistan out of a tight corner. This policy was later enthusiastically embraced by Nazimuddin when he became Prime Minister, but nothing substantial emerged from this shift. Significantly for the ruling group, public opinion, especially in the Punjab, was building up in favour of withdrawal from the Commonwealth. Maulana Shabbir Usmani, the Sheikh-ul-Islam and the President of the Jamiat-ul-Ulama-i-Islam initiated a vociferous anti-Liaquat and anti-British campaign. They argued that Pakistan had to leave the Commonwealth because a Muslim state could invest sovereignty only in *Allah* and not in the King.[35] The press viewed Liaquat Ali as a 'tool' of the Anglo-American bloc, and this fact undermined his position in the Punjab at a critical time in the run-up to the provincial elections in 1951.[36] The opposition was fanned by Mian Iftikharuddin, Faiz Ahmad Faiz and Anis Hashmi who were vocal and persistent critics of government policy, especially in foreign affairs. The build-up of anti-western perceptions, fostered by religious as well as left opposition, was a major internal obstruction. This had to be neutralized before the government could make any move in the direction of a western alliance.

The Punjabi group backed Liaquat Ali's political solution for the formation of a centralized state. This option was accepted because neither the bureaucrats nor the army top brass felt confident enough to pursue any other alternative. The central plank of Liaquat's strategy was the establishment of a constitution to replace the Independence Act of 1947. Fortunately for those in favour of centralization, the cabinet as a whole was in agreement. They felt that some of the major problems (for instance, widening the support for the Muslim League's leadership, the refugee problem and increasing opposition to the government) could be tackled only if the centre assumed some of the powers vested in the provinces. However, the government's attempt to resolve the impasse brought it under fire from all quarters and fractured Pakistani nationalism. Pakistan as a territorial entity had been defined by partition, but two important questions remained unresolved — the position of Islam and regionalism. The proposed constitution attracted hostility from the *ulama*, who objected to the secular character of the state, and the regional elements who opposed the unitary features.[37] Liaquat's solution was to use Islam to widen the support base of the ruling group. He tried to do this by propounding that the Pakistan state would be built on Islamic principles.[38] This was not in contradiction to Jinnah's commitment to secularism and rejection of a state based on confessional faith.[39] Liaquat agreed on the secular approach, but used the term Islam and Islamic socialism rhetorically to describe a society based on social justice and equality.[40] His strategy, however, won him only a small measure of support among the plebeian populace, and this was offset by increasing the expectations of the religious groups.

Partition forced the religious parties to reconsider their old goals and project a new agenda. The religious groups, particularly those who had supported the AIML, had expected that Pakistan would lead to the establishment of the *sharia*. The Jamiat-ul-Ulama-i-Islam, Jamiat-ul-Ulama-i-Pakistan, Majlis-i-Ahrar-i-Pakistan, the Khaksars (now renamed the Islam League) and the Jamat-i-Islami championed the ideal of an Islamic state. The divines were led by Maulana Usmani, the most important *alim* in the ruling hierarchy. Liaquat's reaction was to try to hoodwink the religious opposition, and concede to their demands in appearance but not in substance. The premier called the Objective Resolution the embodiment of the Islamic principle, as it invested all authority in *Allah* and it was accepted by Usmani as a statement of good intent. It was 'nothing but a hoax and...its provisions...particularly those relating to fundamental rights, are directly opposed to the principles of an Islamic State.'[41] Liaquat, however, had misjudged the mood and depth of the opposition, and the publication of the Interim Report provoked a furious response from the *ulama* and Bengal. Khwaja Shahabuddin backed the *ulama's* criticism that the constitution should conform to the Koran and Sunna.[42] The Khwajas of *Ahsan Manzil* extensively patronized the *maulvis, pirs* and *maulanas* for political purposes and could not afford to antagonize them. The centre's nerve and determination remained unshaken, and Liaquat attempted to defuse the issue by appealing to the critics for constructive suggestions.

The premier, however, had not anticipated the arrival of Maulana Nadvi from the Nadwat-ul-Ulama of Lucknow. The latter was able to bring together the two rival groups led by Mufti Shafi and Intisham-ul-Huq into which the JUI had divided on Usmani's death. Despite his leaning towards the Deobandi school, he was accepted by the revivalist elements such as the Ahl-i-Hadith and Jamat-i-Islami as well, and thus he was able to hold a conference of the *ulama* under his presidentship in Karachi, in January 1951. But the refusal by the President of the Constituent Assembly, Tamizuddin, to submit a copy of the Board of Talimat's report gave Maudoodi the opportunity to dominate the proceedings. He had been writing copiously on the principles of an Islamic constitution, and his ideas were accepted by Nadvi and others. The twenty-two principles for the establishment of an Islamic state confounded Liaquat's expectation that the *ulama* were incapable of reaching any agreement. Despite their apparent concurrence on the fundamentals of an Islamic state, the Constitution Sub-committee stubbornly resisted incorporating any of these suggestions into their proposals. To avoid confrontation on this issue Liaquat was forced to delay the proceedings, and was assassinated before he could do anything.[43]

Liaquat's death marked a distinct change in the government's attitude to the religious opposition. Nazimuddin and his supporters in the Bengali cohort were much more sympathetic to the clerics' demands. He tried to remove the religious hurdle to the formulation of a constitution by making concessions that his 'secular'-minded predecessor had been unwilling to make. The Bengali group also included Abdul Rub Nishtar and Mahmud Hussain, and the common denominator which brought these elements together was their sympathy for the *ulama*. Beside their personal religiousness, Nishtar had scholarly interests in Islam, and the Khwaja group was close to the *maulanas* for political reasons.[44] Their ascendancy signalled a shift in leadership from the 'secular-minded' Punjabi cohort to the more conservative Bengali group in the cabinet, and resulted in some gains for the divines. These concessions included the provisions that only Muslims were qualified to be the Head of State, and that an advisory body of the *ulama* would be established to consider whether the laws already approved were compatible with the Koran and Sunna. The divines, however, were not interested in cosmetic changes and wanted a special five-man bench of clerics attached to the Supreme Court to vet laws.[45] They aspired to become the sole arbitrator of Islamic matters, but such a position was unacceptable to the government who saw its implications very clearly.

This basic disagreement as to who should decide what was Islamic was behind the anti-Ahmadiyya controversy that eclipsed the differences over the Final Report. Since 1949, the Ahrar had been hammering away at the Ahmadiyya issue so as to make a political comeback, and by 1952 the public began to respond. The *ulama* argued that the Ahmadiyyas were heretics and Zafrullah should be removed from the government. In May that year an anti-Ahmadiyya board was formed, headed by Maulana Nadvi and Sultan Ahmad of the Jamat-i-Islami. This was followed by two conferences, one held in May and the other in July, where the central issue discussed was that of getting the heterodox Ahmadiyyas declared as non-Muslim. With the Ahrar and the Jamat both vying for leadership of the movement, it forced Maudoodi to launch a direct action campaign, on 26 February 1953, which culminated in the declaration of martial law in Lahore.

Similarly, Liaquat's constitutional proposals aroused considerable opposition from the regional forces. The Interim Report recommended a bicameral system where the provincial delegates to the upper house would be equally represented and the lower house, it was assumed, would be elected on a population basis. The Interim Report left many questions unanswered, such as the size and composition of the lower house, because the recommendations of the Franchise and Judiciary Sub-Committee of the BPC had not been submitted. However, this did not prevent the eruption of the most vociferous anti-centre reaction in East Bengal. Two specific complaints were made in the constituent assembly: the centre was too strong, especially as the powers of the Head of State and the cabinet had been increased at the expense of the provincial chief ministers, and in the upper chamber East Bengal was reduced to a minority.[46] The agitations and protests generated by the Interim Report confused Karachi. The government felt unsure of how to handle the crisis. Liaquat was forced to visit the province to placate the widespread opposition to the proposed constitution, and when this failed he postponed discussion on the BPC Report. This was only a tactical withdrawal and hardly an indication that their demands would be accepted. Abdus Sattar Pirzada warned Bengalis in a radio broadcast that their demand for a majority in both houses of the proposed assembly would be opposed by the other provinces.[47] The premier steered around this highly contentious issue by proposing to the

Constituent Assembly the principle of parity between East and West Pakistan.[48]

The Final Report presented by Nazimuddin made small concessions to regional opposition. It accepted the principle of parity in both houses of parliament. The smaller provinces were given weightages at the expense of East Bengal and the Punjab, and both the houses had equal powers, except on the budget, money bills and votes of no-confidence, all of which were vested only in the lower house. Khwaja Nazimuddin stated that real power was vested in the lower house and the upper house had only a recommendatory role.[49] The Final Report, however, was a collection of compromises cobbled together by Nazimuddin that satisfied no one. It aggravated the internal tension in the Bengali coterie between those in the cabinet (such as Nazimuddin and Fazlur Rahman) and those based in East Bengal (such as Nurul Amin). This was because Nazimuddin refused to devolve the authority of the federal legislature and the executive to the provinces. He also refused to accept the demand for 'maximum autonomy' or the East Bengal Muslim League's call for decentralization regarding trade, communication and transport, and industrial development.[50] The Report infused the opposition in East Bengal with new purpose. The Dacca Bar Association appointed a sub-committee, which reacted strongly to the fact that the demand for greater provincial autonomy and the recognition of Bengali as a state language had not been incorporated. They accepted the principle of parity only in the upper chamber, insisted on representation based on population in the House of the People, disagreed with institutionalization of the '*mullahs*', and wanted that principal organs of the state (such as the Supreme Court and the upper house of the legislature) be established in East Pakistan.[51]

The Final Report also provoked alternative suggestions from West Pakistan. The confederation idea was supported by Mian Iftikharuddin and Shaukat Hayat of the Azad Party. They based their suggestion closely on the Lahore Resolution of 1940 and proposed two autonomous federal states. The East Pakistan state would have a unicameral legislature while the West Pakistan legislature would be bicameral, with its constituent units being autonomous. The two states would merge in a confederation that would be responsible for defence, foreign affairs and inter-zonal communication. The proposal began to gain support in East Bengal as it fitted in neatly with opposition's demands.[52] However, the whole concept was rejected by Nazimuddin who said that it would be the end of Pakistan.[53]

The sharpest reaction to these constitutional proposals came from the Punjab. The Nawab of Mamdot and the other opposition groups in the province called for the withdrawal of the Final Report. Mumtaz Daultana also rejected the constitutional proposals; Daultana regarded federalism as unsuitable and favoured a unitary structure instead. However, this provoked a strong reaction from Qaiyum Khan who, in a speech, rejected the notion that the Pakhtuns would surrender their provincial powers to any central authority. He argued that there should be no further delays or counter-proposals, and early elections should be held under the new constitution. The principle of parity between both wings had been achieved at the Punjab's expense, with Sarhad gaining from the arrangement.[54] Qaiyum's open defiance of the Punjab had the blessing of the Governor of the NWFP, Khwaja Shahabuddin, and Punjabis were horrified by the prospect of losing the political leadership of Pakistan.[55] When, in January 1953, Nazimuddin led a delegation to Lahore to win support for the Final Report, the leadership of the Punjab Muslim League stalled for time. The centre acquiesced and decided not to push the Report through the assembly, thinking that the two League Working Committees of the Punjab and East Bengal could sort out the matter. The breathing space allowed Daultana to tour the districts and unite the provincial League against Nazimuddin's constitution.[56]

However, the centralizing efforts were further hampered by the conflicts within the cabinet itself. Liaquat, supported by the Finance Minister, Ghulam Mohammad, and the Foreign Minister, Zafrullah Khan, was challenged by the Bengali group. The encounter was led by the Interior Minister, Khwaja Shahabuddin, backed by the Chief Minister of Bengal, Nurul Amin, actively aided by Altaf Husain, the editor of *Dawn*, and supported by dissident Punjabi politicians led by the Nawab of Mamdot. The critics also included advocates of an Islamic state and some politicians from Sarhad. The Bengali cohort was not antagonistic to the centralizing process initiated by Liaquat, but realized that there was little point in being in power in East Bengal while all the important decisions concerning the province were decided by the central government. The Jute Board controlled the East Bengal economy and the army and bureaucracy were the biggest employers, all of which were controlled by Karachi. The Bengalis simply wanted to take over the cabinet and redirect the centralizing policies in East Bengal's favour and, towards this end, were prepared to work with other dissident elements in the League.

In the first salvo, Khwaja Shahabuddin's supporters deployed Islamic and anti-Commonwealth rhetoric in their attempt to unseat the Prime Minister. The intrigue was brought into the open in May 1949 while Liaquat Ali Khan was attending the Commonwealth Prime Ministers' Conference in London. Originally, the campaign against the premier was restricted to a series of personal attacks against him and his wife in the Punjab's Urdu press. The opposition then stepped up its campaign by criticising the pro-Commonwealth policy of the Prime Minister and the pro-British camp in the country. *Dawn* persistently printed hostile articles on the Anglo-American bloc, and made veiled threats of seeking aid from 'other quarters'.[57] The ultimate aim of the cabal was to overthrow Liaquat Ali, but to do this successfully the pro-British lobby had to be silenced. The two immediate targets were the removal of the Governor of the Punjab, Sir Francis Mudie, and the closure of the *Civil and Military Gazette*. The *Gazette*, owned by the Hindu magnate, Seth Dalmia, was the largest English-language daily in Lahore and a solid supporter of Liaquat, the pro-Commonwealth policy of the government and Mudie. To silence the *Civil and Military Gazette*, Altaf Husain engineered the suspension of the paper. The matter was finally decided by the cabinet, with Shahabuddin mobilizing sufficient support to overrule the acting premier Ghulam Mohammad.[58] With the *Civil and Military Gazette* out of the way, Governor Mudie no longer had a shield to fend off his critics. The Oust Mudie Campaign was started by the Punjab Muslim League Working Committee, fanned by the *Nawa-i-Waqt* and financed by the Nawab of Mamdot.[59] Ostensibly, the campaign was against the Governor's unwillingness to cooperate with the Muslim League and rumours were spread suggesting that he wanted the return of Khizr Hayat and his Unionist followers. In reality these accusations were a stalking-horse. The actual inspiration was fear and avarice; Mudie's impartial investigation was leading to high places and many prominent persons and officials were apprehensive that they might be implicated.[60]

The Prime Minister became aware of the plot when Altaf Hussain stated in the presence of Hugh Stephenson, the United Kingdom Deputy High Commissioner, A.E. Smith, United Kingdom Information Officer, and Firoz Khan Noon that he would not rest until he 'got rid of Liaquat and his bunch of camp followers.' Firoz Khan Noon rushed to Karachi to meet Liaquat on his return from London and informed him of the intrigue. A London *Times'* article, possibly inspired by the United Kingdom High Commissioner, brought the cabal further out into the open.[61] When exposed, Altaf Hussain immediately capitulated and pledged his loyalty to Liaquat, but the premier's lack of control over the party meant that he could not immediately act against the other ringleaders. Khaliquzzaman, President of the Pakistan Muslim League, was a supporter of the 'stone statue,' the Nawab of Mamdot, and nominated him to the Working Committee in flagrant disregard of the Prime Minister's wishes. Therefore, to crack down on the cabal, Liaquat had to act against the President of the League as well. He engineered the resignation of Khaliquzzaman and inspired a press campaign that requested him (Liaquat) to fill the vacancy. The combination of government and party greatly strengthened Liaquat's hand in dealing with the recalcitrant politicians. It allowed the Prime Minister to replace the Nawab of Mamdot as the President of the Punjab Muslim League with his protégé Mumtaz Daultana. The manoeuvre isolated Shahabuddin, but he continued to oppose Liaquat by rallying his pro-Islamic state supporters against the interim constitution. His fate, however, had been decided and Liaquat prepared to send him to Cairo as ambassador.

Just before further action could be taken, Liaquat Ali Khan was assassinated on October 1951,[62] and his demise resulted in a shift in the cabinet. The important portfolios, such as defence, commerce and education, labour and interior were now in the hands of the Bengali cohort. Their preponderance was consolidated by Fazlur Rahman's takeover of economic affairs, which was separated from the Finance Ministry, and the retention of Shahabuddin as the Governor of the NWFP.[63] The Bengali group's primary interest was simply that their province should be better represented at the centre, and Nazimuddin felt that the best way to accomplish this goal was to quickly ratify the new constitution. With this object in view, he set about forging an alliance, consisting of the smaller provinces of West Pakistan and East Bengal, against the Punjab.[64]

Concurrent with the cabinet reshuffle that accompanied Nazimuddin's co-option as premier and there were certain ominous changes portending the events that followed. The elevation of Ghulam Mohammad, a Punjabi and ex-bureaucrat, to the post of Governor-General was to have important ramifications. His predecessor, Nazimuddin, had acted as a constitutional head of state, but Ghulam Mohammad was to break with this practice and aspired to dominate the cabinet. To succeed in this task, he first had to consolidate his domination over the bureaucracy, and he abolished the post of Secretary General and the parallel 'cabinet' that had acted as the nerve-centre of the civil service. Paradoxically, the return to a segmented bureaucracy meant that it was no longer possible to bypass ministers. The Governor-General now had to confront the cabinet and individual ministers to influence policy.[65] This task was made slightly easier when Chaudhri Mohammad Ali was nominated as Finance Minister strengthening the Punjabi lobby, which consisted of Zafrullah and Gurmani, in the cabinet.

The rivalry between the Bengali and Punjabi groups within the cabinet came to a head with the anti-Ahmadiyya crisis. By July 1952, the centre was convinced that Daultana was not suppressing the agitation but actually encouraging it.[66] However, two diametrically opposed solutions were proposed by the contending groups. Each option was partisan, designed to settle the crisis and deliver a knockout blow to the other side. The Bengali group led by Fazlur Rahman, the power behind the throne, was quite prepared to accommodate the *ulama's* demand. Nazimuddin agreed; he was sympathetic to the clerics and thought it a small price to pay for public tranquillity if the Ahmadiyya sect was declared a non-Muslim minority and Zafrullah dropped from the cabinet.[67] Ghulam Mohammad, who was not prepared to accept any of the sectarian demands of the *maulanas*, called for unity in the cabinet and blocked the Bengali group from carrying out its plan. Nazimuddin was warned that if Zafrullah was removed from the cabinet, Pakistan would not get a grain of wheat from America.[68] Ghulam Mohammad's actions were not based on principles or personal loyalty but on the knowledge that Zafrullah's departure would have been a body-blow to the Punjabi group. It would have tilted the balance of power in the cabinet even more in favour of the Bengali group.

Having blocked Fazlur Rahman's attempt to resolve the crisis, Ghulam Mohammad prepared to counterattack. The first step was to exacerbate the differences that already existed between the Chief Minister of the Punjab and the Prime Minister. These differences with Nazimuddin were exaggerated by the machinations of the Governor-General's supporters, notably Mushtaq Gurmani and Chaudhri Mohammad Ali, and they were able to turn Daultana against the Prime Minister.[69] The dispute on the question of parity only served to intesify Mumtaz Daultana's opposition. He retaliated by fanning the anti-Ahmadiyya agitation, using it as a battering ram against Karachi to overthrow Nazimuddin.[70] Once Daultana had turned against the Prime Minister, the supporters of Ghulam Mohammad attempted to discredit Fazlur Rahman. He was blamed by Ghulam Mohammad for a breakdown in public order. A student demonstration had led to rioting and several deaths and the army had to be called in.[71] This charge was added to the accusation that he was responsible for the economic ills of the country. Nazimuddin, however, refused to dismiss him. Instead, he took away the education portfolio and gave it to another supporter, Dr Mahmud Hussain.

The criticisms against the minister began to swing public opinion against Khwaja Nazimuddin's government, and Ghulam Mohammad increased the pressure on the Bengali group. The latter's action was premised on the knowledge that he had the full confidence of the army. The Commander-in-Chief, General Ayub Khan, stated as early as December 1952 that the army was ready to take-over if the situation became critical[72] and he was not prepared to see either the politicians, particularly Qaiyum Khan and Daultana, 'or the public run the country.'[73] Throughout the first quarter of 1953 the Governor-General made several unsuccessful attempts to persuade the Prime Minister to reconstitute the cabinet. He wanted a surgical action that would remove Fazlur Rahman, Abdul Rub Nishtar, Dr Mahmud Hussain and Abdus Sattar Pirzada from the cabinet and leave the pliable Nazimuddin in place as the nominal leader of the government. These changes were considered necessary by the Punjabi group if they were to make important amendments to the Basic Principles Committee Report. They were opposed to the *ulama's* role in the constitution, which was the immediate worry. The Punjabi cohort was concerned that legitimising them in a constitution with a Prime Minister, whose religious predilections was well known, would create a major stumbling block to any pro-western policy. The other bone of contention was the question of parity in the Final Report, which could possibly lead to Bengali domination. Certainly, this is how the Report was perceived by its opponents, who dubbed the constitutional proposal the Bengal-Peshawar Confederacy Report. The anti-Ahmadiyya agitation gave the Punjabi group a pretext to openly oppose the Final Report's concessions to the religious opposition and, consequently, delay the constitution.[74]

Nazimuddin's inability to defend his policies from the onslaught of the oligarchy so infuriated his own supporters that Fazlur Rahman, Nurul Amin and Altaf Hussain conspired unsuccessfully to remove him from office.[75] Despite their moves being blocked, they continued to castigate the Prime Minister in *Dawn* for not reconstituting the cabinet. In this respect, Fazlur Rahman's intention was similar to the Governor-General's in that he wanted to introduce fresh blood into the cabinet, but at his opponents' expense. Buffeted from all sides by opposing forces within the cabinet, Nazimuddin was unable to decide what to do. However, the paralysis in the decision-making process could not continue indefinitely, and events were beginning to overtake Nazimuddin. The anti-Ahmadiyya agitation had entered a violent phase and Nazimuddin convened a conference, consisting of the highest officials in the administration, on 26 February 1953. The Prime Minister's preferred options for defusing the agitation, such as sacrificing Zafrullah or convening a world conference of the *ulama* to decide the status of the Ahmadiyya community, were strongly resisted. The army was not prepared to see Zafrullah go. His departure would scuttle attempts to steer Pakistan into the US camp. Ghulam Ahmad, the Interior Secretary, urged that the Ahrars should be arrested. When Nazimuddin refused, Gurmani suggested that as law and order was a provincial subject, the provinces should deal with the matter, and this view was backed by Qaiyum Khan and Shahabuddin. This was also resisted by the premier who feared that such action would result in Karachi and the Punjab going up in flames.[76] However, the Ahrar's Direct Action led to disorder in the Punjab and threatened to become a full-scale popular rebellion against the provincial and central governments. Martial law was imposed in Lahore, allowing Ghulam Mohammad and his cohort to liquidate the religious opposition in Nazimuddin's name, he being the strongest sympathizer of the *ulama* in the government.[77] It also eliminated the last stronghold of anti-western resistance in West Pakistan and gave the military-bureaucratic oligarchy a free hand in directing Pakistan's foreign policy. Nazimuddin's conscience could not accept the crackdown. He offered to resign on 10 March, but the cabinet rejected his offer.[78]

A month before Nazimuddin's dismissal, Mirza was freely admitting to the British High Commissioner, Sir Gilbert Laithwaite, that placing a strong man in Lahore was not enough, but that the cabinet itself needed to be reconstituted. The Punjabi coterie was now no longer considering a minor reshuffle but a major purge. At a high-level conference in April 1953, the administration's anxieties over the degree of *'mullah'* influence in the constitution and the recent events in Karachi and Lahore were expressed.[79] The generals and Ghulam Mohammad, supported by Mian Aminuddin and Qaiyum Khan, led the opposition to 'institutionalizing' the *ulama*. Mirza described the manoeuvre as a 'fight to [the] finish' between the conservative and liberal elements.[80] The final assault was made by Ayub Khan, who argued for an immediate change of government if the army's confidence was to be maintained. Ghulam Mohammed obliged by dismissing Nazimuddin's cabinet on 17 April 1953.[81]

As expected, the greatest resistance to the establishment of a unitary structure came from the chief ministers. The premiers of the provinces enjoyed a great deal of autonomy and were unwilling to surrender their power to the centre, especially one that lacked cohesion. They commanded strong personal support independent of the President of the Muslim League and the premier. Only they controlled the League members of the provincial assemblies, nominated provincial representatives to the central legislature, and the Prime Minister's majority in the Constituent Assembly was subject to their goodwill. Karachi's only means of direct control was through PRODA regulation and the implementation of Governor's rule. These cumbersome instruments, in the absence of a constitution, were regularly employed by the governors, who personified the writ of the centre in the provinces. They allowed Karachi to reformulate political combinations, exclude recalcitrant individuals and generally strengthen the hand of the pro-centre elements in the provinces. The centre's hand was further reinforced by the combination of government and party which allowed Liaquat, as President of the party, to assert greater control over the rebellious provincial Muslim Leagues. By wearing both hats, he could dissolve ministries and provincial Leagues, call for elections and distribute tickets to his supporters in the provinces. In practice, however, the intervention by the centre in the provinces was fraught with difficulties and did not necessarily lead to the desired result.

Although the Punjabi group was the driving force behind the centralization process in Karachi, it was resisted by strong centrifugal forces located in Lahore. The Nawab of Mamdot, the premier of the Punjab, led the 'Punjab first' group in resisting Liaquat's cabinet. The centre's intervention over the refugee issue in the province was considered by the 'Punjab firsters' to be an attack against their provincial autonomy. By spring 1948, it was estimated that over 4,880,000 had crossed into west

Punjab from east Punjab.[82] The premier and the Federal Refugee Minister, Ghazanfar Ali Khan, were drawn in due to the international dimensions involving negotiations with India. Mamdot refused to respond to the directives of the central executive and resisted all directives from Karachi. His defiance gained him some kudos since he stood out as the man who defied the Quaid-i-Azad in favour of the Punjab's autonomy.[83] Mamdot was adamant that Karachi should not involve itself on this issue because his family, friends and supporters were cloaking venality in the demand for provincial rights. They had used the administration to obtain possession of evacuee property.[84] Mamdot's group was able to override the administration by acting as a *de facto* kitchen cabinet within the cabinet, but in doing so they made enemies. Mian Iftikharuddin's position as Refugee Minister was reduced to a sham, Mumtaz Daultana complained that Mamdot's 'shadow cabinet,' which included Hamid Nizami, editor of *Nawa-i-Waqt*, were countermanding his decisions,[85] and Francis Mudie despaired at the rampant corruption.[86]

Liaquat had to remove Mamdot if the centralizing process was to be successful in this crucial province. However, he lacked the means to intervene directly and interfered instead in the intra-party rivalry. He backed the attempt of his protégé, Daultana, to capture power. By the summer of 1948, Jinnah had lost confidence in Mamdot and asked him to step down in favour of Daultana. Instead of complying he shrewdly refused and, along with Shaukat, resigned from the cabinet. Daultana realized that without control of the Punjab Provincial League he would be a puppet in the hands of its President, Mamdot. He therefore challenged the premier for the presidency of the Provincial League and narrowly won the contest by eighteen votes in November 1948. From this position of strength he launched a two-pronged attack. A censure motion against Mamdot was instigated as a feint, while he persuaded Liaquat to promulgate Governor's rule. The assumption was that it would be easier for him to take over with the backing of Karachi.[87] But when news of Mumtaz's intrigue leaked out, it brought public censure, forcing the centre to dispatch Khaliquzzaman, the President of the APML, to investigate. The latter, however, was a known supporter of the 'stone statue,' and he forced Mumtaz Daultana to resign in spring 1949 and accept Mian Abdul Bari as President of the Punjab Muslim League.[88]

In order to aid Daultana and regain control of the APML, Liaquat 'combined' the government and party. Now both the national party and bureaucracy were deployed to make Daultana chief minister. His popularity was limited to the districts of Sargodha, Jhang and Mianwali which was not adequate for defeating Mamdot in a straight fight for the presidentship of the League. The balance was tipped in his favour by the judicious deployment of 'gifts, promises of patronage' and the application of pressure by Qurban Ali, the Inspector-General of CID, who was Mumtaz's 'strongman'.[89] This strategy first rewarded him with the recapture of the presidency of the League and cleared the way for him to fulfil his burning ambition of becoming the premier of the Punjab.

To ensure Daultana's victory in the 1951 provincial elections, Liaquat staked his prestige and actively canvassed for the Punjab Muslim League. The party's prospects were boosted by the Pakistan-India Trade Agreement, resulting in the resumption of trade and payments for many small businesses in the Punjab. Liaquat personally supervised the selection of candidates considering scrupulously their 'vote-getting strength' and 'amenability to party discipline.'[90] Daultana was also busy gathering support and promised something to everyone. On the one hand, he promised land reforms to get the backing of the peasantry, and simultaneously entered into complex alliances with the zemindars, such as the Daultana-Gilani pact. The Muslim League won the Punjab elections by a handsome margin, out distancing its nearest rival, the Jinnah Muslim League, by 108 seats.[91] It was as much a victory for the centre as it was for Daultana.

However, the assassination of Liaquat and the nomination of Nazimuddin as Prime Minister left Daultana in the unenviable position of being Liaquat's man, but without any support at the centre. This was a serious setback to Karachi's efforts at centralization. Daultana's troubles were compounded when, in an attempt to fulfil his electoral pledges to both the landlords and the peasantry, he produced a flawed piece of agrarian legislation that resulted in adverse reactions. The peasantry agitated for more radical reforms while the landlords began to use various pretexts to evict their tenants and suspend cultivation. By autumn 1952, the estimated land under cultivation had fallen by over 150,000 acres, precipitating a famine. The government was forced to introduce rationing, and it simultaneously initiated an ineffective procurement drive.[92] The shortages spread to the NWFP and Bahawalpur, and in Lahore it triggered off an *atta* riot.[93] Daultana became desperate and tried to extricate himself from the political mess. He saw the emergence of the anti-Ahmadiyya movement as a godsend, and unwisely used it to divert attention from the food shortages. Ibrahim Chisti, head of the Islamiat Department of the Punjab government, was instructed to surreptitiously fund the Majlis-i-Ahrar, while Mir Nur Ahmad, Director of Public Relations of the Punjab government, placed his printing facilities at their disposal.[94] The police were restrained by Daultana from taking action, and the ban against the agitation was not enforced in Multan for a month, which allowed it to become violent. When arrests (including 377 Muslim Leaguers) were made, the premier personally intervened to release the leaders.[95] Once the agitation gained momentum, Daultana shifted the onus of decision-making from

Lahore to Karachi by asking the centre to decide the issue. However, the anti-Ahmadiyya movement proved to be too volatile. It snowballed into a full-scale rebellion, forcing Daultana to take a firm stand.[96] The agitation exceeded the expectations of the Action Committee, mainly due to the discontent caused by the food shortages and the participation of the left, who wanted to remove the pro-western Zafrullah.[97] Finally the army declared martial law, and the efforts to restore law and order caused 1,000 casualties, not all fatal.[98] At this point Nazimuddin discovered the degree of Daultana's involvement, forced him to resign in disgrace and replaced him with his rival, Firoz Khan Noon.

In reaction to Karachi's intervention, the Jinnah Muslim League was formed to resist the efforts at imposing a central authority. The opposition, however, was not simply centrifugal in its implication, for it had the potential of emerging as an alternative focus of centralizing authority. Mamdot, along with Abdul Bari and Ghulam Nabi, resigned from the Punjab Muslim League, and on 1 November 1950 formed the Jinnah Muslim League. The formation of the new party was hotly debated by Mamdot's advisers. He was pushed by his supporters into leaving the League once they realized that they had little chance of being elected to the Punjab provincial assembly, since the allocation of tickets was controlled by Daultana-dominated Parliamentary Board. The Young Turks were untainted by the venality of the Mamdot ministry and contained popular elements able to win the support of some middle and lower classes. Those who drove Mamdot to withdraw from the League were the same group that urged him to align with Suhrawardy and, in January 1951, the two parties merged to form the Jinnah Awami Muslim League.[99] The new party's first test came with the Punjab elections of 1951. To improve their chances, they cooperated with the Azad Party and Jamat-i-Islami. Suhrawardy claimed that he had the support of Fatima Jinnah.[100] Despite their efforts, the party won only thirty-two seats that mainly went to Mamdot's supporters. The result showed the weakness of the opposition which was greatly aggravated when, in July 1953, Mamdot returned with nineteen followers to the Muslim League.

The other opposition party in the Punjab — the Azad Pakistan Party — was formed when Mian Iftikharuddin fell from grace. He and Shaukat Hayat were expelled from the Muslim League for their incessant criticism of the party in the Constituent Assembly. They were consistent opponents of the excessive centralization which was taking place at the time. In November 1950, after refusing to join Suhrawardy's Awami Muslim League, they formed the Azad Party together with Mahmud Ali Kasuri, Sheikh Mohammed Rashid and Khwaja Mohammed Afzal. The party's position on all major issues was identical with that of the communists. Both were against Liaquat's foreign policy, demanded greater provincial autonomy and wanted socialist economic reforms; but, on Kashmir, Iftikharuddin called for a 'people's revolution.'[101] Most of the communists and sympathizers joined the Azad Pakistan Party when the CPP was banned in 1951, which provided a safe haven for the left, allowing it to make a recovery. By 1952 the Peace Committee, the Democratic Students' Federation and the PWA became active again, and the Azad Party then tried to develop a base in East Bengal by establishing links with the Ganatantri Dal.

In the NWFP, Karachi's efforts to intervene in the province were counter-productive. The centre intervened in the internal affairs of the province almost immediately after partition by dismissing Dr Khan's cabinet and replacing it with a Muslim League government. Qaiyum Khan's ministry, consisting of himself and Khan Abbas Khan, attempted to establish a stable government but was confronted by three problems: the strength of the popular Khudai Khidmatgars, opposition within the party, and the emergence of the Awami Muslim League. Qaiyum, with the blessings of Jinnah, worked at undermining the Red Shirt opposition. He was able to pass the budget in the assembly by winning over supporters of the Khan brothers to the League benches. Mian Jaffar Shah, formerly Ghaffar Khan's principal aide, was elevated to the cabinet in return for crossing the floor with six Red Shirt delegates and joining the Muslim League.[102] By February 1948, only a hardcore of ten delegates, including the Khan brothers, remained on the opposition benches. By March, however, the repressive apparatus was deployed against Ghaffar Khan when he attempted to launch the People's Organization. Qaiyum claimed that Jinnah personally ordered the crackdown against Ghaffar Khan and, in connection with his arrest and the 'Hazara plot,' over 200 Khudai Khidmatgars were jailed. The arrests cut down the ranks of the Red Shirts in the assembly to four, and one of them, Khan Abdul Khan Swati, joined the Awami Muslim League. The use of the state apparatus against political opponents was so pervasive that 'Qayyumitis' infected even petty functionaries who acted harshly against any independent political behaviour.[103]

The removal of the Khan brothers had unforeseen implications for the centre. It allowed Qaiyum to establish an independent support base outside the assembly. He introduced a slimmed-down version of the Khudai Khidmatgars' reform programme, pushed ahead with the available funds, and implemented projects on an *ad hoc* basis. The result was advancement in rural electrification, sugar refining, tanning and elementary education. However, the core of the Red Shirt programme was land reform and the abolition of the *jagirdari* system, and its implementation infuriated the old guard in the League. In 1949, when the bill was introduced in the House, seven Leaguers who were *jagirdars* opposed the motion and entered the ranks of the opposition, but most of them were persuaded to eventually return.

Qaiyum's position became even stronger when, in early 1950, a bill was passed that brought the *auqaf* under the control of the provincial government. Regular salaries were fixed for the *maulanas*, and it was announced that in future only theological graduates would be appointed to any official post. The premier expected a public outcry, but took the risk knowing that it would be a popular move among the masses. There was no break in the ranks of the League and he was able to incorporate religion into the state apparatus in the name of social reform. With his increased authority, he was able to draft the *maulanas* and the religious endowments into the service of his political machine.[104] Most observers agreed that Qaiyum's government had gained significant support among the ordinary people of settled districts, endured in the tribal areas and lost ground among the landlords, the 'service families,' the small group of intellectuals and the divines.[105] It was, however, a short-lived success for the centrist Muslim League.

Abdul Qaiyum's personal popularity increased at the expense of Liaquat's and, as his own position improved, he deserted the centre. The first sign of him turning renegade came in 1948 when he tried to incorporate the tribal areas that were under the centre's control into the province. The tribesmen were then under his sway after he, along with Iskander Mirza, had rallied them (and, to a lesser extent, the inhabitants of the settled areas) to wage *jihad* in Kashmir. To strengthen his claim over the tribal areas, he tried to establish League branches but was thwarted by the Governor. Despite Qaiyum's persistence, the incorporation of these areas into the province was strongly resisted by the Frontier Governor, the central bureaucracy and the army generals. His activities were seen as meddling in a sensitive area, and his only success came when he incorporated the princely state of Amb.[106]

Centrism was further weakened by internal strife in the provincial League. Qaiyum's rise to power upset the old stalwarts in the League. Their displacement from influential positions in the party drove them into leading an internal revolt against him. The inclusion of ex-Red Shirt delegates to the assembly in the Muslim League shifted the balance of power away from the old guard and made the upstart Qaiyum the focus of the alliance. This was opposed by them, but Qaiyum persuaded Jinnah that the reward for defeating the Khudai Khidmatgars in the assembly would justify the risks involved. Thwarted, the old guard, led by Khan Ibrahim Khan of Jaghra and Mohammed Yusaf Khattak, turned their attention to the provincial League, Qaiyum's blind spot. Most of the reorganization and enrolment campaign was conducted by the Khan of Jaghra, who packed the party with their supporters. The Jaghra-Khattak group's position further improved when Yusaf Khattak was first nominated to the Central League Committee and later elected General Secretary of the Pakistan Muslim League. This gave Qaiyum's opponents direct access to the upper echelons of the government and a chance to secure the support of the centre. This was not very difficult. Qaiyum's abrasive and irreverent style had antagonized every elder statesman in Pakistan. He was not on friendly terms with the Governor-General, Nazimuddin, nor with a single member of the Federal Cabinet, except Liaquat. He had also managed to incur the personal hostility of every provincial Governor and most of the provincial politicians.[107]

The League leadership tried to exploit the divisions in the party and oust Qaiyum when, in 1951, he announced elections based on universal suffrage. The Khan of Jaghra was the figurehead of the opposition, with Yusaf Khattak the power behind the throne.[108] They had assembled a majority in the Provincial Muslim League Council and were ready to oust Qaiyum's nominee, Badshah Gul, and replace him with the Khan of Jaghra as President of the League.[109] Qaiyum's reaction was to mobilize the entire state machinery against his opponents, cajoling, coaxing and threatening them. Jalaluddin was weaned away from the Jaghra-Khattak group. The alliance tipped the scales in Qaiyum's favour, and he was elected President of the League with Jalaluddin as Vice-President.[110] In the next test of strength, the centrist League clashed openly with Qaiyum when he distributed tickets for the elections only to his supporters. This was overruled by the Central Parliamentary Board, of which Jaghra was a member, and out of the rejected nominations, six tickets were awarded to the Jaghra-Khattak group. Nine of the candidates rejected by the Board ran as independent candidates, tacitly supported by Qaiyum Khan; and seven of them (including the opponents of Jaghra and Khattak) were successful. The Muslim League won a landslide victory claiming sixty-seven seats out of the eighty-five, with thirteen of the independents also prepared to join the League. This left Jaghra and Khattak in the embarrassing position of being office-holders of the All-Pakistan Muslim League but lacking any local support.[111]

By opposing the Jaghra-Khattak faction, Qaiyum Khan had humiliated the League high command and got away with it. Khalilur Rahman, General Secretary of the Punjab Muslim League, summed up the centre's feelings: the province was far too sensitive an area bordering Afghanistan and Kashmir for Karachi to take strong action against Qaiyum and risk losing control of the province.[112] Qaiyum, emboldened by his success, allied himself with others who wanted to control the centre. The premier, Nazimuddin, gave Qaiyum a free hand at home so as to fashion the Peshawar-Dacca axis against the Punjabi cohort at the centre.[113] Consequently, when Ghulam Mohammed dismissed Nazimuddin, he offered

Qaiyum a position in the central cabinet in order to forestall a hostile response. The latter fell for this bait and ensured his own downfall, deserting his power base which he had built up so adroitly.

The intra-party disputes linked Sarhad politics with the emergence of an all-Pakistan opposition. When Jinnah offered Qaiyum the premiership, the Pir of Manki Sharif was offended at being passed over.[114] He formed a parallel League consisting of seven League members of the assembly. This survived until November 1949, when Liaquat ordered the reorganization of the party in the province. The ministerial group, represented by Badshah Gul, dominated the Organizing Committee and prevented the Pir and his supporters from rejoining the provincial League.[115] Thus the Pir of Manki Sharif and Khan Ghulam Mohammad, the Khan of Lundkhwar, together founded the Awami Muslim League, and they were later joined by the Pir of Zakori Sharif and others. Once he had been pushed out of the party, Qaiyum Khan turned the full force of the administration against them. By June 1949, the Pir was externed from the province, and nine Awami supporters (including Taj Ali Khan, ex-President of the Provincial Muslim League, and two former members of the provincial assembly) were in jail.[116] At this stage Suhrawardy joined the opposition, but the coalition was not strong enough to effectively challenge a Chief Minister armed to the teeth with executive powers, such as the Frontier Crimes' Regulation Act and the North West Province Public Safety Act. Suhrawardy, the Pir and the Khan of Lundkhwar were allowed only limited access to the province before the elections.[117] However, Suhrawardy's intervention began an association that culminated in the merger of their organization into the All-Pakistan Awami Muslim League.

The picture in Sind was similar. The League, with its policy of centralization, continually intervened in provincial affairs, provoking a strong backlash. Sindi politics were always fluid, but the intervention by Karachi exacerbated the situation and revived, unwittingly, the issue of regionalism and pushed it back into the centre stage. Ever since independence, resentment against the central government had been growing over such issues as the settlement of refugees and inadequate representation in the legislature and government. Of the sixty-nine members of the Constituent Assembly only four were from Sind, and the province went unrepresented in Liaquat Ali's cabinet. The underlying tension came to a head when the Chief Minister, Mohammad Ayub Khuro, clashed with Jinnah over the question of jurisdiction over Karachi. In the communal riots of January 1948, refugees and civil servants looted, attacked and even killed Sindi Hindus and Sikh refugees. The Sind government initiated steps to maintain law and order and investigated the incident. The riots highlighted the precarious condition and insecurity of the central government. It demonstrated that it had no juridical control over the capital and was dependent on the goodwill of the Sind government. As a result, the Federal government objected to the exercise of police authority against its secretariat, and retaliated. In February it amended the India Act of 1935, bringing the offence committed in Karachi under federal jurisdiction, and Khuro was sacked for his audacity in challenging Jinnah.[118] The centre followed up these actions by separating Karachi from Sind, placing the capital under its own control and replacing Sindi with Urdu as the language of administration in the province. These actions were strongly resented by Sindis, and provoked a revolt by the Sind League. This, in turn, led to the increase of anti-centre feelings fuelled by the fear that political and economic power was slipping out of local hands. This was reflected in the Sind Muslim League's resolution which demanded that at least 50 per cent of the province's import business should be in local hands and that the *waderas* should be fully protected.[119] The Premier, Pir Ilahi Buksh, issued statements designed to soothe public concern, but he himself was troubled by the centre's action. Jinnah tried to pacify the Sind League by urging them to seek financial compensation for the separation of Karachi but this fell short of their demand that a New Karachi should be established along the lines of New Delhi.[120]

The continued interference by the centre aggravated the tensions created by the failure to accommodate the provincial leadership. In June 1948, the League leadership instigated PRODA proceedings against Khuro, but he used local grievances against the centre as a launching pad for a political come-back. He presented himself as the champion of Sindi ethnicity and, backed by Yusaf Haroon, captured the leadership of the Sind Provincial Muslim League just before the special court of inquiry had reached a verdict. His victory, however, precipitated an indignant press reaction, which he shrewdly deflected by stepping down from the presidentship until the outcome of the proceedings against him were announced. The centre could not hide its intense distaste and disappointment when the PRODA proceedings were declared by the Sind High Court to be *ultra vires*, and they realized that they were unable to halt Khuro's return to power.[121]

Khuro's premiership, however, was marked by bitter in-fighting, and it eventually provided the central government with the opportunity to remove him. The Sind government split into two groups. Khuro's only support came from Sayed Miran Mohammed Shah, and he was opposed by Kazi Fazlullah, Mir Ghulam Ali Talpur and Ghulam Nabi Pathan. Despite being in a minority in the cabinet, he was able to maintain power due to his majority in the Sind League. However, a damaging cabinet dispute arose between the two groups, ostensibly over Khuro's interference in the departmental affairs of his ministers. Particular reference was made to his intervention in the murder investigation involving Sardar Khan, a member of the Sind assembly. He had overruled Kazi Fazlullah, the Home Minister, and was reported to have assisted in Sardar Khan's release on bail. Fazlullah used this as a pretext to lead a challenge against the Chief Minister. The attempt to oust Khuro produced a flurry of PRODA petitions and counter-petitions by all the parties concerned.[122] This allowed the Governor, Sheikh Din Mohammed, to demand the resignation of Khuro and Fazlullah while judicial proceedings were being initiated to examine the validity of the various PRODA petitions.

With Khuro out of the way, the fortunes of the League and its programme for centralization were temporarily revived. The Prime Minister, Khwaja Nazimuddin, threw his support behind Ghulam Ali Talpur hoping that he could lead a united Sind Provincial Muslim League into the elections. Nazimuddin backed Talpur's appointment as head of the caretaker government in return for his support for the Final Report. The Bengali group had the support of Bengal and the NWFP, but lacked the support of the Punjab, and sought the backing of Sind as a counter-weight.[123] However, the fly in the ointment was Khuro. He opposed the centre's nominee Ghulam Ali Talpur from assuming the presidentship of the Sind Muslim League and, when this failed, he advocated the imposition of Governor's rule. He patently felt that his chances of dominating the province would improve if his opponents did not control the reins of government, and did his best to create a chaotic situation. The Prime Minister reluctantly recommended the imposition of Section 92A in December 1952 when all attempts at a compromise solution to end the bickering failed.[124]

Later, in March 1953, Khuro was also removed by Nazimuddin from the presidentship of the Sind Provincial Muslim League. The former's immediate response was to challenge his removal and concurrently issue PRODA writs against Ghulam Ali Talpur, the leading candidate for the presidentship of the provincial League. By doing this he prevented Karachi's man from participating in the impending elections.[125] Relations between Nazimuddin and Khuro deteriorated still further. Khuro, in defiance of the premier, formed the Sind League and issued tickets for the elections to be held in the spring of 1953. Nazimuddin retaliated by recommending to the All-Pakistan Muslim League Working Committee that Khuro should be expelled from the party. In reply Khuro resorted to taking out a series of restraining orders against the Prime Minister from the Sind High Court. For the ruling group this unseemly squabble could not have happened at a worse moment, at a time when they were urging unity in the run-up to the elections.[126] The issue, however, became academic as Nazimuddin was summarily dismissed by Ghulam Mohammad and PRODA proceedings were instigated against Ayub Khuro.

The continuous intervention by the ruling group resulted in the emergence of an anti-centre opposition. The fragmented opposition attempted to exploit the internal strife of the Sind Muslim League. The Sind Awami Mahaz was a coalition of the Sind Jinnah Awami Muslim League, the Hari Committee and the Sind Awami Jamat, which was formed to contest the Sind elections. G.M. Sayed and Abdul Majid Sindhi were ardent Sindi nationalists, and the former became associated with left wing organizations, such as the Pakistan-Soviet Cultural Association (of which he was President), so as to further his anti-centre activities. Their main support was located in the *mofussil* areas. But, lacking organization and funds and subject to government harassment, they failed to make much headway. The party won seven seats in the elections. All were won by the Awami Jamat, but three of the successful candidates left the party. After the elections, Hyder Baksh Jatoi and Khan Mohammed Leghari withdrew the Hari Committee and the Jinnah Awami Muslim League respectively from the coalition.[127]

Karachi's efforts to impose central authority on the province were also responsible for the re-emergence of Bengali ethnicity. The centre's control of the economy and its inflexibility on the language and constitutional controversies became key issues in East Pakistan. The centre's policies on these questions eroded the credibility of the provincial Muslim League and acted as a catalyst for the centrifugal forces. However, unlike his counterparts in West Pakistan, the Chief Minister Nurul Amin did not want to break with the centre. Instead, he backed the Bengali group's unsuccessful attempts to take control of the administration in Karachi so that policies more palatable to the region could be implemented.

Partition brought East Bengal's economic life to a standstill. The East Bengal government was dealt a weak hand that it played badly. Khwaja Nazimuddin, the Chief Minister, was weak, indecisive and lacking in leadership qualities. He could not induce his cabinet to provide the investment funds necessary for rejuvenating the ailing economy, nor did he have any policy to attract foreign entrepreneurs. The provincial government's ineffectiveness was compounded by the fact that all financial and economic policy decisions were in the hands of Karachi. This was to remain a permanent headache for Dacca, even when Nazimuddin had been kicked upstairs.[128] The Jute Board, headed by Ghulam Farooq, Secretary for Industry, and including non-Bengalis such as M.A. Ispahani, literally ran the provincial economy, and was under the centre's direct control. It controlled transport and communications, and its recommendation on the jute acreage indirectly affected the acreage of the rice crop and consequently its price. When Nurul Amin protested to Farooq that his ministry had not been consulted on the jute policy, he was brusquely

informed that 'the Government of East Bengal had nothing to do with
it.'[129] Industrial planning was another contested area. It was a central
subject and Karachi refused Nurul Amin's government permission to
establish jute and paper mills, although jute exports were the biggest
earner of foreign exchange.[130]

With this millstone around the ministry's neck, it could not initiate any
policy to gain popularity. Instead, its unpopularity increased due to
Karachi's insistence that Urdu should be the only state language. The
Khwaja group's *ashraf* background made them naturally inclined to
support the centre's position on the language question. The ill-conceived
move, however, offended Bengalis and set them on the path of linguistic
nationalism. The prising apart of Bengali regionalism that up to now had
co-existed with Muslim nationalism, was to have very profound effects
in the long term. However, it would be simplistic to attribute this parting
of ways only to the pride and attachment of Bengalis to their literary and
cultural heritage. Underpinning the dispute was the competition for jobs
with non-Bengalis. The overwhelming number of employees in the
provincial government — particularly in the upper echelons but also in
the district administration, post offices and railroads — were from Bihar,
the United Provinces and the Punjab, as well as Urdu speaking groups
from Calcutta.[131] This fact deflated the expectation among the indigenous
population that the East Bengal government would provide them with
employment. The consequent resentment was inflamed by the attempt to
impose Urdu, as it would have prevented most aspiring Bengalis from
entering the public services by introducing a linguistic handicap.

Widespread opposition began to manifest itself almost as soon as plans
were drawn up to replace Bengali with Urdu in the schools of the province.
The Tamaddun Majlis, formed by members of Dacca University, spearheaded the language movement. It demanded that Bengali should be the
language of the provincial administration and courts, the medium of
instruction in schools and one of the official state languages alongside
Urdu.[132] On 1 March 1948, Nazimuddin capitulated to the opposition and
accepted the central demands of the State Language Action Committee.
This, however, was immediately repudiated by Jinnah, who unequivocal-
ly supported Urdu as the state language of Pakistan. He reiterated this
position on his visit to Dacca, which resulted in widespread protest. The
Language Action Committee submitted a memorandum to him demanding that Bengali should be one of the state languages.[133] The Muslim
League turned a deaf ear to the opposition, and Nazimuddin introduced a
watered down resolution in the provincial assembly, which made Bengali
a medium of instruction but not a state language.

The publication of the Interim Report only served to stoke the fires of
discontent. Divisions within the party emerged. Akram Khan, President

of the East Bengal Muslim League, issued secret instructions to his paper, *Azad*, to fight the constitutional proposals.[134] The issue receded into the background when Liaquat postponed discussion on the Interim Report, only to be revived by Nazimuddin's tactless statement. In a public speech in January 1952, the Prime Minister categorically asserted that Urdu would be the state language. Observers commented that Nazimuddin, for no practical reason, not only antagonized the audience with his declaration but rubbed salt into the wound. He delivered his speech in highly Persianized Urdu rather than in the 'street' language, and gratuitously pointed out the progress made in desanskritizing the Bengali language. Local politicians of all persuasions were appalled by the gaucheness of the speech, and it triggered off vocal protests. Nazimuddin was subject to intense criticism in all the newspapers; the student body unanimously went out on strike and Bhashani's call for all-party meetings drew support from pro-League intellectuals.[135]

Nurul Amin's government, confronted with an internal revolt as well as the deteriorating law and order situation, tottered. Tafazzal Ali and other members of Amin's cabinet were in touch with Fazlul Huq, and a straw poll showed that the latter's majority in the house was quickly evaporating. Nurul Amin was bitter that Karachi had 'hung him out as a punching bag on the language issue' and was, therefore, ready to resign. But Aziz Ahmad, the Chief Secretary, leading a group of officials, persuaded Amin that all would be lost if Fazlul Huq took over, and that they would resign if the ministry fell. Yusaf Ali Choudhury, General Secretary of the East Bengal Muslim League, threw his weight behind Aziz Ahmad by getting the Working Committee to endorse Nurul Amin's cabinet. Thus fortified, the premier prorogued the assembly and launched a determined crackdown. The opposition leadership, including five members of the provincial assembly (including Abul Hashim and Hamidul Huq Choudhry) were rounded up. The university was singled out for the most rigorous treatment. Students and lecturers were arrested and the offices of the Youth League and the Communist Party were raided.[136] Once the back of the opposition was broken, the government regained its confidence and reconvened the assembly. However, although most of the Muslim League assembly members who had resigned in the heat of the moment returned to the government benches, thirteen of the dissidents did not, and formed themselves into the Awami League bloc.[137] The provincial League was now only a party on paper with little grass-roots support, and it was further weakened by the factional rivalry between Nurul Amin and Yusaf Ali Choudhury, caused mainly by the latter's dismissal as General Secretary on charges of corruption.[138]

Karachi's inappropriate and insensitive attempts to incorporate East Bengal into a centralized framework triggered off violent opposition that favoured a weak centre and greater regional autonomy. Moreover, there were many who had been dissatisfied at the way they had been treated by the Muslim League. For, along with Suhrawardy and Abul Hashim, many thousands of supporters had been purged from the party. The President of the All-Pakistan Muslim League, Khaliquzzaman, admitted that membership could be enlarged quite easily, but was deliberately restricted so as to prevent members of the Suhrawardy and Mohammad Ali group from joining.[139] The opposition in Bengal had already demonstrated their strength by defeating the League candidate in the Tangail bye-election. On 23-24 June 1949 in Dacca, Raghib Ahsan presided over the meeting, which resulted in the establishment of the East Pakistan Awami Muslim League, with Maulana Bhashani as President, Ataur Rahman as Vice-President and Shamsul Huq as Secretary.

The Awami Muslim League created an array of organizations to maximize its influence. However, many of these, such as the East Pakistan Muslim Students' League, the East Pakistan Peace and Rehabilitation Committee, the East Pakistan Jute Traders' Association, the Pakistan Jute Federation, the Krishak Proja Samiti, and the Pakistan Railwaymen's League existed only on paper. Through these organizations and its newspaper *Insaf*, the Awami League hammered away at issues such as low jute prices, the Korean war and both the provincial and federal governments.[140] The Awami League, however, only became a major threat to the provincial government when it played a leading role in the language and anti-BPC agitation. It was the most organized party in East Bengal and, through Suhrawardy, it was the only one that attempted to become a national party. The Awami League also collaborated with Communist front organizations, such as the Democratic Youth League, the East Pakistan Students' Federation and the Peace Committee that worked mainly with students and intellectuals.[141] The Peace Committee was backed by Ataur Rahman, and the Democratic Confederation was also supported by the Awami League.[142] Consequently, many US embassy officials saw Suhrawardy as a 'fellow traveller.'

The other major actor in the anti-centre opposition was Fazlul Huq, whose oratorical panache stole the show. He used the agitation to refloat his political career, founded the Krishak Sramik Party and was joined by several politicians, including Yusaf Ali Choudhury. In reality, however, the party was a one-man show. It had no internal machinery, and no party officials were named until December 1953. The charismatic Fazlul Huq, despite being an octogenarian, had a formidable reputation, and now stood forth in his familiar role as a man of the people. The fact that he was the most effective public speaker in East Bengal compensated for the lack of party organization and catapulted him to the head of the anti-government agitation. Unlike the Awami League, the Krishak Sramik Party became associated with the religious groups.[143]

The opposition groups merged to form the rickety Jukta Front to present a combined opposition to the Muslim League. A single candidate was nominated to contest each constituency. The relevant negotiations presented no insurmountable difficulty. However, the rivalry over leadership between Bhashani, Suhrawardy and Huq created more serious problems. This dispute was eventually settled in Fazlul Huq's favour. The other area of friction within the Jukta Front was the question of working with the Communist Party. Fazlul Huq, supported by the Nizam-i-Islam Party,[144] the Khilafat-i-Rabani[145] and a group of Awami Leaguers, led by Abdus Salam Khan and Abdur Rashid Tarkabagish, opposed the inclusion of communists,[146] while Maulana Bhashani, Suhrawardy and Sheikh Mujibur Rahman favoured working with them. Under Huq's threat of setting up his own 'joint front,' Bhashani was forced to back down.[147]

One of the few areas on which there was an agreement, in principle, between the Punjabi and Bengali groups in the cabinet was on the question of establishing a unitary structure. The leadership, rather than trying to achieve their goals by establishing a broad consensus, concentrated on robust action against all potential opposition, particularly at the all-Pakistan level. It was equally harsh in quelling internal dissent within the provincial Leagues. They used administrative levers and instruments of sanction within the party to subdue recalcitrant chief ministers and replace them with pliant supporters. The frequent interventions, however, by the state institutions in the body politic retarded the emergence of an alternative leadership and fragmented the Muslim League into numerous opposition parties. Ultimately, this systematic destruction of the political fabric affected the balance of power between the two contending groups in the cabinet. It undermined the political base of the Bengali group and strengthened the hand of the military-bureaucratic oligarchy. Simultaneously, the centre's interference in civil society prepared the ground for the Governor-General's assault on parliamentary democracy itself.

Ghulam Mohammad's dismissal of Nazimuddin's cabinet was on the grounds that it had failed to deal with the serious law and order situation arising from the Punjab disturbances. However, it was only a pretext to justify the ejection of the Bengali cohort from power. Daultana's hand in the anti-Ahmadiyya agitation was known to the centre, but the responsibility for the breakdown in law and order was pinned on the premier and his supporters. The Punjabi group were concerned that their opponents in the cabinet would resolve the crisis with compromises which were highly prejudicial to their interests. Nazimuddin and his supporters had already disturbed the military-bureaucratic combine with the Final Report. It opened the possibility of Bengali domination by giving them an overriding influence in the all-important lower house. The Punjab was checkmated in both houses as Bengali representatives aligned with the minority provinces of western Pakistan.

Moreover, Ghulam Mohammed and his cohort were made even more anxious by the probability that Nazimuddin would reach a compromise with the *ulama* and thereby prevent Pakistan from joining the western alliance. After the rounding up of the communists, the divines alone were left to offer determined opposition to a pro-western foreign policy. They had great influence over Nazimuddin and were determined that he should pursue a pan-Islamic, neutral foreign policy more rigorously. The ambivalence of the Bengali coterie towards a pro-US foreign policy was apparent in their willingness to sacrifice Zafrullah to the wolves. These demands, together with the concessions to the divines already made in the Final Report, raised the possibility that they might acquire undue influence over government policy and stop Pakistan from aligning with the west. The military-bureaucratic oligarchy wanted to detach Nazimuddin and his supporters in the cabinet from the *ulama* by persuading him to violently suppress the anti-Ahmadiyya agitation. As a result, the last impediment to alignment with the west was removed and the only people who might have rallied to Nazimuddin support when he was dismissed were crushed in his name.

The emergence of Ghulam Mohammad's cohort as the new masters of Pakistan radically altered the political equilibrium. The strategies for creating a centralized structure were now firmly and exclusively under the control of the Punjabi-dominated military-bureaucratic combine. The political careers of Nazimuddin and his supporters were now doomed. The usurpers, however, had only limited political support in Lahore, and were surrounded by strong currents of anti-centre politics emanating from East Bengal, the NWFP and Sind. The political configuration established by Muslim nationalism was now being reformulated. As in the 1930s and early 1940s, Muslim politics were again marked by strong centrifugal tendencies. The Punjab, previously a major advocate of provincial autonomy, now emerged as the staunchest champion of a strong centre. However, a substantial opposition in the Punjab led by Daultana had to be won over to the view that their interests would be best protected by extra-constitutional strategies and not through parliamentary politics. Daultana wanted to capture political power, but the mandarins and the praetorian guard were working to strengthen the institutional structures at the expense of the political parties. In their lust for power, the Punjabi group destroyed the fragile unity established by Muslim nationalism and stoked the fires of discontent that generated strong centrifugal impulses in the provinces.

NOTES

1. A. Jalal, *The State of Martial Law*, pp. 26-31.
2. The Pakistan authorities were housed in 'tin shacks,' lacked skilled technical and experienced administrative personnel and operated without pens, paper, typewriters and telephones. Ibid., pp. 30-31.
3. NAP, QAP, F 10/51-54, 'The Organization of the Pakistan Government by Liaquat Ali Khan', 6 July 1947.
4. Ibid.
5. H. Alavi, 'Authoritarianism and Legitimation of State Power in Pakistan,' pp. 41-42.
6. *Pakistan Economic Survey, 1972-73* (Islamabad, 1973), statistical section, p. 114.
7. 'Pakistan's Request for US Material and Assistance to the State Department, October-November 1947,' in K. Arif, ed, *America-Pakistan Relations: Documents, i* (Lahore, 1984), p. 7.
8. R. Braibanti, *Research on the Bureaucracy of Pakistan* (Durham, 1966), p. 49.
9. S.P. Cohen, *The Pakistan Army* (Berkeley, 1984), pp. 44-57.
10. *Speeches by Quaid-i-Azam Mohammed Ali Jinnah, Governor-General of Pakistan* (Karachi, 1948), p. 68.
11. NAUS, Microfilm on Internal Affairs of Pakistan, Roll 1, 845F.00/4-3048, Alling to the Secretary of State, 30 April 1948 (hereafter Microfilm).
12. M.R. Afzal, *Political Parties in Pakistan, 1947-1958*, p. 91.
13. *Dawn*, 13 May 1948.
14. NAUS, Microfilm, Roll 1, 845F.00/7-2648, Lewis to the Secretary of the State, 26 July 1948. This view was given greater credence by the fact that G.M. Sayed was only confined to his home village of Sann and the Congress members remained free.
15. NAUS, Microfilm, Roll 1, 845F.00/6-2148, Cootes to the Secretary of State, 21 June 1948.
16. Two new left parties emerged shortly after partition: one was the Socialist Party, founded in 1947, led by Mohammed Yusaf and Mubarak Saghar, and the other was the Communist Party of Pakistan. Sajjad Zaheer, a member of the Communist Party of India's Central Committee from the United Provinces, was sent in 1948 to form the party which, by 1950, had approximately 300 members and sympathizers. PRO, DO35/2591, Appendix A, Report on Communist Activities in West Pakistan, January to June 1951. Ibid., Appendix AI, Chief Events in Past History of the CPP.
17. NAUS, Microfilm, Roll 1, 845F.00/7-2648, Lewis to the Secretary of State, 26 July 1948.
18. The plot was essentially an attempted coup d'état led principally by Major General Akbar Khan, Brigadier M.A. Latif and other officers who were dissatisfied with the government's policy on Kashmir. Akbar's wife, Nasim Akbar, an active member of the Peace Committee, persuaded him to widen the support for the coup d'état by including the CPP. Faiz Ahmad Faiz, Sajjad Zaheer and Mohammed Hussain Atta were the only members of the central committee who knew of the plot, and they had postponed taking any action. This interpretation of events is reinforced by the fact that most of the army officers and the East Pakistan Communist Party had no idea of the involvement of the CPP. PRO, DO35/2591, Communists in Pakistan, 14 July 1951. Ibid., Appendix A, Report on Communist Activities in West Pakistan, January to June 1951.

19. NAUS, RG 59, Box 4145, 790D.00/5-1251, Metcalf to the Department of State, 12 May 1951.
20. NAUS, RG 59, Box 4144, 790D.00/9-150, Withers to the Department of State, 1 September 1950.
21. NAUS, RG 59, Box 4144, 790D.00/4-2150, Preston to the Department of State, 21 April 1950.
22. NAUS, RG 59, Box 4145, 790D.00/10-1050, American Embassy, Karachi, to the Department of State, 10 October 1950.
23. NAUS, RG 59, Box 4144, 790D.00/4-2150, Preston to the Department of State, 21 April 1950.
24. *Dawn*, 30 March–3 April 1951.
25. M.R. Afzal, *Political Parties in Pakistan*, p. 100.
26. 'Memorandum of the Government of Pakistan to the US State Department on the requirement of financial and military assistance, October 1947,' in K. Arif, ed, *America-Pakistan Relations: Documents, i* (Lahore, 1984), p. 5.
27. H.W. Brands, 'India and Pakistan in American Strategic Planning, 1947-54: Commonwealth as Collaborators,' *Journal of Imperial and Commonwealth History*, 15, 1 October (1986), pp. 42-43.
28. PRO, DO 134/3, Brigadier Walker to Major General Ward, 30 July 1948. Ibid., telegram from Delhi to CRO, 28 July 1948.
29. Ibid., Mc Cullagh to Stevens, 18 July 1948.
30. PRO, FO 371/101198, Olver to Burrows, 20 March 1952.
31. I. Stephens, *Pakistan* (London, 1967), p. 217.
32. PRO, FO 371/101198, Norris to Bromley, 5 April 1952.
33. Ibid., Reeve to Scott, 27 December 1951.
34. Ibid., Note on Pakistan's Foreign Policy, 3 June 1952.
35. PRO, FO 371/7601, Minutes, 15 May 1949. *Sind Observer*, 6 May 1949.
36. NAUS, RG 59, Box 4145, 790D.00/1-451, Preston to Secretary of State, 4 January 1951.
37. NAUS, Microfilm, Roll 1, 845F.00/7-2648, Lewis to the Secretary of State, 26 July 1948.
38. *Pakistan News*, i, No. 30, 17 December 1948.
39. 'Inaugural Speech of Quaid-i-Azam in the Constituent Assembly,' G.W. Choudhury, ed, *Documents and Speeches on the Constitution of Pakistan* (Dacca, 1967), p. 21.
40. *Weekly Pakistan News*, i, No. 35, 19 February 1949.
41. *Report of the Court of Inquiry Constituted Under the Punjab Act II of 1954 to Enquire into the Punjab Disturbances of 1953* (Lahore, 1954), p. 203.
42. PRO, FO 371/84204, United Kingdom High Commission to CRO, 17 November 1950.
43. L. Binder, *Religion and Politics in Pakistan* (Berkeley, 1961), pp. 214-18.
44. PRO, DO 35/3185, Memo on the Mullahs and their Influence in Pakistan, 14 February 1951.
45. PRO, DO 35/5102B, extract from Pakistan opdom 3/53, 4 February 1953.
46. M.R. Afzal, *Political Parties in Pakistan*, p. 45.
47. NAUS, RG 59, Box 4145, 790D.00/1-2651, Withers to Department of State, 26 January 1951.
48. This climb-down merely maintained the prevailing status quo that had emerged after partition, with the nomination of at least eight non-Bengali delegates to represent East

Pakistan in the Constituent Assembly. Their presence had effectively reduced the majority of the Bengali representatives, and this was institutionalized with the parity proposal. M.H.R. Talukdar, ed, *Memoirs of Huseyn Shaheed Suhrawardy* (Dhaka, 1987), p. 79.

49. I. Rehman, *Public Opinion and Political Development in Pakistan, 1947-58* (Karachi, 1982), p. 48.

50. NAUS, RG 59, Box 4145, 790D.00/2-2752, Withers to the Department of State, 27 February 1952.

51. PRO, DO 35/5107B, Extract from Fortnightly Report No. 12 from the Deputy High Commissioner, 19 June 1952.

52. I. Rehman, *Public Opinion and Political Development in Pakistan*, pp. 53-54.

53. *Dawn*, 13 January 1953.

54. NAUS, RG 59, Box 4146, 790D.00/1-553, American Consulate, Lahore, to the Department of State, 5 January 1953.

55. NAUS, RG 59, Box 4146, 790D.00/1-1953, American Consulate, Lahore, to the Department of State, 19 January 1953.

56. PRO, DO 35/5107B, extract from Lahore Report 2/53, 30 January 1953. NAUS, RG 59, Box 4146, 790D.00/1-2653, American Consulate, Lahore, to the Department of State, 26 January 1953.

57. NAUS, Microfilm, Roll 1, 845F.00/5-2849, Newsom to the Department of State, 28 May 1949.

58. Altaf was able to plant an article in the paper which reported that Liaquat and Nehru had agreed in London to divide Kashmir along the existing cease-fire line and drop the idea of a plebiscite. On publication of the article, the editor of *Dawn* filed a complaint with the government for the confiscation of the *Gazette's* property and demanded that its presses be turned over to *Dawn* to be used for its Lahore edition. The view that the whole affair was engineered was strengthened by the revelation that Mahmood Haroon offered to buy both the Lahore and Karachi editions of the *Civil and Military Gazette* from Seth Dalmia ten days before the suspension order informing him that the paper was to be suspended. Ibid.

59. Ibid. IOR, Mss. Eur. F 164/49 (Mudie Collection), Mudie to Liaquat, 12 May 1949.

60. NAUS, Microfilm, Roll 1, 845F.00/5-2749, American Embassy, Karachi, to the Secretary of State, 27 May 1949. At least eighteen MLAs were considered corrupt and charges were prepared against Husain Iftikhar Khan, the ex-premier, Deputy Commissioner Hasan Akthar and Commissioner Khwaja Rahim. QAA, PC- ARN-4 (Abdur Rub Nishtar Collection), Mudie to Nishtar, 1 August 1949. Ibid., Mudie to Liaquat, 20 April 1949.

61. NAUS, Microfilm, Roll 1, 845F.00/5-2849, Newsom to the Department of State, 28 May 1949.

62. There was much speculation that Liaquat's assassination was hatched in high places, which continued despite an investigation by a Scotland Yard detective, who found no plot. However, the assassin, Said Akbar, was an employee of the NWFP government and had been used by Governor Chundrigar to spread anti-Afghan and pro-government propaganda among the tribes. He had tried to see Liaquat earlier, in Karachi, to complain that he had not been adequately rewarded for his services. The money found at his home, which had been attributed by the media to Afghanistan, was, in fact,

Pakistan government payments. PRO, FO 371/101219, Inspector-General Police, Grace, his views on Liaquat's assassination, 8 October 1952.

63. *Manchester Guardian*, 25 October 1951.

64. NAUS, RG 59, Box 4146, 790D.00/4-1653, Withers to the Department of State, 16 March 1953.

65. H. Alavi, 'Authoritarianism and Legitimation of State Power in Pakistan,' p. 43.

66. PRO, DO 35/5371, Hunt to Bottomely, 7 June 1954.

67. PRO, DO 35/5370, Keeble to Howes, 26 February 1953. Nazimuddin had already unsuccessfully tried to muzzle those newspapers that were hostile to the agitation, but was restrained from taking action by the persuasive and strong intervention of the bureaucracy. NAUS, RG 59, Box 4146, 790D.00/9-2752, Perkins to the Department of State, 27 September 1952.

68. PRO, DO 35/3185, UK High Commission to Pericvale Liesching, CRO, 9 August 1952. *Report of the Court of Inquiry Constituted Under the Punjab Act II of 1954 to Enquire into the Punjab Disturbances of 1953*, p. 296.

69. L. Ziring, 'The Failure of Democracy in Pakistan: East Pakistan and the Central Government, 1947-1958' (Columbia Univ. Ph.D. thesis, 1962), pp. 142-45.

70. PRO, DO 35/5370, Recent Disturbances in the Punjab, report by Laithwaite, 9 March 1953.

71. L. Ziring, 'The Failure of Democracy in Pakistan,' pp. 142-45.

72. NAUS, RG 59, Box 4146, 790D.00/12-2352, Memo of conversation between General M. Ayub Khan, C.-in-C., Pakistan Army, and Gibson, 23 December 1952.

73. NAUS, RG 59, Box 4146, 790D.00/2-1353, Memo of conversation between Ayub Khan and Raleigh Gibson, 13 February 1953.

74. PRO, DO 35/5107B, UK High Commission to CRO, 7 January 1953. DO 35/5300, Murray to Swinton (CRO), 12 January 1953.

75. NAUS, RG 59, Box 4146, 790D.00/2-1253, Withers to the Department of State, 12 February 1953.

76. PRO, DO 35/5370, Keeble to Howes (CRO), 26 February 1953. NAUS, RG, 59, Box 4146, 790D.00/4-1653, Emmerson to the Secretary of State, 16 April 1953.

77. PRO, DO 35/5106, U.K. High Commission to CRO, 18 April 1953.

78. PRO, DO 35/5370, Laithwaite to Liesching, CRO, 11 March 1953. Note of conversation with Zafrullah Khan, 10 March 1953.

79. PRO, DO 35/5370, Laithwaite to Liesching, CRO, 12 March 1953. Note of conversation with Iskander Mirza.

80. NAUS, RG 59, Box 4146, 790D.00/4-1653, Emmerson to the Secretary of State, 16 April 1953.

81. PRO, DO 35/5106, UK High Commission to CRO, 19 April 1953.

82. IOR, Mss. Eur. F 164/27 (Mudie Collection), Note on the Loss of Muslim Life Due to Disturbances in East Punjab and the States by Fazal-i-Ilahi, Superintendent of Refugee Census Operation.

83. IOR, Mss. Eur. F 164/51 (Mudie Collection), Mudie to the Governor-General, Nazimuddin, n.d.

84. The stakes were high as it was estimated that the non-Muslim population had left behind twenty-two to twenty-five lakh acres of agricultural land and about 50,779 houses in the towns. NAP, QAP, F/804, Note on Rehabilitation by the Minister for Refugees and Rehabilitation, Mian Iftikharuddin, to Jinnah, 9 November 1947.

85. NAUS, RG 59, Box 4144, 790D.00/9-1250, Candreva to the Department of State, 12 September 1950.
86. He was unable to effectively discipline officials such as Khwaja Abdur Rahim, Commissioner of Rawalpindi district and Kashmir Affairs and Hasan Akthar, District Commissioner of Montgomery district, who were hand in glove with the Chief Minister of Punjab. IOR, Mss. Eur. F 164/52 (Mudie Collection), Mudie to Nazimuddin, 31 January 1949.
87. NAUS, RG 59, Box 4144, 790D.00/9-1250, Candreva to the Department of State, 12 September 1950.
88. NAUS, Microfilm, Roll 1, 845F.00/3-1849, Doolittle to the Secretary of State, 18 March 1949.
89. NAUS, RG 59, Box 4144, 790D.00/9-1250, Candreva to the Department of State, 12 September 1950.
90. NAUS, RG 59, Box 4145, 790D.00/3-851, Perkins to the Department of State, 8 March 1951.
91. *Dawn*, 31 March 1951.
92. NAUS, RG 59, Box 4145, 790D.00/2-2152, American Consulate, Lahore, to the Department of State, 21 February 1952. Box 4146, 790D.00/9-1552, American Consulate, Lahore, to the Department of State, 15 September 1952. In Multan the shortfall was 60,000 tons, but Daultana refused to take action against hoarders and profiteers who were mainly his supporters. Ibid.
93. NAUS, RG 59, Box 4145, 790D.00/2-2752, American Consulate, Lahore, to the Department of State, 27 February 1952.
94. NAUS, RG 59, Box 4146, 790D.00/3-1753, Gibson to the Department of State, 17 March 1953.
95. NAUS, RG 59, Box 4146, 790D.00/8-3052, American Consulate, Lahore, to the Department of State, 30 August 1952.
96. Maulana Abdus Sattar Niazi barricaded himself in the Wazir Khan Mosque in the heart of the labyrinthine walled city of Lahore and led the plebeian population in turning it into a no-go area, an act reminiscent of the Shahidganj agitations of the 1930s.
97. NAUS, RG 59, Box 4146, 790D.00/2-2053, American Consulate, Lahore, to the Department of State, 20 February 1953.
98. PRO, DO 35/5370, Laithwaite to Liesching, CRO, 11 March 1953.
99. NAUS, RG 59, Box 4145, 790D.00/11-350, Preston to the Department of State, 3 November 1950.
100. NAUS, RG 59, Box 4145, 790D.00/2-951, American Consulate, Lahore, to the Department of State, 9 February 1951.
101. NAUS, RG 59, Box 4145, 790D.00/11-1650, Perkins to the Department of State, 16 November 1950.
102. NAUS, Microfilm, Roll 1, 845F.00/4-3048, Alling to the Secretary of State, 30 April 1948.
103. NAUS, RG 59, Box 4145, 790D.00/6-1451, Memo by Bowling on the internal political situation in the NWFP, 14 June 1951.
104. Ibid.
105. Ibid.
106. Ibid.
107. Ibid.

108. The driving force was Abdul Rub Nishtar, Governor of Punjab, with the tacit backing of I.I. Chundrigar, Governor of the NWFP. It was widely rumoured that Liaquat Ali Khan had also given his approval. Ibid.

109. It was planned that once the Khan of Jaghra was installed, the Pir of Manki Sharif would be invited to return to the fold and share power with the conspirators. Ibid.

110. Ibid.

111. NAUS, RG 59, Box 4145, 790D.00/12-1951, Perkins to the Department of State, 17 December 1951.

112. NAUS, RG 59, Box 4145, 790D.00/1-1452, Perkins to the Department of State, 14 January 1952.

113. NAUS, RG 59, Box 4146, 790D.00/1-553, American Embassy, Karachi, to the Department of State, 5 January 1953.

114. NAUS, Microfilm, Roll 1, 845F.00/7-1149, Wolf to the Secretary of State, 11 July 1949. The Pir of Manki Sharif, whose crucial role in the plebiscite in 1947 was an acknowledged fact, was at the height of his success and felt that he could use his prestige to manipulate the ministry from outside. However, Qaiyum pulled the rug from under him by sending tribal *laskers* into Kashmir. The Pir of Manki Sharif, in his fury, attempted unsuccessfully to halt the flow of tribesmen, egged on by the vision of booty, which greatly undermined his authority. NAUS, RG 59 Box 4145, 790D.00/6-1451, Memo by Bowling on the internal political situation in the NWFP, 14 June 1951.

115. NAUS, Microfilm, Roll 1, 845F.00/2-1849, Lewis to the Secretary of State, 18 February 1949.

116. NAUS, Microfilm, Roll 1, 845F.00/7-1149, Wolf to the Secretary of State, 11 July 1949.

117. NAUS, RG 59, Box 4145, 790D.00/12-1951, Perkins to the Department of State, 17 December 1951. Moreover, thirty-one nomination papers, including those of the Pir of Manki Sharif and Zakori Sharif, the Khan of Lundkhwar and Fazal Huq Shaida, were rejected. Only Ahmed Gul, the brother of the Pir of Manki Sharif, Arbab Ataullah Khan, Asaf Khan Arbab and Samin Jan Khan were elected, all from the Peshawar district constituencies. Ibid.

118. L. Binder, *Religion and Politics in Pakistan*, pp. 131-33.

119. NAUS, Microfilm, Roll 1, 845F.00/7-1948, American Embassy, Karachi, to the Department of State, 19 July 1948.

120. NAUS, Microfilm, Roll 1, 845F.00/6-2548, Lewis to the Secretary of State, 25 June 1948.

121. NAUS, Microfilm, Roll 1, 845F.00/12-1348, Lewis to the Secretary of State, 13 December 1948.

122. It was claimed that Khuro was counting on the future influence that the defendant would have if he assumed the tribal leadership in place of the murdered man. NAUS, RG 59, Box 4145, 790D.00/12-1551, Perkins to the Department of State, 15 December 1951.

123. NAUS, RG 59, Box 4146, 790D.00/4-1653, American Embassy, Karachi, to the Department of State, 16 April 1953.

124. NAUS, RG 59, Box 4145, 790D.00/1-452, Perkins to the Department of State, 4 January 1952.

125. NAUS, RG 59, Box 4146, 790D.00/2-1253, Withers to the Department of State, 12 February 1953.

126. NAUS, RG 59, Box 4146, 790D.00/4-1653, American Embassy, Karachi, to the Department of State, 16 April 1953.
127. NAUS, RG 59, Box 3859, 790D.00/5-2155, Memo of Conversation with Sind Mahaz Leaders, 15 May 1955.
128. NAUS, Microfilm, Roll 1, 845F.00/3-648, Derry to the Secretary of State, 6 March 1948.
129. NAUS, RG 59, Box 4144, 790D.00/6-1250, A.M. Warren to the Department of State, 12 June 1950.
130. NAUS, RG 59, Box 4145, 790D.00/11-1850, Withers to the Department of State, 18 November 1950.
131. NAUS, RG 59, Box 4145, 790D.00/2-2752, Withers to the Department of State, 27 February 1952.
132. 'Tamaddun Majlis' Claim for Bengali as a State Language,' in H.H. Rahman, ed, *History of the Bangladesh War of Independence*, i, p. 49.
133. Memo to Jinnah from the State Language Action Committee on the Question of Language, 24 March 1948. Ibid., p. 89.
134. NAUS, RG 59, Box 4145, 790D.00/10-2050, American Consulate, Dacca, to the Department of State, 20 October 1950.
135. NAUS, RG 59, Box 4145, 790D.00/2-252, American Consulate, Dacca, to the Department of State, 2 February 1952.
136. NAUS, RG 59, Box 4145, 790D.00/2-2352, Wilson, American Consulate, Calcutta to the Department of State, 23 February 1952. Box 4145, 790D.00/3-152, Bowling to the Department of State, 1 March 1952.
137. NAUS, RG 59, Box 4145, 790D.00/3-2952, American Consulate, Dacca, to the Department of State, 29 March 1952.
138. NAUS, RG 59, Box 4147, 790D.00/5-1353, American Consulate, Dacca to the Department of State, 13 May 1953.
139. NAUS, Microfilm, Roll 1, 845F.00/3-549, American Embassy, Karachi, to the Department of State, 5 March 1949.
140. NAUS, RG 59, Box 4144, 790D.00/9-150, Withers to the Department of State, 1 September 1950. In its manifesto, the party called for the nationalization of key industries and the abolition of the zemindari system without compensation and declared that the country should be declared a 'socialist welfare republic.' NAUS, RG 59, Box 4147, 790D.00/1-854, Bream to the Department of State, 8 January 1954.
141. NAUS, RG 59, Box 4144, 790D.00/9-150, Withers to the Department of State, 1 September 1950.
142. PRO DO 35/2591, Note on Communist Activity in Pakistan, July 1951 to January 1952.
143. NAUS, RG 59, Box 4147, 790D.00/1-854, Bream to the Department of State, 8 January 1954.
144. Atahar Ali, the head of the Jamiat-i-Ulama-i-Islam, had been flirting with the United Front. His willingness to throw in his lot with the opposition split the organization, and a sizeable number of the *ulama*, led by Maulana Abdul Aziz and Maulana Din Mohammed, repudiated Atahar Ali, forcing him to form the Nizam-i-Islam Party. Later, a difference between Huq and Atahar Ali over the nomination of candidates emerged, leading the Nizam-i-Islam Party to withdraw and contest the elections separately. Ibid. NAUS, RG 59, Box 4147, 790D.00/3-154, Bream to the Department of State, 1 March 1954.

145. Abul Hashim formed the short-lived Khilafat-i-Rabani which, for a while, was associated with the Huq wing of the United Front. Differences with Huq led to the Khilafat-i-Rabani pulling out from the Front and fighting the elections independently. It did badly in the provincial elections, and Hashim drifted back into the Muslim League, accepting Mohammed Ali Bogra's invitation to all previous League members to return. NAUS, RG 59, Box 4147, 790D.00/1-854, Bream to the Department of State, 8 January 1954. Box 4147, 790D.00/3-154, Bream to the Department of State, 1 March 1954.

146. The Ganatantri Dal was excluded from participating in the elections and fought independently. However, it supported Jukta Front candidates in those constituencies which it was not contesting.

147. NAUS, Box 4147, 790D.00/3-154, Bream to the Department of State, 1 March 1954.

5

REGIONAL PULLS AND THE DISINTEGRATION OF CONSTITUTIONAL POLITICS, 1954–58

Ghulam Mohammad and his cohort were faced with an awkward question: How were they going to stabilize their open domination of Pakistan? Their victory was a hollow one, as they were confronted with a Constituent Assembly that they did not control. Without the support of the delegates from East Bengal and the minority provinces of western Pakistan, the military-bureaucratic oligarchy could not carry out the intended changes in government policies. As a sop to the Bengali opposition, Mohammad Ali Bogra was made Prime Minister but, on its own, this move was not going to widen the support for the regime. The crux of the problem was that Ghulam Mohammad needed to secure and ratify a constitution that would consolidate the predominance of the bureaucracy and the army and exclude any feature that would act as an impediment to Pakistan joining the western alliance. The administration, however, insisted on maintaining the fiction of constitutional politics and rejected the alternative of some form of authoritarian rule. The material weakness of the government made it incapable of resisting a combined opposition, and it lacked the resources to mould a potentially hostile public opinion. In recognition of these facts, the Punjabi group continued the myth of constitutional rule — an act of expediency taken to gain time so that the balance of power could be made more favourable. A two-pronged strategy was launched. On the one hand, the United States was courted to secure the funds necessary to fortify the bureaucracy and the army. On the other, there were efforts to gather support for the new Prime Minister in the Constituent Assembly to legitimize the regime.

The only part that went according to plan was persuading the Eisenhower administration to become directly involved in the region. Even before Nazimuddin's unceremonious dismissal, the Pakistan army had established direct contact with US embassy officials in the country. Ayub Khan had made it clear that he wanted to strengthen Pakistan's defence with American assistance, and was prepared to enter a US-sponsored regional defence organization or 'a bilateral agreement' immediately.[1] These surreptitious contacts became unnecessary when the enthusiastically pro-American Mohammad Ali Bogra became Prime Minister. Readily backed by the military, he was prepared to make a sharp and sudden change in foreign policy and steer 'Pakistan into full co-operation with the United States.'[2] John Foster Dulles' visit to Karachi in May 1953, resulted only in modest aid. By the winter of 1953, Ayub Khan had returned from Washington after meeting Admiral Radford, confident that Pakistan would receive substantial military aid.[3]

The idea that Pakistan would receive military aid from the US was met with widespread approval. There was opposition from the left wing organizations (such as the Communist Party, the Azad Party and the Ganatantri Dal), but the major opposition groups (such as the United Front) remained silent and did not make it an issue in the East Bengal provincial elections of March 1954. In private, the opposition approved of the development, and the degree of assent was even greater among the Muslim League and government officials. This was a surprising turnaround in public opinion as, only a year earlier, there had been considerable resistance to such moves. One principal factor in establishing a favourable atmosphere was Nehru's strong opposition to the proposals. This reaction was based on the perception that Nehru and India never accepted an independent Pakistan and that their hostility to military aid was informed by their desire to prevent Pakistan from being able to 'stand up to' India.[4]

The other significant factor that swung public opinion to the American side was the non-military assistance that Pakistan began to receive. This was composed of wheat grants, technical assistance and economic aid programmes. These aid packages became more prolific after Pakistan entered the various security pacts sponsored by the US.[5] Of these, the Baghdad Pact was the most important. Once these protocols were ratified, then the political health of the Government of Pakistan became the concern of the US officials in the country.[6] These various programmes were used in a partisan manner and were not simply designed to increase the popularity of the US with the Pakistani public. Ghulam Mohammad received crucial US support when he dissolved the Constituent Assembly: 'Department believes wise for US Government proceed with military, economic assistance planning for Pakistan, in order maximise chance pro-US group remaining in power.'[7]

Immediate assistance was used as a stop-gap measure by the US to strengthen Ghulam Mohammad's group in the short term while the major military and economic aid programmes were in the pipeline. By the late 1950s, the various treaties with the western alliance provided approximately $500,000,000 of military and $750,000,000 of economic aid.[8] The input of US military and economic aid significantly strengthened the centralizing processes. It provided the pro-US ruling group with the necessary means to subdue the opposition and tilt the equilibrium in the centre's favour.

With the tilt in foreign policy, the military-bureaucratic combine simultaneously launched a political initiative designed to widen its support base and undermine the remaining opposition that still backed Nazimuddin in the Constituent Assembly. To achieve this, Mohammad Ali Bogra needed to win over the Chief Ministers. His supporters now included Firoz Khan Noon, Abdus Sattar Pirzada and Qaiyum Khan. However, the premier of East Bengal, Nurul Amin, could not be bought off so easily and demanded a higher price. He wanted a resolution on the language question that would be acceptable to Bengal. He also wanted the Governor-General's authority to be curtailed so that a repetition of Nazimuddin dismissal would not occur.[9] Mohammad Ali was forced to defer to Nurul Amin in recognition of his strong influence over the Bengali bloc of the Central Parliamentary Party. Without Amin's support, he could not expect his nomination for the Presidentship of Muslim League to be ratified.[10] The immediate result of horse-trading was the complete subordination of the party to governmental authority. The only resistance to this development came from Nazimuddin who, as President of the Muslim League, appointed a Working Committee without consulting the Prime Minister. This was a belated attempt to consolidate his support and resist Bogra's move to accept the Presidentship. The government, however, had isolated the President of the party by winning over the provincial premiers. In the process, it had reduced the party to a supine body.[11] 'The council meetings are summoned merely to elect ministers as League presidents. ....Formerly, ministers regarded it a unique honour to be nominated in the League working committee. But now they pride [sic] in wooing the authority.'[12]

The Prime Minister's next step was to cut the Gordian knot and ratify a constitution. Once this was done, he could go to the polls in East Bengal and attempt to secure a mandate. The government's weakness, however, forced it to give further ground to the Bengali camp in the assembly. To get the consent of the Bengali delegates, various concessions concerning the Islamic content of the constitution were made. Paragraphs specifying that the official name of the state would be the 'Islamic Republic of Pakistan,' that no law repugnant to Islam would be passed and an organization would be established to propagate Islam, represented a victory for the East Bengal members who were led by Khwaja Nazimuddin, Nurul Amin and Fazlur Rahman. These compromises were felt necessary to improve the Bengal Muslim League's chances in the elections to be held in the spring of 1954.[13] These carefully laid plans collapsed when the Muslim League suffered a humiliating defeat in the Bengal provincial elections. The government used the rioting in Karnaphuli and Narayanganj to dissolve the Bengal Provincial Assembly and impose Governor's rule. It was hoped that by doing this, and standing firm at the centre and refusing to compromise with the United Front, it could regain control in the general elections. However, to balance the arbitrary measure, the premier had to make further concessions to the Bengalis. The Mohammad Ali formula was designed to settle the language controversy and conceded the right of regional languages, as well as Urdu and Bengali, to be state languages. It also provided for a compromise procedure for the passing of motions of confidence and no-confidence.[14] The Punjabi members of the assembly, however, rejected the formula. They feared that unless West Pakistan was made into a unitary structure, Bengal, in alliance with Sind and the Frontier, would dominate the central government. Firoz Khan Noon argued instead for a 'zonal federation' of West Pakistan, which was opposed in the house by Qaiyum Khan, Ghaffar Khan, Pirzada and Nazimuddin. In reality, the zonal scheme was a red herring, and its aim was to delay the introduction of the constitution that was being hastened through the assembly.[15]

Punjabi politicians, however, were not only the ones unhappy with the new constitution. For some time members of the military-bureaucratic oligarchy had become anxious about the constitutional concessions made by Bogra. They decided that changes in the government were necessary to resist Bengali resurgence in the Constituent Assembly. They claimed to the Americans that their actions were designed to prevent Pakistan becoming a 'mullahocracy.'

> Our Embassy has been told by two informants of a tentative plan bringing about a change of regime, possibly around the end of the year. (The informants are General Iskander Mirza and Wajid Ali, brother of the Pakistan Ambassador to the United States.) This change would involve dissolution of the Constituent Assembly by the Governor-General and the institution of what appears to be a sort of constitutional dictatorship. The active cooperation of the Governor-General and the

present Prime Minister, Mohammad Ali, would be sought, and it appears there would be relatively little change in the individuals now heading the Government.[16]

By December, however, the plan had to be watered down due to press stories predicting a 'military grab for power.' Pressure was then exerted on the premier to remove Qaiyum Khan from the cabinet as he still had links with Nazimuddin's group.[17] Bogra rejected the demands for a change in his cabinet and the matter was dropped till after the elections in East Bengal.[18]

By now, the nearly-completed constitution had become an even more serious challenge to Ghulam Mohammad and his supporters. It had become clear that the final document would greatly reduce the power of the Governor-General and make the executive responsible to the legislature. For the bureaucrats and the military top-brass the situation was grave, but they had no intention of letting power slip out of their hands. First, Firoz Khan Noon led the Punjabi delegates in the Constituent Assembly to adopt delaying tactics against the ratification of the constitution. Next, Mirza was brought into the Cabinet as Defence Minister in the role of the much-needed strongman.[19] Furthermore, Ghulam Mohammad had declared Governor's rule in Bengal and prepared PRODA proceedings against leading members of the opposition in the Constituent Assembly. Nazimuddin, however, got wind of the intrigue and led a group of opposition delegates in a night raid against the central authorities. On 21 September 1954, the last day of the Constituent Assembly session, Khwaja Nazimuddin, supported by Fazlur Rahman, Nurul Amin, Abdus Sattar Pirzada and Qaiyum Khan, in ten minutes railroaded through the Constituent Assembly an amendment that stripped the Governor-General of his authority and placed the locus of power in the legislature. Mohammad Ali Bogra was presented with an ultimatum the night before, and he joined the conspirators.[20] Nazimuddin's cohort, however, made a major tactical error and the adjournment of the Constituent Assembly for five weeks gave the military-bureaucratic oligarchy time to regroup and counter-attack. Ghulam Mohammad called on the Law Minister, Brohi, to prepare the legally dubious justification for the dissolution of the Constituent Assembly. The army and the civil service were solidly behind Ghulam Mohammad, and Mirza made it clear that if Nazimuddin's group went too far 'we' the state 'will stop them.'[21]

On 24 October, an emergency was declared, the cabinet dismissed and the Constituent Assembly dissolved. Bogra just managed to keep his job, only due to the pressure exerted by Mirza and Ayub on Ghulam Mohammad, but he was a broken man. The cabinet was reorganized and the key positions were taken up by the Governor-General's supporters who, up to now, had operated in the background. The Punjabi group was now openly represented by Ghulam Mohammad, Iskander Mirza, Mohammad Ayub Khan, Chaudhri Mohammad Ali, Mushtaq Ahmad Gurmani and Sayed Wajid Ali. Most of them were members of different branches of the executive, except Wajid Ali who was a non-official confidant. None had any popular support. To widen the support for the oligarchy and simultaneously weaken potential opposition, outsiders such as Suhrawardy and Dr Khan Sahib were inducted into the cabinet. In this manner, they managed to gain the support of the Awami League and split the United Front, while Dr Khan Sahib's inclusion resulted in some gains in Sarhad. Before the end of the year, the general aims of the Punjabi-dominated faction became clear. First, they wanted to promulgate the long-delayed constitution providing for a strong executive but with a presidential system instead of a cabinet type government.[22] They intended to do this by holding a carefully managed convention of trusted men who would rubber-stamp the government proposals. The centre-piece of the constitution would be the merger of West Pakistan into One Unit. This was designed to consolidate the Punjabis' hold over western Pakistan and give them a stronger constitutional bulwark to counter a resurgent Bengal. On the political level, the ruling group wanted to improve the centre's position in East Bengal by capitalizing on the internal dissension within the Jukta Front and retaining control of the province until a *modus vivendi* with a section of the opposition could be established.[23]

The establishment of constitutional autocracy, however, had been a hastily executed measure, and Ghulam Mohammad had not fully thought-out the implications of his actions. The Speaker of the Assembly, Tamizuddin Khan, instigated legal proceedings, questioning the legality of the dissolution. The proceedings exposed how poorly thought-out the Governor-General's actions were and the military-bureaucratic camp became entangled in a tussle with the courts. Ghulam Mohammad declined the option of simply ignoring the courts and ruling by decree. This hardline advocated by Iskander Mirza and Ayub Khan was opposed by Chaudhri Mohammad Ali, who argued that they should first try all means to legitimize the government's action. If this failed, they could then resort to the Mirza-Ayub line and carry on the coup from where it had been dropped. The Governor-General then made the mistake of going to the courts without rigging them first. The Sind High Court ruled in favour of Tamizuddin, stating that the Governor-General had no power or prerogative to dissolve the Constituent Assembly, and to appoint ministers who were not members of the assembly was illegal.[24] Immediately, the Government of Pakistan appealed to the Federal Courts. During the hearing the Chief Justice, Mohammad Munir, was quick to suggest that the dispute was political and the parties should reach a compromise. A compromise solution, however, was not possible due to the unwillingness of the government to settle, except on its own terms. The failure to reach a settlement put the Chief Justice in a difficult situation. He was unwilling to declare the Governor-General's action as illegal because such a move would force Ghulam Mohammad to declare martial law.[25] Justice Munir eventually awarded the judgement in favour of the Government of Pakistan by declaring that the Sind High Court had no jurisdiction to issue writs. The main issue — whether Ghulam Mohammad had the power to dissolve the Constituent Assembly — was never decided.[26]

Ghulam Mohammad's supporters thought they had been give a *carte blanche* by the courts, and the Governor-General issued the Emergency Power Ordinance on 28 March 1955. He intended to call a Constituent Convention and frame a constitution by ordinance. The courts, however, had taken seriously the government's implied promise that they would quickly establish a new assembly as soon as the case was out of the way. When Chief Justice Munir realized that the government had reneged on its promise to establish a validating machinery, he used the Yusaf Patel case to retaliate. The court's decision debarred the Governor-General from framing a constitution and unifying the provinces of West Pakistan into One Unit. These functions, the court decided, were the exclusive preserve of the Constituent Assembly. Again, the merits of disregarding the law were debated in the cabinet and Chaudhri Mohammad Ali, backed by most of the ministers, was able to resist Mirza and Ayub. The Governor-General now approached the Federal Court for advice on how to legitimize his actions. The Chief Justice pointedly enquired why the convention's name, power and composition was different from the old Constituent Assembly. Justice Munir's deliberations forced the government to issue orders for the re-establishment of the Constituent Assembly.[27] Consequently, the actions of the Federal Court forced the Punjabi group, who had ended parliamentary democracy, to return to some form of representative government. The original plans were derailed by the courts and the group was forced to present, for scrutiny, the blueprint for One Unit to an Assembly that was not of their choosing.

To bypass the various impediments to their plans, the ruling group resorted to a combination of obfuscation and brute force. This was apparent from the documents prepared by Daultana for the government on the unification of West Pakistan.[28] He argued that if the plan for One Unit was to be successful, 'We must clear the decks before we launch our political campaign' and 'silence and render inoperative all opposition.' The fear among the smaller provinces of western Pakistan that One Unit would lead to Punjabi domination had to be laid to rest. The 'Punjab must be kept quiet. At a later stage Punjab will have to take the lead. At that time I hope an effective intelligent Punjab leadership will have been put in place both at the Centre and at Lahore.'[29] However, in their impatience, the oligarchy used strongarm tactics rather than persuasion in implementing One Unit. The attitude was best exemplified by Mirza who stated: 'I am against all compromises;' the 'One Unit steam-roller' will not be stopped by 'small pebbles.'[30] The provincial legislatures of Sind and the NWFP were at the receiving end of the One Unit 'steam-roller' and were bulldozed into passing resolutions supporting the unification of West Pakistan.

The Bengali members of the Constituent Assembly saw the new constitution as going some way towards meeting their twenty-one points.[31] The Murree Pact that Suhrawardy had persuaded the East Bengal delegates to accept, stipulated that in exchange for the amalgamation of West Pakistan and parity between the two wings, East Bengal would be granted full regional autonomy, Bengali would be a state language on a par with Urdu and the principle of joint electorates accepted.[32] However, when Chaudhri Mohammad Ali led the Muslim League into a coalition with the United Front, the Awami League, along with others opposed the One Unit Bill. Sardar Abdur Rashid, the former Chief Minister of Sarhad, like Suhrawardy, had previously favoured unification, but both opposed the plan after they realized that they had been misled by the Punjabi group. The Awami League's opposition increased when the documents prepared by Daultana were revealed in the Constituent Assembly by Sardar Rashid and Mian Iftikharuddin. It caused great embarrassment to the coalition government of Chaudhri Mohammad Ali, who vigorously denied the accusations that it was a plan for Punjabi domination, insisting that the reforms were purely administrative.[33]

Despite the combined opposition to One Unit, the Muslim League – United Front coalition was able to marshal a clear majority to ratify the legislation and form a unitary West Pakistan. The Prime Minister was backed by the religious parties who played a significant role in getting the new constitution accepted, especially in East Pakistan. They backed the proposal because of the Islamic provisions, such as the appointment of a 'Commission to advise the enactment of Islamic law' and that no law would be enacted which was repugnant to the Koran or Sunna.[34] The controversial issue of joint versus separate electorates was left to be dealt with later. The All-Party Islamic Front, consisting of the East Pakistan Jamat-i-Islami, the Nizam-i-Islam, Jamiat-ul-Ulama-i-Islam and the Jamiat-ul-Ulama-Pakistan, was formed to campaign for the acceptance of the constitution. Maulana Maudoodi and Mian Tufail Mohammad toured East Pakistan extensively and successfully countered the opposition. The Awami League and the Ganatantri Dal attempted to counter the Islamic Front's activities. When they failed they, along with Mian Iftikharuddin and the Hindu members, boycotted the Assembly the day the Constitution was adopted.[35]

Concurrent with the constitutional developments, Suhrawardy made a bid for premiership. He wanted to forge a mainstream all-Pakistan consensus but was unsuccessful in establishing a significant presence in West Pakistan. The imposition of Governor's rule in East Pakistan made it clear to him that without the support of the military-bureaucratic combine, he could not become premier. The other consideration was that by making a bid at the centre, he would outfox his rival Fazlul Huq. Thus, when Ghulam Mohammad promised that he would head the next coalition government in return for his support for the parity principle, he accepted.[36] Bogra, however, resisted Suhrawardy's attempt to take over. First, with Mirza's consent, he lifted Section 92A in East Pakistan and installed a Krishak Sramik government, paving the way for a Muslim League–Krishak Sramik coalition at the centre.[37] Fazlul Huq agreed, realizing that if Suhrawardy became Prime Minister, not only would he dominate the centre but he would also capture power in Bengal. The other action taken by the premier was to support the replacement of Ghulam Mohammad by Iskander Mirza, on 5 August 1955, as acting Governor-General.[38] In the resulting cabinet reshuffle, Chaudhri Mohammad Ali was elected President of the Muslim League and Mohammad Ali Bogra asked to step down, to be cast out into political limbo. Mirza was extremely hostile to the suggestion that Suhrawardy should become Prime Minister, and pressurized Chaudhri Mohammad Ali into leading the Muslim League into a coalition with the Krishak Sramik Party and becoming Prime Minister.

However, without Ghulam Mohammad's leadership, the unity of the Punjabi group broke up. There were very serious differences between the principal leaders of the ruling cohort. Mirza believed that Pakistan required a 'strong hand...indefinitely.' Already, with the backing of Ayub, he had 'used, at least tacitly, threat of force to obtain [his] own position and...used it again to coerce' Chaudhri Mohammad Ali 'into accepting the premiership.'[39] His rival Chaudhri Mohammad Ali also believed in a strong centre, but wanted to consolidate the ruling group's position through political means and the government to be based on consent. There followed a tussle between the Prime Minister and the Governor-General over the future direction of the country. Chaudhri Mohammad Ali assured the Constituent Assembly that it would not be dissolved, and firmly stated that 'no power here will be able [to] destroy democracy.' Mirza, however, was not a man to be impressed by moral suasion, and it required something more solid to deter him. The United States exerted pressure on Mirza because it did not want to be associated with an autocracy. It cryptically told him to restrain his impatient authoritarian impulses while giving its support to the Prime Minister.[40]

His plans frustrated, Mirza was forced to take the more difficult option of using political means to dominate Pakistan. His task was made easier by the fact that the President in the new constitution was not a figurehead and had the power to appoint the Prime Minister. He wielded his authority to become the ultimate arbitrator of the composition of the cabinet. Mirza's intention was to develop an obedient cabinet headed by a subservient Prime Minister so that he could continue as President after the general elections were held. This approach of Mirza and Ayub was ultimately responsible for the disintegration of constitutional politics. The process was initiated when the Muslim League refused to accept Dr Khan Sahib as the Chief Minister of West Pakistan. Not being a member of the Muslim League and refusing to become one, the party, led by Abdur Rub Nishtar, rebelled against Mirza and caused the downfall of Chaudhri Mohammad Ali. The President struck back by splitting the League and forming the Republican Party led by Dr Khan Sahib. Despite Mirza's public denials, he was the real force behind the Republican Party.[41] The manoeuvre highlighted the difficulty of the political option for Mirza. In attempting to use his authority to establish some kind of political base, he was atomizing Pakistani politics.

The departure of Chaudhri Mohammad Ali forced Mirza into accepting a Republican–Awami League government headed by Suhrawardy. The immediate problem he had to face was the electorate issue involving the religious parties. The Islamic rhetoric was just a camouflage. The introduction of separate electorates was aimed at reducing East Bengal, with its relatively large number of Hindus, into permanent inferiority. Predictably, the West Pakistan Assembly voted for separate electorates, with the Republican Party divided on the matter and the Sind Awami Mahaz opposing it. However, to persuade the East Pakistan Assembly to adopt separate electorates, the Muslim League and the various religious parties formed a committee of action, but the manoeuvre was unsuccessful. A compromise solution with President Mirza's approval was evolved to break the deadlock. Separate electorates were recommended for West Pakistan and joint electorates for East Pakistan. Suhrawardy waited till the spring of 1957 when he persuaded the Republicans to change their decision and accept joint electorates for West Pakistan as well.[42]

In the Awami League, there was an expectation that Suhrawardy, as premier, would alter Pakistan's foreign policy, demand greater autonomy for Bengal and dismantle One Unit. Suhrawardy, however, was a pragmatic politician and his position differed quite substantially from that of his supporters. He had become convinced that US aid was essential for Pakistan, and concluded that he could not be Prime Minister without US support.[43] Thus Suhrawardy opened and closed the debate in the National Assembly on foreign policy, which was the first of its kind. He justified

Pakistan's pro-American policy as a deterrent against India adding that the high level of economic aid was entirely due to Pakistan's membership of the Baghdad Pact. His emphasis on the economic benefits allowed him to persuade the house to accept the government's position, despite the hostility against the west generated by the Suez crisis.[44]

Foreign policy, however, was secondary. He was concerned with building up a credible domestic track record before the general elections, and so he was prepared to accept the constitutional status quo. His opposition to One Unit had been based on the fact that it was an engine of Punjabi domination but, as premier, he was willing to support it. Similarly, on the question of autonomy, his Bengali constituency wanted full provincial autonomy, but his object was to form a national government supported by both wings which would initiate a programme of social amelioration.[45] Relations, however, between the two wings were at a nadir and he could not afford to make a mistake on this problem: 'It's (*sic*) the major issue because should the country's leaders fail to hit on the right solution, Pakistan will inevitably, in course of time, be something less than what it is today.'[46]

Suhrawardy's greatest success was in the improvement of relations between the two wings of the country, as he was the first Prime Minister to act as if East Pakistan was important. The Bengalis began to feel and wanted to be more Pakistani. The slogan of provincial autonomy was still potent in the region, but intellectuals no longer considered it to be the most important solution to the province's problem, although there was still some political mileage in raising the demand. By now most leaders knew that the premier's policies had secured the maximum level of investment in industry possible under the circumstances. Moreover, the political alliances formed in both provinces forced parliamentarians to work together, and the increased presence of East Pakistanis in the federal cabinet gave them new insights into the central government's problems. Suhrawardy's tenure was responsible for the reduction in tension between Karachi and Dacca. Hostility to the centre persisted, but not to the same degree as before.[47]

Suhrawardy became the inter-wing bridge in Pakistani politics, briefly confirming the ascendancy of the Bengali politicians over the military-bureaucratic oligarchy led by Mirza.[48] The President became extremely hostile to his Prime Minister, whose growing stature was reducing the possibility of the former contesting successfully for another term of office. The political development made Mirza extremely impatient, and he began to consider the option of introducing executive rule as early as the summer of 1956.[49] Thus, when Suhrawardy lost the support of the Republicans in October 1957, it gave Mirza the opportunity to force his resignation; he did this by refusing to convene the assembly so that a vote could decide whether Suhrawardy's opponents had a majority.[50] The premier's allies deserted him. They feared losing control of the Government of West Pakistan to the Muslim League if they did not form an alliance with the National Awami Party and agree to the dissolution of One Unit. The Prime Minister insisted that the dissolution of One Unit should take place after the general elections. He was against dissolution for the important reason that it would reopen the whole question of parity between the wings in the National Assembly.[51]

Mirza had patiently nursed contacts with the Muslim League for just such an emergency, and he now formed an alliance with the support of the Raja of Mahmudabad. Ismail Ibrahim Chundrigar was selected as the Prime Minister, but was unable to hold the unstable League-Republican -Krishak Sramik-Nizam-i-Islam coalition together. The new Prime Minister was not represented in either of the two provincial governments, while Suhrawardy sat on the opposition benches at the centre and controlled the ministry in East Pakistan. This development was viewed unfavourably by East Pakistan because the composition of the cabinet showed a clear bias in favour of West Pakistan. All the important portfolios (such as the premiership, Foreign Affairs, Finance and Defence) were allocated to West Pakistanis. In contrast, Bengalis were given Commerce, Labour, Agriculture and Communication and Works.

Another issue that antagonized East Pakistan was the ideological tactic that the Muslim League was employing. The party, during their tenure in opposition, resorted to playing the 'Islam in danger' card so as to turn the tide in their favour. The agitation in Karachi over the book *Religious Leaders*[52] which was published in India, or the demand for separate electorates, was used to maintain political activity.[53] The same tactic was continued by the new cabinet. The premier, Chundrigar, Fazlur Rahman, the Minister of Commerce, and other ministers made various statements urging that the nation's laws should be based on Islamic ideology. The Islamic argument revived the electorate issue, which again turned into a controversy underlining east-west tensions. On this occasion, however, the President supported the implementation of separate electorates so as to undermine Suhrawardy's electoral chances in the expected general elections. Consequently, the Chundrigar coalition also contributed to the increase in tension between the centre and Bengal.[54]

His government, however, lasted only two months. The withdrawal of Republican support was in defiance of Mirza and a revolt against his leadership. The perception had developed within the party that the President had cast in his lot with the Muslim League and intended to follow a course of action inimical to the Republican Party's existence. Mirza had been pressing them to accept separate electorates, but they feared that if they agreed there would be no reason for them to remain a separate party.

Mirza commissioned Chundrigar to form another government, hoping that under greater pressure the Republicans would agree to separate electorates. The recalcitrant Republicans, however, refused and forced the President to call on Firoz Khan Noon, the Republican leader, to form a government. His cabinet had the support of fifty of the seventy-eight members of the National Assembly. His supporters were a heterogeneous group that only persisted due to the fear that if the Republicans were not supported then some form of executive rule would be imposed.[55] Suhrawardy refused to accept any cabinet position for his party in return for the support he gave Firoz Noon. Instead, he was promised that elections would be held as soon as possible, and the premier announced February 1959 as the latest date for the elections.[56]

The struggle in Karachi between those seeking to implement the centre's control and centrifugal forces was paralleled by similar developments in the provinces. The Government of Pakistan asserted its authority in the regions by backing pro-centre candidates. The Punjabi group simply manipulated provincial Muslim League politics to produce loyal and winnable combinations, but Karachi's increasing interference in provincial politics was counterproductive. This approach to regional politics was only possible as long as there was no shift in political loyalties. However, the general effect of treating provincial Leagues as appendages of a distant centre was to lead to the collapse of their credibility and viability. Thus, provincial Leagues witnessed an exodus of their membership, varying in magnitude from area to area, and the concomitant rise in the strength of the opposition. In both wings of the country, the old political patterns were replaced by a new equilibrium. In the case of Bengal, Sind, the NWFP and Baluchistan, the constitutional and political options being forced on them by the executive provoked a strong centrifugal backlash. The politics of the periphery went back into the melting-pot and produced new political combinations which resisted the centralizing processes emanating from Karachi. The polarization was not a simultaneous reaction; its tempo was influenced by developments in local politics. A clear theme, however, becomes increasingly apparent — the Punjab, trying to capture and impose central authority, versus Bengal, Sind, Sarhad and Baluchistan seeking ways of escape. This development resulted in a deep change in the body politic not only at the provincial but also at the all-Pakistan level.

The greatest problem for Ghulam Mohammad's cohort came from Bengal. Here, the political continuum had been broken by events of the early 1950s, with the emergence of a strong centrifugal current in the form of the United Front. The Muslim League's chances in the provincial elections had been weakened by the failure of the East Bengal government and the rise of linguistic politics. Nurul Amin tried to improve his position by campaigning against the Jukta Front on an Islamic agenda in the spring elections of 1954.[57] The League leadership, however, was perceived to be distant from the local people. The Prime Minister personally intervened in the campaign, but was unable to sell his constitutional compromise as something beneficial to Bengal. To make matters worse, Mohammad Ali Bogra imported West Pakistanis to run the campaign, and failed to address the source of discontent. He presented no remedy for the recurrent shortages of essential commodities, spiralling inflation and the low price of agricultural products that resulted in deep dissatisfaction among the masses. His appeal for unity and patriotism and the promise of a better economic future fell on deaf ears.[58]

The elections produced an overwhelming victory for the Jukta Front and decimated the Muslim League Parliamentary Party. The League's organizational structure remained intact but, with only ten seats, it was no longer a political force in the province. The United Front won 223 seats, not including the seventeen seats won by candidates of the Ganatantri Dal and Communist Party contesting non-Muslim constituencies.[59] The anti-centre forces in East Bengal were successful because the United Front's twenty-one point programme encapsulated the feeling that the centre did not have East Pakistan's interests at heart. The demand for greater provincial autonomy was the basis for an agenda to repair the damage done to the province by policies of the central government. The jute policy, the distribution of revenue and the lack of industrialization were cited as the most glaring examples of central neglect.

Was there any truth in the accusations made by Bengal against Karachi? The Bengalis were hardly represented in the armed forces, and only a small number of them were officers. As a result, the western wing received the lion's share of the military expenditure, with barely 2 per cent of the total given to East Bengal.[60] Similarly, the Bengalis were poorly represented in the upper echelons of the bureaucracy. They were unable to influence economic policy, and their attempts to remind the centre of the importance of hard currency earned from jute exports had no effect.[61] The eastern province was allocated only Rs 50 crore for industrial development, out of a budget of Rs 800 crore.[62] The result of these inequitable policies was that Rs 210,000,000 per annum were transferred from East Pakistan to West Pakistan by 1955. This accounted for the greater industrialization of West Pakistan at the expense of Bengal.[63] Consequently, the demands raised by the Jukta Front attracted the urban professionals, students and *jotedars* who felt that the introduction of provincial autonomy and making Bengali a state language would improve their economic prospects. The twenty-one points also included class demands (such as the abolition of the Permanent Settlement, the nationalization of the jute trade and the industrialization of the province) which mobilized workers and peasants.[64] Fazlul Huq, however, considered the twenty-one points to be just an 'election stunt.' Other moderate politicians admitted the manifesto to be extravagant but, under pressure from the left wing of the Jukta Front, they dared not admit this in public. Even Bhashani privately said that it would take at least five years to carry out the whole programme.[65]

Table 5.1

East/West Representation in the Upper Echelons of the Civil Service of Pakistan, 1955

Rank	West	East	East as % of Total
Secretary	19	Nil	Nil
Joint Secretary	38	3	7.3
Deputy Secretary	123	10	7.3
Under Secretary	510	38	7.3

Source: Rounaq Jahan, *Pakistan: Failure in Integration* (New York, 1972), p. 28.

Table 5.2

East/West Representation in the Army, 1956

Rank	West	East
General	1	–
Lieutenant-General	3	–
Major-General	20	–
		(Was one but retired)
Brigadier	35	1
Colonel	50	–
Lieutenant-Colonel	198	2
Major	590	10

Source: *Constituent Assembly of Pakistan, Debates*, i, no. 51, 16 January 1956, p. 1844.

The resounding defeat of the Bengal League did not lead to any changes at the centre. Bogra attempted to improve the centre's position by patching up the differences with Fazlul Huq and exploiting the differences within the Jukta Front. As premier of East Bengal, Huq expressed great satisfaction at the conciliatory attitude of the centre when he visited Karachi at the end of April 1954. He informed the Prime Minister of his desire to cooperate, and urged him not to be unduly concerned by statements made by him for political reasons. The Prime Minister's intention was to detach Huq from the leftist elements in the coalition. On the understanding that he would be given a free hand in the province, Huq would enter into a coalition with the Muslim League in the Constituent Assembly.[66] This enterprise was not improbable given the ideological differences and conflicting personal ambitions of the various leaders of the Jukta Front. The main areas of contention were the composition of the cabinet, the role of the left in the Front and relations with the central government. Fazlul Huq's original cabinet excluded members from the Awami League, and this was a source of friction until they were included.[67] The other point of difference was the strident demand of Suhrawardy and Bhashani for the dissolution of the Constituent Assembly. Once he became Chief Minister, Huq realized that he needed the cooperation of Karachi, and became silent on this question. There was also friction over the relationship between the Front and the communists and the Ganatantri Dal. The Krishak Sramik Party and the Nizam-i-Islam opposed their inclusion while Awami League claimed that the Ganatantri Dal was a member, and was prepared to work with the communists.[68]

Mohammad Ali's strategy, however, foundered on opposition from within the Punjabi group who perceived the United Front to be dominated by radical elements. To neutralize this threat, hardliners such as Ayub Khan, Mushtaq Gurmani and Wajid Ali advocated the dismissal of Huq's ministry. The pretext for intervention came with the rioting that took place at the Adamjee Jute Mills. The incident was used as a stick to beat with both communists and the Front. What was essentially an ethnic conflict between Bengalis and non-Bengalis was claimed by Karachi to be a communist plot. Fazlul Huq was given a last chance to clear the province of communists, which patently he could not do. There were leftist sympathizers in his own cabinet and Bhashani, a radical, was the third member of the United Front triumvirate.[69] Eventually, the army's view prevailed with the Governor-General. Mirza was sent as Governor of East Bengal, the Jukta Front government dismissed and Governor's rule instituted. His brief was to 'isolate known communists and certain pink civil service employees and the police, replacing them with dependable personnel,' mainly West Pakistanis.[70] More than a thousand persons were arrested, including thirty members of the provincial legislative assembly.[71] Only after this action was the Governor-General prepared to establish a dialogue with the United Front. The alliance's unacceptable price for cooperation was the restoration of parliamentary democracy, the release of political prisoners and the removal of the ban on Bhashani. However, the antagonism between the Awami League and the Krishak Sramik Party reached such proportions that they parted company, undermining the opposition to the centre. The Awami League's *de facto* departure from the United Front occurred when Suhrawardy joined the 'cabinet of talent' as the Law Minister. Fazlul Huq was not consulted by Suhrawardy on the question of joining the government. Consequently, when the centre wanted to counterbalance Suhrawardy's influence, Huq allowed his nominee, Abu Husain Sarkar, to be included in the cabinet. This step eventually paved the way for an alliance with the Muslim League.

The League coalition with the Krishak Sramik Party at the centre was accompanied by the abrogation of Governor's rule and the formation of a provincial ministry headed by Abu Husain Sarkar. Once in power, however, the Front began to disintegrate slowly. For one, it simply lacked organizational cohesion. Further, the selection of Sarkar as Chief Minister was not acceptable to many, and the fact that Fazlul Huq was not trusted by his colleagues compounded the instability of the party.[72] The cabinet's aim of playing down the significance of the food crisis was countered by the Awami League's campaign on the issue, which successfully embarrassed the government. But, in the end, the controversy over the Islamic provisions in the constitution proved to be the major factor that undermined the government. The United Front's support for the constitution resulted in the departure of the non-Muslim groups. Many members of the National Congress, the United Progressive Parliamentary Party, some members of the Scheduled Castes Federation and the Ganatantri Dal deserted the United Front and joined the campaign against Islamic provisions, led by the Awami League and Democratic Party. The Jukta Front government was considerably weakened by the departures, and was consequently unwilling to have its strength tested in the provincial assembly. When Sarkar finally did convene the house, it was adjourned by the speaker on a point of order raised by the opposition. To give the Chief Minister breathing space, the Governor, Fazlul Huq, prorogued the assembly and instituted Governor's rule. Later, Sarkar's reinstatement frustrated the Awami League's plan to replace him. Suhrawardy then launched an extensive campaign focusing popular discontent against the provincial ministry, culminating in hunger marches, which were fired on by the police. Sarkar had great difficulty in keeping his coalition together, and it eventually fell apart forcing him to resign in favour of Ataur Rahman, on 30 August 1956. By 1958, the United Front had ceased to exist and the Krishak Sramik Party, an amorphous collection of personalities, was deeply divided. The latter's major asset had been Fazlul Huq, whose personal popularity more than compensated for the lack of organization and discipline. It was speculated for a while that he might step down as Governor to revive the party's fortunes, but the octogenarian could no longer actively participate in politics.[73] Once in opposition, the divisive forces in the Krishak Sramik Party took their toll and it began to disintegrate. A splinter group led by Kafiluddin Ahmad had joined the Awami League. The main body was divided into the Sayed Azizul Huq and Hamidul Huq Choudhry's factions. This latter group seriously considered establishing itself as a separate party, but the two factions unified again under the leadership of Abu Husain Sarkar in the spring of 1958.

Similarly, the Awami League suffered from intra-party disputes once it was no longer in the opposition, but it was better equipped to deal with the difficulties. Suhrawardy's assumption of office as Prime Minister created tensions with the Awami League's left wing. Maulana Bhashani called for the abrogation of Pakistan's military agreements and the adoption of a 'neutral' foreign policy. These views were reinforced by statements made by Oli Ahad, Organizing Secretary, and Abdul Hai, Publicity Secretary. Even Ataur Rahman bluntly stated: 'We want to get out of the Baghdad Pact.' Its allies, the National Congress, the Ganatantri Dal and communist sympathizers were also against the pro-American foreign policy. Suhrawardy, however, was able to use the party machinery to come to grips with the revolt. Sheikh Mujibur Rahman issued a press statement calling for a halt to public discussions of foreign policy. Internal differences were put aside during the by-elections of December 1956 and the Awami League focused all its energies on the hustings.[74] Later at Kagmari, on 2 February 1957, a temporary truce was reached between Suhrawardy and Maulana Bhashani. The Prime Minister was endorsed as the leader and no resolution condemning foreign policy was moved, but Bhashani was left free to criticize Pakistan's foreign policy. Suhrawardy was displeased that he had been unable to get a positive endorsement. But he was prevented from taking a stronger stand against Bhashani because he considered his support essential for the impending general elections. Bhashani was also dissatisfied with the compromise, and began to raise the issue of provincial autonomy to snipe at the premier. He warned that if East Pakistan's genuine grievances were not rectified, then the province would be forced to say *'assalam alaikum'* to West Pakistan. He did not believe that the Awami League, hamstrung by the Republican Party at the centre, could introduce the necessary changes.[75] However, only after Suhrawardy had successfully completed the National Assembly debate on foreign policy did Bhashani and his supporters switch their attack on the premier moving from foreign policy to the issue of provincial autonomy. In March that year, Bhashani raised the demand for full provincial autonomy with only defence, currency and foreign affairs to be under central control, and called for members of all parties to support the provincial autonomy resolution in the assembly.[76]

The showdown between Shaheed Suhrawardy and Maulana Bhashani for control of the party took place at the Awami League Council meeting in Dacca on 13-14 June 1957. The premier received an overwhelming endorsement from the council on the federal government's international policy, and his supporters (such as Ataur Rahman and Mujibur Rahman) consolidated their position in the party. Oli Ahad was expelled and nine of Bhashani's supporters on the Working Committee were forced to resign, leaving only Bhashani. Resolutions were passed preventing members of the Awami League from being members of the pro-Bhashani Youth Leagues, but Bhashani himself was requested by the council to withdraw his resignation. Suhrawardy wanted him to remain as a figurehead.[77] Bhashani was anticipating the worst, and when the crucial council meeting ended he was in touch with his West Pakistani counterparts. He suggested that the National Party, Democratic Party, Youth League and the Bhashani group of the Awami League should combine to form a new all-Pakistan opposition party to contest the next general elections. From West Pakistan, a hundred delegates (including Ghaffar Khan, G.M. Sayed, Mian Iftikharuddin, Mahmudul Huq Usmani, Abdul Majid Sindhi and Abdul Samad Achakzai) attended the Democratic Workers' Convention on 25 July 1957 where the National Awami Party was founded. It proposed the break-up of One Unit for West Pakistan, full provincial autonomy for the eastern wing and an independent foreign policy.[78]

The National Awami Party's position on provincial autonomy influenced the peasantry and sections of the middle class. However, the party lost its initial gains in East Pakistan due to its policy of supporting the Awami League government of Ataur Rahman. The price for supporting the Awami League was the five-point programme: the break-up of One Unit, a neutral foreign policy, regional autonomy for the provinces, early elections based on joint electorates and the implementation of the fourteen unfulfilled items of the twenty-one point programme. However, the agreement broke down over two issues: foreign policy and the breaking up of One Unit. The National Awami Party's reaction was to remain neutral during a vote on 18 June, causing the defeat of Ataur Rahman's ministry. By holding the balance of power, it persuaded Sheikh Mujibur Rahman to reach an accommodation with Mahmood Ali based on the five-point programme. The understanding between the National Awami Party and the Awami League brought down Sarkar's government within two days. The Governor then advised the centre that no stable cabinet could be formed, and President's rule was implemented in the province.[79]

Suhrawardy and other leaders of the Awami League were embarrassed by their association with the National Awami Party, and argued that the party did not accept the five-point programme. There was some justification for this position. Haji Danesh, President of the Parliamentary Group of the National Awami Party, said that the 'mutual understanding of the two general secretaries is yet an unpublished document' and asked for restraint in the criticism of the agreement to prevent a Muslim League-Krishak Sramik-Nizam-i-Islam coalition taking over.[80] Maulana Bhashani was against supporting the Awami League but was forced to accept the decision in order to preserve the integrity and solidarity of the organization in East Pakistan.[81]

The alliance resulted in great strains in the National Awami Party and a concomitant loss in popularity. The West Pakistani section of the National Awami Party was hostile to Suhrawardy because he refused to repudiate One Unit, a burning issue in Sind and Sarhad. In East Pakistan, the party's members in the assembly were divided on the issue. However, the dominant group, the Danesh-Samad faction, maintained control and threw its weight behind the Awami League, allowing it to form a government on 25 August. This was done in the belief that democracy would be strengthened. The National Awami Party was invited to enter the cabinet and three seats were offered.[82] Fearing a split in the party, Bhashani rejected the offer but continued to support the Awami League government. Despite the tensions that the relations with the Awami League caused within the National Awami Party, it became apparent that an electoral alliance was in the offing.[83]

Unlike Bengal, politics in Sind moved in the opposite direction — from a semblance of unity to disunity. Highly volatile initially, it only began to solidify in reaction to the imposition of One Unit. The centre's interventions in Sind politics were successful in the beginning in promoting centralization. The Governor-General succeeded in getting Abdus Sattar Pirzada elected as the President of the party and leading the Sind government. This was highly irregular as Pirzada was not a member of the Sind Legislative Assembly and was only elected to that body nine months later. Once in power, three factors worked in his favour. The first was that he was the choice of Ghulam Mohammad, and not of the premier, Mohammad Ali Bogra. The strong backing from the military-bureaucratic oligarchy made him less susceptible to the vicissitudes associated with the premiership. Next, Khuro's supporters deserted him for the 'in' group, and were joined by ten Hindu members and eight independent delegates. Finally, the premier was able to form a working alliance with G.M. Sayed's Sind Awami Mahaz. Although Sayed reserved the right to criticize the cabinet, he agreed to support the government in view of the joint agreement reached between the two over the Minister's programme for Sind. Pirzada assured Sayed that the League ministry would abolish *jagirdari* and that the illegal ejectment of *haris* would be prevented by the efficient administration of the Sind Tenancy Act.[84]

At first the Chief Minister stoutly defended the centre against the trenchant criticisms levelled against it by the Sind Awami Mahaz. G.M. Sayed's thesis that Pakistan was a multinational state in which Sindi was a distinct nationality and that the central government's powers should be limited to certain reserved subjects, such as defence, foreign affairs and communications, struck a deep chord among the Sindis. There were other powerful grievances — the central government's excessive interference in the provincial ministry's 'internal affairs,' inadequate representation in the Constituent Assembly, absence of compensation for the loss of Karachi and insufficient financial assistance for refugee settlement in Sind. These charges, however, were refuted by Pirzada. He admitted that some problems were due to poor administration, but blamed the Sindis themselves for failing to take up past opportunities due to 'factionalism'. He was appalled by the idea of Sindi nationality, arguing that it threatened to undermine national unity, and personally favoured Urdu as the state language.[85]

The Punjabi group reciprocated by backing Pirzada when Ayub Khuro threatened to overthrow the cabinet. Khuro had managed to win over several delegates to the Sind Legislature, including three cabinet ministers. A showdown between the two took place during March and June 1954. The opposition threatened to overturn the Pirzada's ministry by passing a no-confidence motion, but the centre intervened by proroguing the assembly.[86] Separate negotiations with the Talpurs and Khuro followed, but were unsuccessful. Fifty-nine Muslim Leaguers resigned. The Sind premier overcame the opposition when the central government sanctioned the enlargement of the cabinet. The judicious distribution of portfolios was a significant factor in winning over most of the opposition, and allowed him to survive the no-confidence motion when the assembly was reconvened.[87]

The political balance, however, was disturbed by Karachi's push for centralization. The new equilibrium in Sindi politics that gradually emerged was focused on regional nationalism. The various political groups subordinated their personal and ideological differences and took a common stand against the central government. The strongest opposition came from the Sind Awami Mahaz. G.M. Sayed's resolution for the reunification of Karachi with Sind in March 1954 generated popular support in the assembly. It was supported not only by other opposition leaders (such as Pir Mohammad Ali Rashidi) but also by the Chief Minister.[88] Pirzada increasingly became responsive to this development, and later promised that he would secure the proper place for the Sindi language in education and the administration.[89] In the same month, the Muslim League, Sind League, Sind Awami Mahaz and the Sind Hari Committee formed a common front called 'Security of Sind' to resist unification.[90] The hostility to One Unit reached such a pitch that nearly three-quarters of the Sind Assembly, led by Pirzada, stated their opposition to it in writing. Ghulam Mohammad, Iskander Mirza and the Governor of Sind, Mamdot, conferred on 8 November 1954 and dismissed Pirzada and his cabinet supposedly for maladministration. To get the Sind Assembly to support the resolution on One Unit, Ayub Khuro, Kazi Fazlullah and others were freed from PRODA disqualifications by the Governor-General. Khuro, who was neither a member of the League nor of the Sind Assembly, was appointed Chief Minister, and he nominated Pir Ali Mohammad Rashdi and Moula Baksh Soomro to his cabinet. The opposition to unification, however, was so strong that many refused to cooperate. Ghulam Mohammad Talpur said that no one from his group would join. Moreover, Fazlullah deserted the supporters of unification and declared that his cohort would oppose any merger plan. The Sind Awami Mahaz's executive committee passed a resolution on 5 November rejecting any federal constitution that did not grant maximum autonomy to the provinces. It becomes plain that there was genuine hostility to One Unit, and that Pirzada was depending on the legislators opposed to the proposal as well as his own supporters to prevent any resolution on merger being passed by the assembly.[91]

Khuro, however, bulldozed the same intransigent assembly into passing the One Unit resolution on 11 December 1954, with an overwhelming majority. The delay in the implementation of the new constitution and its centre-piece, One Unit, due to the Tamizuddin case, necessitated another session of the legislature to ratify the provincial budget. The result was that anti-centre forces in Sind regrouped to overthrow the Khuro-Rashdi cohort. Ghulam Ali Talpur resigned as minister from the central cabinet and resumed his old position as Speaker of the Sind Assembly so as to re-enter Sind politics. The Chief Minister attempted to block this move but was restrained by a court injunction. However, Khuro and Rashdi acted promptly and they struck at the leadership of the opposition a day before the legislature was due to meet in order to consider the budget. Rashdi announced the discovery of a plot 'which had for its objective the assassination of Sind Ministers and the creation of widespread disorders between Sindis and Punjabis'. Ghulam Ali Talpur and Pir Ilahi Baksh were charged with the conspiracy and arrested.[92] The budget was brought forward to be considered before the *habeas corpus* was heard, and the Sind Assembly building was surrounded by police to intimidate the delegates into passing the budget.[93]

When elections for the Constituent Assembly took place in June 1955, there were many irregularities committed by Khuro's group. Only Ayub Khuro, Pir Ali Mohammad Rashdi, Moula Baksh Soomro, Ghulam Mohammad Talpur and Sirumal Kirpaldas were elected. Sheikh Abdul Majid Sindhi, President of the Sind Awami Mahaz, complained to the Governor of the province that G.M. Sayed had been threatened with dire consequences if he did not withdraw his candidature, and that the police had been ordered to escort members of the Sind Legislature to Hyderabad to vote. Kazi Fazlullah accused the premier of instigating a reign of terror in Sind. He alleged that his arrest on charges of involvement in the bomb plot to blow up the Sind Assembly was designed to prevent him from participating in the elections. These methods, described as Khuroism, only aggravated the deep hostility to the merger, which assumed a new form in the context of the unified province of West Pakistan.[94]

Sindi sensibilities were deeply injured by One Unit. Even before this innovation was proposed, Sindi politics had strong centrifugal currents that emphasized the region's distinctiveness. The politics of ethnicity now fed into the opposition to One Unit. The antipathy to amalgamation was stated in ethnic terms, underlining the Sindi fear that they would be swallowed up by the Punjab. Tension between the provinces was compounded by the age-old friction over Punjabi settlers in Sind and the question of sharing the Indus waters. The completion of the Kotri and Guddu barrages resulted in the opening up of irrigated land, and it was feared that unification would lead to an influx of Punjabi settlers into these areas at the expense of the indigenous population.[95] The other old rivalry was over the question of distribution of the Indus waters between the two provinces. Sind lost the right to veto the allotment of the Indus waters based on pre-independence agreements. Thus the centralization process brought together two strands — one based on Sindi identity and the other based on hostility to the Punjab. These were now combined into a powerful centrifugal force opposed to attempts at centralization.[96]

Developments in the Frontier were similar to those in Sind, except that the pace of the opposition to One Unit was slower. In Sarhad, Karachi first consolidated its hold over the province when Qaiyum Khan's nominee Sardar Abdur Rashid, the Inspector-General of Police, replaced him as Chief Minister. Qaiyum, however, retained the presidency of the Muslim League, hoping to control the party from Karachi. Abdur Rashid, however, asserted his independence and Qaiyum was forced to resign from the presidentship in October 1954. The former continued his predecessor's policy of maintaining a tight grip over the Muslim League and the province. The Pir of Manki Sharif became so exasperated with the way freedom of political action was being strangled in the province that he felt that the Awami Muslim League should resign from the NWFP Legislative Assembly in protest. The pro-centrist group wooed Rashid, seeking his support for One Unit. His support, so vital in Sarhad, was received on the understanding that the capital of West Pakistan would be in the province.[97]

The opposition's ambiguous response to unification helped the centralizing process. The ambivalence was due to the centre's co-option of Dr Khan into the central cabinet. He was a popular figure in the Frontier, and genuinely believed that the formation of One Unit was beneficial. He was the only political figure who actively campaigned for amalgamation. His support was considered essential by Karachi if the Pakhtuns were to be brought into line with the Punjabis and others who favoured unification.[98] Consequently, Ghaffar Khan's opposition was muted. He argued that he was not against unification in principle but urged that national elections should be held immediately. Similarly, the leadership of the NWFP Awami Muslim League wanted to fudge the issue. The Pir of Manki Sharif took up a similar position when faced with the strong opposition to One Unit in the party. With time, the opposition's mild criticism became more vocal and strident. This was partly due to Pakhtun nationalism and the realization that many power holders would lose to the Punjab once West Pakistan was promulgated.[99] The opposition boycotted the assembly and were joined by Leaguers such as Saifullah Khan. The Prime Minister, Sardar Abdur Rashid, supported by his ministers Sardar Mohammad Ayub Khan, M.R. Kayani and Khan Mohammad Farid Khan steered the One Unit resolution through the Frontier Assembly.[100] The Chief Minister's hold over the provincial assembly was so solid that only he himself and his colleagues, Mian Jaffar Shah, M.R. Kayani and Jalaluddin Khan, were elected to the Constituent Assembly.[101] However, when Lahore was announced as the capital of West Pakistan, Abdur Rashid realized that the Punjabi group was finalizing a scheme that was quite different from the one canvassed earlier. He resigned from the One Unit Committee, headed by Gurmani, and began to oppose it. The centre, however, dismissed him as Chief Minister on 18 July 1955, and replaced him with Sardar Bahadur Khan.[102] Rashid retaliated by revealing the contents of the Daultana document but, despite the stir caused by its revelation in the Constituent Assembly, he could not prevent the introduction of One Unit.[103]

In the Punjab, unification plans were carried out without much difficulty. In contrast to the other provinces, the divisions in the province were not along the lines of for or against unification, but along party and factional lines. The first concern of Karachi was to consolidate its position in the province by backing Firoz Khan Noon and to deal with the opposition in the Punjab Muslim League led by Daultana. The Governor-General appointed his confidant Aminuddin as Governor of the Punjab, who supported Firoz Khan Noon in his dispute with Daultana.[104] Noon's pro-zemindar cabinet wanted to dismantle the land reforms that had been introduced by the previous cabinet. Daultana had the support of the district committees of the League and formed a secret alliance with Iftikharuddin. The Azad Party, Pakistan National Party and the communists backed the liberal wing of the Muslim League in their defence of agrarian legislation.[105] Daultana then unsuccessfully challenged Noon in the party. However, Ghulam Mohammad's position changed after he had dissolved the Constituent Assembly in October 1954 and now needed to widen his support base. Therefore, he released Mumtaz Daultana from PRODA proceedings. Daultana reciprocated by throwing his weight behind the plans for unification, and said that he was in full accord with any plan that would 'fortify the unity and solidarity of Pakistan'.[106] His star was again on the rise as he was the architect of the One Unit plan used by the military-bureaucratic oligarchy.[107]

Although by this action Ghulam Mohammad had increased the quantum of support for One Unit in the Punjab Muslim League, it lined up two antagonistic groups that became locked in a struggle for the spoils of unification. The dispute became intertwined with Noon's rivalry with Daultana. The two were involved in a bitter conflict over the question of patronage. This was specifically expressed by their disagreement over how members of the Punjab Muslim League Parliamentary Party should be nominated to the Constituent Assembly. The premier of the Punjab was willing to set aside six seats to be filled by nominees of the central leadership as demanded by Karachi, but wanted a free hand in the selection of the remaining candidates. Daultana, with nothing to lose, was willing to give the centre a free hand. No compromise could be worked out to resolve the resulting deadlock. The new Governor, Gurmani, decided to cut the Gordian knot, dismissed Noon's cabinet and asked Sardar Abdul Hamid Khan Dasti, a Daultana supporter, to form a new cabinet. He nominated himself and his sympathizers to the Constituent Assembly, and the Noon group was denied any Muslim League nominations. Later, in August 1955, the whole group resigned when Noon. Muzaffar Ali Qizilbash, Choudhry Ali Akbar and Raja Ahmad Ali were expelled from the Muslim League.[108]

The rump of the Jinnah Awami Muslim League, led by Mian Abdul Bari, also approved of One Unit. They urged that national elections should be held within a year but, unlike their counterpart in the Frontier, they did not link this issue with One Unit. Khwaja Abdur Rahim, a leading figure in the Punjab Awami Muslim League, said that the Punjab branch urged Suhrawardy to accept any offer of inclusion in the federal cabinet. He added that here was an opportunity to demonstrate their loyalty to Pakistan by giving full support to the government's efforts to establish a strong administration.[109]

The only opposition to One Unit in the Punjab came from the Azad Party, led by Mian Iftikharuddin. He supported the United Front's demand for the dissolution of the Constituent Assembly and argued for a confederal Pakistan where the centre retained only minimal powers. The organization's ability to act as an effective opposition to the process of amalgamation was greatly hindered when two of its leading members, Shaukat Hayat and Sardar Asadullah Jan, rejoined the Muslim League, and its Karachi offices were raided and sealed following the ban on the Communist Party of Pakistan in July 1954. Only Iftikharuddin was elected to the Constituent Assembly, and he supported Sardar Rashid's description of One Unit as an instrument of Punjabi domination.[110]

The establishment of West Pakistan was an inherently flawed legislative act that juxtaposed antagonistic forces within a single legislature, not by consent but by a combination of subterfuge and force. Rather than enhancing the stability of the provincial government, it created greater political disequilibrium, and the diverse regional political groups formed a common platform against One Unit. The centrifugal elements within and without the assembly exploited the unharmonious politics of the Muslim League and the Republican Party, being prepared only to support those who were ready to accept the dissolution of West Pakistan. As central executive pressure brought about the establishment of West Pakistan, it remained the only bonding factor, and the structure continued to survive only due to external pressure rather than any internal cohesion.

In party terms, there were three groups in the newly-formed legislature. Initially, the West Pakistan Legislature was dominated by the Muslim League. This dominance, however, was brought to an end when Dr Khan's credentials as Chief Minister were challenged by Nishtar, the President of the All-Pakistan Muslim League. Dr Khan eventually convened the Republican Party, which originally only attracted opponents of Daultana and Khuro. Its position was also bolstered by the backing it received from President Mirza and Governor Gurmani. Failing to secure a clear majority, the Chief Minister offered seats in the cabinet as an incentive towards ensuring adequate support. Ghulam Ali Talpur, Sardar Rashid, Nur Muhammad Khan and Firoz Noon joined the Republican Party in return for, or in anticipation of, ministerial positions.[111] Despite these measures, the party's majority was not assured and it was forced to turn to the Pakistan National Party for support.

The Pakistan National Party exploited the rift between the Muslim League and the Republican Party and the dissensions within each party to press for the dissolution of One Unit. The organization had emerged from the Anti-One Unit Front formed to oppose unification. It consisted of Ghaffar Khan of the Red Shirts, the NWFP Awami League led by the Pir of Manki Sharif, the Vror Pakhtun of Abdul Samad Achakzai, the Ustaman Gal led by Prince Abdul Karim and G.M. Sayed's Sind Awami Mahaz. Later, the Azad Party of Mian Iftikharuddin also joined, after its attempt to merge with the Awami League collapsed. The Pakistan National Party's strongest influence was outside the assembly. It was assessed by its convenor, Mahmud Ali Kasuri, as being strong in big cities and weak in small towns, and Iftikharuddin was more popular in East Pakistan than in the western wing.[112] In the West Pakistan Assembly, the National Party had only twelve seats — eleven belonging to the Sind Awami Mahaz and one to the Azad Party. However, the influence of the anti-One Unit lobby was further increased when it merged with the Bhashani wing of the Awami League in July 1957 to form the National Awami Party.

The Republican Party faced dissension in its ranks, mainly from Sindi and tribal members, and was concerned that this would be exploited by the Muslim League. For a while the Sindi delegates were reassured by Dr Khan's statement that their grievances would receive sympathetic consideration. His position, however, was eroded by the activities of the National Party, which previously had cooperated with the Republicans over joint electorates.[113] The National Party's inflexible posture in the face of the Muslim League's blandishments was a part of the political posturing between the two over the question of cooperating in overthrowing the West Pakistan government. On 19 March 1957, the Muslim League forged its long-expected alliance with the National Party with a pledge to oppose One Unit. The unpopularity of the measures had increased steadily. Some groups, such as the Sind Awami Mahaz, had always opposed One Unit, but disenchantment among the Republican ranks and the independents over the issue had increased. The unholy alliance tried to submit the Republicans to a test of strength on 20 March. However, when he realized that all was lost, Dr Khan advised the Governor to invoke his emergency powers and suspend the West Pakistan Legislature and cabinet.[114] With the dissolution of the Assembly, National Awami Party-Muslim League co-operation also ended. The Governor, Gurmani, accepted Dr Khan's resignation on 16 July and appointed Sardar Rashid as Chief Minister of West Pakistan.

Besides the change in premier, there was no major change in the cabinet, and the Republican strategists pursued the previous policy of parcelling out ministerships to anyone who had a significant following. However, they feared losing control of West Pakistan and, in desperation, they allied themselves with the National Awami Party on their terms. On 18 September, the Republican and National Awami Party alliance passed a resolution recommending the reconstitution of West Pakistan as a sub-federation of four or more fully autonomous provinces. The leaders of the National Awami Party, Maulana Bhashani, Abdul Ghaffar Khan and G.M. Sayed applauded the resolution. It was also endorsed by the Pakistan Socialist Party, the Sind Hari Committee and by leaders of the Republican Party, such as Ghulam Ali Talpur, and Firoz Khan Noon.[115] Sardar Rashid was also in favour of dissolution although he was more guarded in his public statements.[116] A parallel wave of support came from the former princely states of Kalat, Swat and Bahawalpur and from Baluchistan demanding the restitution of their autonomy. However, the Awami League, the Republican Party's coalition partner at the centre continued to defend One Unit along with thirty-two Punjabi members.[117] The agreement between the National Awami Party and the Republican Party had been approved by Iskander Mirza. But, almost immediately, Mirza made a public pronouncement in support of One Unit. The leadership of the National Awami Party concluded that the premier had repudiated their understanding to dissolve One Unit. Ghaffar Khan, the President of the National Awami Party, then took the party into an alliance with the Muslim League. Despite their ideological differences, an agreement was reached with the Muslim League on a sixteen-point socio-economic programme and the decision to press for early general elections. G.M. Sayed said that there was a secret section of the agreement that bound the Muslim League to accepting joint electorates and the dissolution of West Pakistan. However, the Republican high command was able to stave off defeat by replacing the Chief Minister, Sardar Rashid, with Muzaffar Ali Qizilbash.[118] The Muslim League's failure to capture power, and the election of Qaiyum Khan as the president of the party, made the understanding with the National Awami Party redundant.

The issue of dismemberment of One Unit, however, was to create a cleavage within the National Awami Party itself. The West Pakistan section of the party was opposed to the pro-Awami League policy of the East Pakistan section because Suhrawardy refused to support the break-up of West Pakistan into its original provinces. The east-west split in the National Awami Party was approximately in line with its division between a left wing and a right wing. Sayed claimed that he had presented an ultimatum to Bhashani that if he did not distance himself from the pro-communist elements who favoured cooperation with the Awami League, the party would split. G.M. Sayed had already fired Sobo Gianchandani, the editor of *Naeen Sind*, and other communist sympathizers from the staff of the paper. Ghaffar Khan had taken similar action, and both were urging Bhashani to follow suit.[119] Maulana Bhashani was able to placate Ghaffar Khan and avert a split in the National Awami Party by pointing out that the eastern section of the party had passed a resolution stating that the condition for supporting the Awami League was the dismemberment of One Unit.[120]

The little support for unification, originally to be found in Sarhad, Sind and Baluchistan, quickly evaporated when it became clear that One Unit had become a vehicle for Punjabi domination. The office-holders and politicians from the former provinces became unhappy at the loss of patronage and power which accompanied the merger. The sense of injustice was aggravated by the fact that the disparity in education between Punjabis, Sindis and Pakhtuns (partly because Urdu was the language of culture and education of the former province) gave Punjabis a clear advantage in the competition for government jobs in West Pakistan. Pakhtun resentment was not expressed in the same manner as that of the Sindis, but they were deeply concerned that, on the question of water and power, they would lose out to the Punjab.[121] Despite the prominent role played by the Pakhtuns in the West Pakistan government, there was growing bitterness between them and the Punjabis.[122] However, since the Sindis had lost more than any other minority, they were the most hostile to the process of centralization. The province was dominated by Punjabis and Muhajirs, most businesses were in non-Sindi hands, the indigenous population was neglected in the distribution of import permits, government projects were concentrated in the Punjab and Sind treasury surpluses were used outside the region.[123]

Table 5.3

Ethnic Representation in the Civil Service of Pakistan and the Government of West Pakistan

| | | | | *(Percentage)* |
Mother Tongue	In Pakistan	In CSP	In West Pakistan	In West Pakistan Government
Bengali	55.48	32.00	0.12	–
Punjabi	29.02	35.00	66.39	51.00
Sindi	5.51	5.00	12.59	8.63
Pashto	3.70	7.00	8.47	9.40
Baluchi	1.09		2.49	0.50
Urdu	3.65	21.00	7.57	26.80
Others	1.55	–	2.37	6.67

Source: *Census of Pakistan, 1961,* i, Statement 5.1, iv, p. 31. R. Braibanti, *Asian Bureaucratic Traditions Emergent from the British Imperial Tradition* (Durham, 1966), p. 269. *Census of West Pakistan Government Employees,* 1962, pp. 28-29, Table 9.

Table 5.4

Distribution of Muslim Industrial Investment and Population by 'Community', 1959

| | | *(Percentage)* |
Community	Industrial Investment	Population*
Halali Memon	26.5	0.16
Chinioti	9.0	0.03
Dawoodi Bohra	5.0	0.02
Khoja Ismaili	5.0	0.06
Khoja Isnashari	5.5	0.02
Other Muslim Trading Communities	5.5	0.08
Sayed and Shaikh	18.0	–
Pakhtun	8.0	7.0
Bengali Muslim	3.5	43.0
Other Muslims	14.0	37.5

Source: Gustav F. Papanek, *Pakistan's Development: Social Goals and Private Incentives* (Cambridge, Mass., 1967), p. 42.

* Rough estimates of community size.

On 7 October 1958, President Mirza and General Ayub Khan abrogated the Constitution, dismissed the central and provincial governments, dissolved the constituent and provincial assemblies, banned all political parties and proclaimed martial law. The two leaders simultaneously announced that they intended to re-establish constitutional government once the situation had been stabilized.[124] The alternative, however, that Mirza was considering was a 'controlled democracy' with a strong executive and administration, limited franchise and restricted political activity.[125] The ostensible reason given for the takeover was the collapse of law and order, such as the disgraceful scenes of violence in the East Pakistan Assembly resulting in the death of the Deputy Speaker, the inflammatory statements of Qaiyum Khan and the attempted secession by the Khan of Kalat. These reasons were just a fig-leaf for the military coup. It seems likely that the plan to seize power was decided around 15 September, before the incident in the East Pakistan Assembly and the rebellion by the Khan of Kalat.[126] Mirza was motivated by the realization that there was no way he could be re-elected President as he was increasingly becoming the main target of popular resentment.[127] His popularity among West Pakistanis had fallen after the autumn crisis of 1957, and he was actively resented by the leaders of East Pakistan.

On the other hand, his chief enemy Suhrawardy, in preparation for the general elections in March 1959, had established a base in East Pakistan and was confident that the Awami League would emerge as the largest single party there. In West Pakistan the situation was quite different, and the Awami League's attempted revival was not successful despite Suhrawardy's efforts. Here the Muslim League, under the presidentship of Qaiyum Khan, had conducted an efficacious mass contact campaign in the Punjab. In Sind, however, its position was weak as Khuro's Sind League had detached itself from the Muslim League and formed the Anti-One Unit Front, reducing the League's strength to mainly the Muhajir population of the urban areas. In these areas, it had to compete with the alliance formed between Jamat-i-Islami and the Nizam-i-Islam for the urban vote.[128] Despite these setbacks, however, there was a possibility that the Muslim League might win a small majority in the provincial assembly and among the West Pakistani delegates to the National Assembly; that is, if elections went according to schedule and were fair. In East Pakistan, the League was still in disgrace and had little chance. The National Awami Party also was preparing itself for the hustings. It had established itself in the Frontier and East Pakistan, and made major inroads in Sind as well. It was probably destined to play a more influential role than its size would suggest due to its involvement in the anti-One Unit campaign.[129]

For Mirza, however, the emerging scenario of the Muslim–Awami League coalition was quite unacceptable. But the political alternatives were exhausted. The other major contender in East Pakistan — the Krishak Sramik Party — was disintegrating, a fact publicly admitted by its leaders,[130] while in West Pakistan it was patent that the Republicans were not keen on early elections. They were organizationally weak and their only activity was in moving loyal officials into vital places in the administration so that they could rig the votes. Politically motivated transfers of police and civil servants were taking place and their men were packing the 'advisory committees' formed to appoint local bodies.[131] To make matters worse for the powers that be, the centre's position in West Pakistan was further undermined by the rise of the anti-One Unit lobby. It represented a broad spectrum, consisting of sections from the Republican Party, Muslim League and the National Awami Party, and was becoming stronger as the general elections approached. The Republican Party was hopelessly divided between those for and against One Unit. The Sindi delegates of the Republican Party formed a Parliamentary Board in conjunction with G.M. Sayed and Khuro's Sind League. To overcome these difficulties, the Republican Party arrived at a formula by which members from Sind were allowed to be anti-One Unit and those from the Punjab could support unification. The equivocal stance taken by the Republican leadership headed off a major rebellion by Sindi delegates.[132] The other anti-One Unit element was the National Awami Party which, except for the rank and file from the Punjab, was solidly for the break-up of West Pakistan. It had extracted a commitment from the Republicans that dissolution would take place if most of the delegates from the smaller units voted against One Unit. The Awami League's position, however, was that a clear majority of the West Pakistan Legislature must vote for dismemberment.[133]

It now seemed almost certain that the general elections in West Pakistan would bring to power a political combination committed to the break-up of One Unit. Suhrawardy would perhaps be successful in East Pakistan and come to terms with the new political reality and form a coalition with the Muslim League if he wanted to become Prime Minister. The military-bureaucratic combine's hostility to Suhrawardy was garbed in ethnic terms, but the issue was one of power and domination. It was not simply a Bengali-Punjabi clash but part of a wider conflict between the Punjab and the rest of the country. The Bengalis concurred with the non-Punjabi population of West Pakistan that the centralizing process had established the Punjabi domination of Pakistan and were prepared to dismantle it.[134] Consequently, the declaration of martial law was designed to perpetuate the policies of the ruling group.[135] It was feared that a viable political alternative would emerge that would be inimical to their interests. Thus, constitutional politics had to be terminated. However, President Mirza himself, within a short while, was removed by Ayub. The reason for Ayub distancing himself from Mirza was his intimate involvement in the disintegration of Pakistani politics: 'Mirza, for about five years had been up to [his] elbows in political manoeuvres " [*sic*]" and was an "inveterate ...intriguer."[136] No doubt, the army group felt that he was a liability, too closely linked with the 'corruption and maladministration' associated with the politicians. Another reason for the army wanting to get rid of Iskander Mirza was the controversial promotion of Lt General Musa, an Afghan Shiah from Hazara, to the post of Chief of Staff over the heads of several more senior officers. This promotion caused extensive discontent among the senior officers towards Mirza and his supporters.[137] Finally, President Mirza had become aware that Ayub's loyalty was uncertain, and tried to involve Air Commodore Rabb, the Chief of Staff of the Air Force in a plot against him. This backfired as Ayub was notified of the conspiracy. He removed Mirza and took over directly.[138]

The State Department was acutely aware that a *coup d'état* was in the offing. As early as 1956 and on several occasions in May and June 1958, President Mirza told the US embassy officials that he was prepared and ready to takeover.[139] Ambassador Hildreth, frustrated with dealing with a succession of ministers, felt that dictatorship was the only way out. However, the State Department's officials in Washington disagreed with this view. They saw no Mustafa Kemal Ataturk on the horizon. Neither Mirza nor Ayub had the character and vision to lead Pakistan into the future. On the contrary, they argued, dictatorship would continue to divert the country's limited resources to the military at the expense of social and economic development, probably resulting in economic deterioration and an increased pressure for aid from the US. It was also considered possible that under such economic pressures the military might go to war with India to regain Kashmir as the only other way out.[140] Another question considered by US officials was the viability of Pakistan in view of the hostility that the coup would generate in East Pakistan. It was incorrectly assumed that the implementation of military rule would be violently opposed in East Pakistan.[141] Despite the lack of resistance, there was evidence to suggest that separatist feelings were developing in East Pakistan. What was remarkable was that Suhrawardy predicted a scenario where local discontent would combine with Indian involvement in the future and result in the separation of East Pakistan, as actually happened in 1971.[142] Ayub Khan's regime suppressed the centrifugal forces and refused to recognize the legitimacy and depth of hostility of his policies. Thus, he sowed the dragon's teeth which ripened into the Bangladesh war of liberation.

The US realized that military rule in Pakistan would lead to internal and external confrontation. Consequently, the preferred option was that elections should be held and that Suhrawardy, who was closely associated with them, should be allowed to come to power.[143] It is difficult to estimate the involvement of the intelligence wing of the US government in the coup. There were links between the intelligence agencies of the two countries, and Sardar Bahadur Khan, Ayub's brother, claimed that the

Central Intelligence Agency was involved in the takeover.[144] However, the official position of the United States was summed up by an embassy memorandum: 'No American should be led to believe that the United States, officially or unofficially, had anything whatever to do with the establishment of dictatorship in Pakistan. The United States did not.'[145]

The collapse of constitutional politics was due to the polarization between centrifugal and centripetal forces. This dichotomy formed the framework within which inter-party and intra-party disputes took place. Poor leadership, weak party organization and the lack of programme only aggravated the political volatility caused by the military-bureaucratic oligarchy's determination to dominate Pakistan. Karachi was unwilling to concede ground to the opposition and reach a political solution. The compromise formula of Mohammad Ali Bogra was a dead letter even before it had been completed. Khwaja Nazimuddin's legislative coup was a counteraction based on the realization that Ghulam Mohammad and his cohort had no intention of accepting a constitution that would weaken their authority. Ghulam Mohammad's cohort, however, was surprised by Nazimuddin's ambush, and the counter-coup became entangled in a legal thicket. The consensus in Ghulam Mohammad's camp was to go along with the courts, but if crucial verdicts were given against them, they would then resort to the mailed fist. Time was on the side of the centre. John Foster Dulles had decided to support the pro-US camp — a fact of paramount importance. This backing was in recognition of the responsibility of the Ghulam Mohammad group in changing the foreign policy of Pakistan and bringing it into the western alliance. The concomitant influx of military and economic assistance consolidated the military-bureaucratic camp's position, both in the short and the long term.

The objective of the Punjabi group was to promulgate a unitary structure with One Unit as its centre-piece. There were no differences over the objectives but only over how they could be achieved. The hardline approach of Mirza and Ayub — their intention to bypass constitutional processes and rule through executive fiat — was overruled by the US who preferred Chaudhri Mohammad Ali's political option. The Constitution, however, was not a product of consensus and accommodation between the disparate parties. Support for it was marshalled in the assembly through a combination of Machiavellian and bulldozing tactics, and there lay its essential flaw. The military-bureaucratic oligarchy achieved success by imposing its will on the opposition, and the structures that it created could only be sustained by the continuation of executive pressure. Mirza used the presidency to pulverize and manipulate the fragile policy of Pakistan into smaller units, so that he could recombine them into new coalitions which were loyal to him. When it became clear that the capricious disequilibrium was inimical to the mandarins and praetorian guard and to him personally, he began to consider alternatives. Consequently, Mirza's intervention in the political arena, and the military support for it, were based on the assumption that the collapse of the democratic process would justify martial law.

Ironically, the provocative activities of the centre contributed to the revival and unity of the centrifugal opposition. The emergence of the Republican Party because of the split in the Muslim League undermined, perhaps, the only organization that could have legitimized the attempts at centralization. The League, however, was torn asunder and reduced to a rump, and its influence limited to the Punjab. Yet it still was expected to be the largest party in the West Pakistan assembly. The unexpected end product that emerged from the political melting-pot was the combined opposition in West Pakistan. In the minority provinces of West Pakistan, the anti-centrist opposition cut across party lines to form the Anti-One Unit Front which had support from members of the Muslim League, the Republican Party and the most implacable opponent of unification — the National Awami Party. The opposition to One Unit also could count on the support of the East Pakistan National Awami Party, which emerged as an influential organization. Suhrawardy, undoubtedly, led the single most effective all-Pakistan party that was well placed for electoral success in the eastern wing. However, it was clear that without accommodating the Muslim League and the Anti-One Unit Front he could not take office as the next premier. Thus, whatever political permutation was to emerge after the general elections, Suhrawardy probably would lead a coalition that was determined to scrap the constitutional structures that had been imposed by the Punjabi group.

Precisely in order to defend their gains which had been secured through centralization, Mirza and Ayub imposed martial law. It was feared that the resurgent centrifugal forces would undermine the position of the army, and the alleged collapse of law and order became a cover for their activity. Ultimately, Pakistan's constitutional politics perished, not due to any inherent weakness but because of the coercive power of those who feared its success. The constitutional process did not die a natural death but was the victim of political assassination. However, Mirza himself became a victim of the military group and was ousted from power. He had become too closely associated with the political turmoil, and his rash attempt to remove Ayub only confirmed that he was an incorrigible intriguer who was best exiled. The army rejected the anti-centre demands of the opposition, and pursued policies that maximized the possibility of conflict both internally and externally. Ayub Khan's strategy was fraught with danger. It heightened the possibility of conflict with India and of secessionist movements within Pakistan. It established the hallmark of Pakistani politics as Punjabi domination imposed on the rest of the country. The fundamental tension between centrist structures and policies, meant to shore up that domination, and centrifugal forces were at the root of the discontent that led to the emergence of Bangladesh. The same tensions underlie the basic political problems of post-1971 Pakistan as well. Their roots go back to the pre-partition decades — the unresolved tension between all-India organizations which claim the allegiance of all Muslims and the regional interests fostered by the devolution of power to the provinces.

NOTES

1. NAUS, RG 59, Box 4146, 790D.00/3-1553, Memorandum of Conversation with Ayub Khan, 28 February 1953.
2. NAUS, RG 59, Box 4148, 790D.00/9-2554, Emmerson to the Department of State, 25 September 1954.
3. NAUS, RG 59, Box 4147, 790D.00/11-2153, Memorandum of Conversation with Sayed Wajid Ali, 18 November 1953.
4. NAUS, RG 59, Box 4146, 790D.00/1-753, Bream to the Department of State, 1 July 1953.
5. Between 1954 and 1955, Pakistan became a signatory to the US-Pak Mutual Defence Assistance Treaty and the Mutual Defence Assistance Programme, and entered the Turco-Pakistan Pact and the South-East Asia Treaty Organization (SEATO).
6. NAUS, RG 59, Box 4148, 790D.00/7-154, Emmerson to the Secretary of State, 1 July 1954.
7. NAUS, RG 59, Box 4148, 790D.00/9-2954, Dulles to American Embassy, Karachi, 29 September 1954.
8. NAUS, RG 59, Box 3876.26, 790D.5MSP/8-1059, 10 August 1959.
9. NAUS, RG 59, Box 4147, 790D.00/5-1353, Bream to the Department of State, 13 May 1953.
10. NAUS, RG 59, Box 4147, 790D.00/5-153, Davis to the Department of State, 1 May 1953.
11. NAUS, RG 59, Box 4147, 790D.00/7-1753, Withers to the Department of State, 17 July 1953.
12. QAA, PC-ARN-7 (Abdur Rub Nishtar Collection), Manzar-i- Alam to Nishtar, 20 July 1953.
13. NAUS, RG 59, Box 4147, 790D.00/11-753, Withers to the Department of State, 7 November 1953.
14. He proposed a bicameral legislature with equal powers, and that no motion could be passed unless 30 per cent of the members from both West and East Pakistan supported it. Talukder Maniruzzaman, *The Politics of Development: The Case of Pakistan, 1947-1958* (Dacca, 1971), pp. 47-58.
15. NAUS, RG 59, Box 4148, 790D.00/10-2354, Memorandum of conversation with Khwaja Nazimuddin, 23 October 1954.
16. NAUS, RG 59, Box 4147, 790D.00/11-253, Communication from Near Eastern and

African Affairs, Mr Byroade to the Under Secretary to the Department of State, Mr Murphy, 5 November 1953.

17. NAUS, RG 59, Box 4147, 790D.00/12-3053, Hildreth to the Secretary of State, 30 December 1953.

18. NAUS, RG 59, Box 4147, 790D.00/11-553, Hildreth to the Secretary of State, 5 November 1953. Box 4147, 790D.00/12-3053, Hildreth to the Secretary of State, 30 December 1953.

19. NAUS, RG 59, Box 4148, 790D.00/9-1654, Emmerson to Hildreth at the Department of State, 16 September 1954.

20. NAUS, RG 59, Box 4148, 790D.00 9-2554, Emmerson to the Secretary of State, 25 September 1954.

21. NAUS, RG 59, Box 4148, 790D.00/10-154, Aldrich, London, to the Secretary of State, 15 October 1954.

22. NAUS, RG 59, Box 4148, 790D.00/12-2254, Hildreth to the Secretary of State, 22 December 1954.

23. NAUS, RG 59, Box 3860, 790D.00/6-1755, Soulen to the Department of State, 17 June 1955.

24. Ibid.

25. Ibid. NAUS, RG 59, Box 3859, 790D.00/3-2255, Hildreth to the Secretary of State, 22 March 1955. Munir was most concerned that the authoritarian direction should be arrested. He deplored the present situation where those at the helm in Karachi were 'responsible to no one' since they had dissolved the legislature. NAUS, RG 59, Box 3859, 790D.00/4-1455, Memorandum of Conversation with Mohammad Munir, 14 April 1955.

26. NAUS, RG 59, Box 3860, 790D.00/6-1755, Soulen, to the Department of State, 17 June 1955.

27. Ibid.

28. Khalid B. Sayeed, *The Political System of Pakistan*, p. 77.

29. 'One Unit Document', Section B, p. 1; Section D, p. 6.

30. NAUS, RG 59, Box 3859, 790D.00/2-2555, Hildreth to the Secretary of State, 25 February 1955.

31. NAUS, RG 59, Box 3860, 790D.00/7-1355, Williams to the Department of State, 13 July 1955.

32. 'M.L. Acceptance of Regional Autonomy Reported (Muree [sic] Pact), 10 July 1955,' H.H. Rahman, ed, *History of the Bangladesh War of Independence*, i, p. 430.

33. NAUS, RG 59, Box 3860, 790D.00/9-1555, Soulen to the Department of State, 15 September 1955.

34. Keith Callard, *Pakistan: A Political Study* (London, 1957), Appendix I, The Constitution of the Islamic Republic of Pakistan, p. 339.

35. M.R. Afzal, *Political Parties in Pakistan, 1947- 1958*, pp. 172-75.

36. Ibid., pp. 164-65.

37. NAUS, RG 59, Box 3860, 790D.00/6-455, Memorandum of Conversation with Mirza, 3 June 1955.

38. M.R. Afzal, *Political Parties in Pakistan*, pp. 164-65.

39. NAUS, RG 59, Box 3860, 790D.00/9-1955, Gardiner to the Secretary of State, 19 September 1955.

40. Ibid.

41. *Pakistan Observer*, 6 April 1956. The Republican Party's leadership was dominated by Shiahs. Mirza did not favour them for religious reasons, but was trying to use them as well as big landholders for political ends. His political technique was to place trusted men, loyal only to him, in key positions in the government and the party. But to the Sunni majority it appeared that he was favouring the Shiah community. NAUS, RG 59, Box 3864, 790D.00/4-1658, Lewis to the Department of State, 16 March 1958.

42. M.R. Afzal, *Political Parties in Pakistan*, pp. 186-88.

43. NAUS, RG 59, Box 3860, 790D.00/9-255, Memorandum of Conversation with Suhrawardy, 2 September 1955.

44. NAUS, RG 59, Box 3862, 790D.00/2-2657, Hildreth to the Secretary of State, 26 February 1957.

45. NAUS, RG 59, Box 3860, 790D.00/9-255, Memorandum of Conversation with Suhrawardy, 2 September 1955.

46. NAUS, RG 59, Box 3860, 790D.00/1-1156, Williams to the Department of State, 11 January 1956.

47. NAUS, RG 59, Box 3864, 790D.00/4-2458, Williams to the Department of State, 24 March 1958.

48. NAUS, RG 59, Box 3862, 790D.00/5-3157, USARMA Karachi to the DEPTAR Washington, 31 May 1956.

49. NAUS, RG 59, Box 3861, 790D.00/5-2456, American Embassy, Karachi, to the Department of State, 24 May 1956.

50. NAUS, RG 59, Box 3863, 790D.00/11-157, Langley to the Secretary of State, 1 November 1957. Box 3863, 790D.00/11-1557, Lewis to the Department of State, 15 November 1957.

51. NAUS, RG 59, Box 3863, 790D.00/10-157, Lewis to the Department of State, 11 October 1957.

52. Henry Thomas and Dana Lee Thomas, *Living Biographies of Religious Leaders*, Bombay, 1956.

53. NAUS, RG 59, Box 3862, 790D.00/9-2256, American Embassy, Karachi, to the Department of State, 22 September 1956.

54. NAUS, RG 59, Box 3863, 790D.00/11-1557, Lewis to the Department of State, 15 November 1957. Box 3863, 790D.00/10-2457, Williams to the Department of State, 24 October 1957.

55. NAUS, RG 59, Box 3863, 790D.00/12-1957, Office Memorandum of US Government, Bartlett, South Asian Affairs, to Rountree, Near Eastern Affairs, 19 December 1957. Mohammad H.R. Talukdar, ed, *Memoirs of Huseyn Shaheed Suhrawardy*, pp. 65-66, 125.

56. Ibid., p. 65.

57. NAUS, RG 59, Box 4147, 790D.00/11-753, Withers to the Department of State, 7 November 1953.

58. NAUS, RG 59, Box 4147, 790D.00/3-3054, Bream to the Department of State, 30 March 1954.

59. Keith Callard, *Pakistan*, p. 57.

60. *Constituent Assembly of Pakistan, Debates*, i, No. 51, 16 January 1956, p. 1844.

61. NAUS, RG 59, Box 3863, 790D.00/2-2858, Telegram from Langley to the Department of State, 28 February 1958.

62. *Pakistan Observer*, 22 May 1956.

63. Safdar Mahmood, *Pakistan Divided* (Lahore, 1984), pp. 13-14.
64. 'Twenty-One Points of the United Front', M.R. Afzal, *Political Parties in Pakistan, 1947-1958*, Appendix I, pp. 225-26.
65. NAUS, RG 59, Box 4147, 790D.00/3-3054, Bream to the Department of State, 30 March 1954.
66. NAUS, RG 59, Box 4148, 790D.00/5-1554, Emmerson to the Department of State, 15 May 1954.
67. Huq expanded the original four-man cabinet into one consisting of seven members from the Krishak Sramik, five from the Awami League and two from the Nizam-i-Islam Party.
68. NAUS, RG 59, Box 4148, 790D.00/5-1554, Emmerson to the Department of State, 15 May 1954.
69. NAUS, RG 59, Box 4148, 790D.00/5-2254, Memorandum of Conversation with Ayub Khan, 22 May 1954, Memorandum of Conversation with M.A. Gurmani, 21 May 1954, Memorandum of Conversation with Wajid Ali, 21 May 1954.
70. NAUS, RG 59, Box 4148, 790D.00/5-2154, USARMA, Karachi, to the Secretary of State, 21 May 1954.
71. *Constituent Assembly (Legislature) of Pakistan, Debates*, i, no. 23, 28 June 1954, p. 1376.
72. NAUS, RG 59, Box 3859, 790D.00/3-2455, American Consulate, Dacca, to the Department of State, 24 March 1955.
73. NAUS, RG 59, Box 3864, 790D.00/8-2858, American Consulate, Dacca, to the Department of State, 28 August 1958.
74. NAUS, RG 59, Box 3862, 790D.00/12-1456, Williams to the Department of State, 14 December, 1956.
75. NAUS, RG 59, Box 3862, 790D.00/2-2857, Williams to the Department of State, 28 February 1957.
76. NAUS, RG 59, Box 3862, 790D.00/3-1257, Williams to the Secretary of State, 12 March 1957.
77. NAUS, RG 59, Box 3862, 790D.00/6-2757, Painter to the Department of State, 27 June 1957.
78. *Dainik Sangbad*, 26 July 1957, in H.H. Rahman, ed, *History of the Bangladesh War Of Independence*, pp. 611-12. Maulana Bhashani's Address at the All-Pakistan Democratic Workers' Conference, in Dacca, 25-26 July 1957, ibid., pp. 765-66.
79. M.R. Afzal, *Political Parties in Pakistan, 1947-1958*, pp. 209-10.
80. NAUS, RG 59, Box 3864, 790D.00/7-258, Caprie to the Department of State, 25 July 1958.
81. NAUS, RG 59, Box 3864, 790D.00/7-1458, Caprie to the Department of State, 14 July 1958.
82. NAUS, RG 59, Box 3864, 790D.00/9-258, Caprie to the Department of State, 2 September 1958.
83. NAUS, RG 59, Box 3864, 790D.00/9-3058, American Consulate, Dacca, to the Department of State, 30 September 1958.
84. NAUS, RG 59, Box 4147, 790D.009/9-2853, Withers to the Department of State, 28 September 1953.
85. Ibid.

86. NAUS, RG 59, Box 4147, 790D.00/3-2754, American Embassy, Karachi, to the Department of State, 27 March 1954.
87. M.R. Afzal, *Political Parties in Pakistan*, p. 72. Imdad Husain, 'The Failure of Parliamentary Politics in Pakistan, 1953-58' (Oxford Univ. D. Phil. thesis, 1966), pp. 95-97.
88. *Dawn*, 7 March 1954.
89. *Dawn*, 17 March 1954.
90. M.R. Afzal, *Political Parties in Pakistan*, p. 145. *Dawn*, 26 August 1954.
91. NAUS, RG 59, Box 4148, 790D.00/11-1354, Soulen to the Department of State, 13 September 1954.
92. NAUS, RG 59, Box 3859, 790D.00/3-2555, Soulen to the Department of State, 4 April 1955.
93. NAUS, RG 59, Box 3859, 790D.00/4-455, Soulen to the Department of State, 30 June 1955.
94. NAUS, RG 59, Box 3860, 790D.00/6-3055, Soulen to the Department of State, 30 June 1955.
95. This had already occurred under the British where newly irrigated land was distributed among retired soldiers from the Punjab.
96. NAUS, RG 59, Box 4148, 790D.00/7-3154, American Embassy, Karachi, to the Department of State, 31 July 1954. Box 3859, 790D.00/5-2155, Memorandum of Conversation with G.M. Sayed, Sheikh Abdul Majid Sindhi and Ghulam Mustafa Bhurgiri, 15 May 1955.
97. Imdad Husain, 'The Failure of Parliamentary Politics in Pakistan, 1953-58' (Oxford Univ. D.Phil. thesis, 1966), pp. 97-98, 101, 245-46. *Dawn*, 6, 17 January, 16 November 1954.
98. NAUS, RG 59, Box 3860, 790D.00/7-155, American Embassy, Karachi, to the Department of State, 1 July 1955. Box 3862, 790D.00/1-1057, Fisk to the Department of State, 10 January 1955.
99. NAUS, RG 59, Box 4148, 790D.00/11-2254, Fisk to the Department of State, 22 November 1954.
100. *Dawn*, 26 November 1954.
101. Qaiyum Khan, who could not get elected, accused the NWFP government of terrorist tactics. He disclosed that great pressure was brought to bear on the delegates by the authorities, and that he himself was followed by the CID who threatened his supporters. NAUS, RG 59, Box 3860, 790D.00/6-3055, Soulen to the Department of State, 30 June 1955.
102. Imdad Husain, 'The Failure of Parliamentary Politics in Pakistan, 1953-58' (Oxford Univ. D.Phil. thesis, 1966), p. 246.
103. NAUS, RG 59, Box 3860, 790D.00/9-1555, Soulen to the Department of State, 15 September 1955.
104. Imdad Hussain, 'The Failure of Party Politics in Pakistan', p. 85.
105. NAUS, RG 59, Box 4147, 790D.00/5-2853, American Consulate, Lahore, to the Department of State, 28 May 1953. Box 4147, 790D.00/5-2153, American Consulate, Lahore, to the Department of State, 21 May 1953.
106. NAUS, RG 59, Box 4148, 790D.00/11-2254, Fisk to the Department of State, 22 November 1954.
107. Khalid B. Sayeed, *The Political System of Pakistan*, p. 77.

108. Nur Ahmad, *From Martial Law to Martial Law: Politics in the Punjab, 1919-1958,* by Craig Baxter, ed, (Boulder, 1985), p. 348. M.R. Afzal, *Political Parties in Pakistan,* pp. 162-63.
109. NAUS, RG 59, Box 4148, 790D.00/11-2254, Fisk to the Department of State, 22 November 1954.
110. NAUS, RG 59, Box 3860, 790D.00/9-1555, Soulen to the Department of State, 15 September 1955.
111. M.R. Afzal, *Political Parties in Pakistan, 1947-1958*, pp. 178-79.
112. NAUS, RG 59, Box 3861, 790D.00/3-156, American Consulate, Lahore, to the Department of state. Box 3862, 790D.00/6-1757, American Embassy, Karachi, to the Department of State, Memorandum of Conversation with Mahmud Ali Kasuri, 17 June 1957.
113. NAUS, RG 59, Box 3862, 790D.00/2-1557, Spengler to the Department of State, 15 February 1957.
114. NAUS, RG 59, Box 3863, 790D.00/10-157, Lewis to the Department of State, 1 October 1957.
115. Ibid.
116. NAUS, RG 59, Box 3863, 790D.00/12-557, American Consulate, Lahore, to the Department of State, 5 December 1957.
117. NAUS, RG 59, Box 3863, 790D.00/10-157, Lewis to the Department of State, 1 October 1957.
118. NAUS, RG 59, Box 3864, 790D.00/5-658, Memorandum of Conversation with G.M. Sayed, 18 April 1958.
119. NAUS, RG 59, Box 3864, 790D.00/9-1758, Mallory-Browne to the Department of State, 17 September 1958.
120. *Dawn,* 21 September 1958.
121. NAUS, RG 59, Box 3860, 790D.00/7-855, American Embassy, Karachi, to the Department of State, 20 June 1958.
122. NAUS, RG 59, Box 3864, 790D.00/6-458, American Embassy, Karachi, to the Department of State, 4 June 1958.
123. NAUS, RG 59, Box 3863, 790D.00/10-457, Memorandum of Conversation with Pir Pagro, 4 October 1957.
124. NAUS, RG 59, Box 3864, 790D.00/10-2858, Knight to the Department of State, 28 October 1958.
125. NAUS, RG 59, Box 3864, 790D.00/10-2958, Langley to the Secretary of State, 29 October 1958. These musings became the principles on which Ayub Khan's Constitution of 1962 was based.
126. NAUS, RG 59, Box 3864, 790D.00/10-2858, Knight to Department of State, 28 October 1958.
127. NAUS, RG 59, Box 3864, 790D.00/6-2058, American Embassy, Karachi, to the Department of State, 20 June 1958.
128. NAUS, RG 59, Box 3864, 790D.00/8-2958, American Embassy, Karachi, to the Department of State, 29 August 1958.
129. NAUS, RG 59, Box 3862, 790D.00/2-2857, American Embassy, Karachi, to the Department of State, 28 February 1957.
130. NAUS, RG 59, Box 3864, 790D.00/9-958, American Embassy, Karachi, to the Department of State, 9 September 1958.
131. NAUS, RG 59, Box 3864, 790D.00/9-1858, Mallory-Browne to the Department of

State, 18 September 1958. Box 3864, 790D.00/7-258, American Embassy, Karachi, to the Department of State, 2 July 1958.

132. *Dawn*, 27, 29, 30 September 1958.

133. *Dawn*, 27 September 1958.

134. NAUS, RG 59, Box 3863, 790D.00/9-2457, American Consulate, Dacca, to the Department of State, 24 September 1957.

135. NAUS, RG 59, Box 3864, 790D.00/10-2858, Knight to the Department of State, 28 October 1958.

136. NAUS, RG 59, Box 3864, 790D.00/10-2958, Langley, Karachi, to the Secretary of State, 29 October 1958.

137. The Deputy Chief of Staff, Major General Sher Ali, resigned in opposition. He argued that the President promoted Shiahs to key position in order to ensure the loyalty of the army in an emergency. NAUS, RG 59, Box 3864, 790D.00/4-1658, Lewis to the Department of State, 16 April 1958.

138. Rabb had over a thousand troops stationed under his command in Karachi and was ordered by Mirza to arrest four army generals, including Major General Yayha Khan and Major General Sher Bahadur, who were in the city. NAUS, RG 59, Box 3866, 790D.00/4-159, Carle to the Department of State, 1 April 1959.

139. NAUS, RG 59, Box 3861, 790D.00/5-2456, American Embassy, Karachi, to the Department of State, 24 May 1956. Box 3864, 790D.00/5-2058, Langley to the Secretary of State, 20 May 1958. Box 3864, 790D.00/6-1258, Langley to the Secretary of State, 12 June 1958.

140. NAUS, RG 59, Box 3876.26, 790D.5 MSP/4-1557, Evaluation of Pakistan Program by Office of the Assistant to the Director of Evaluation, 1 February 1957, pp. 36-37.

141. NAUS, RG 59, Box 3864, 790D.00/5-2958, Williams to the Department of State, 29 May 1958.

142. NAUS, RG 59, Box 3864, 790D.00/12-658, Memorandum of Conversation with H.S. Suhrawardy, 21 November 1958.

143. NAUS, RG 59, Box 3864, 790D.00/4-758, Office Memorandum from Bartlett, South Asian Affairs to Rountree, Near Eastern and African Affairs, 7 April 1958.

144. NAUS, RG 59, Box 3875, 790D.05/12-1357, American Embassy, Karachi, to the Department of ⁄ State, 13 December 1957. Tariq Ali, *Pakistan: Military Rule or People's Power* (London, 1970), p. 88.

145. NAUS, RG 59, Box 3864, 790D.00/10-1558, Memorandum from the Ambassador [Langley] to all Embassy personnel, 15 October 1958.

CONCLUSION

The parameters of South Asian Muslim politics were firmly set by the India Act of 1935. Muslim political loyalties were divided between strong regional parties and weak organizations with centralizing ambitions. Subcontinental parties such as the Congress and the Muslim League, with some exceptions in the case of the former, had little influence. They were confronted by regional parties in the Muslim majority provinces keen on maximizing their autonomy at the periphery. Of these, the Unionists were the most powerful. Their position was reinforced by the activities of communitarian parties, which further undermined all-India political organizations. The opposition between the two forces established a historical continuity that stretched across the chasm of partition.

However, the success of the Congress in the 1937 elections initiated a major political shift. The regional Muslim or Muslim-dominated parties feared that the Congress would corral them within a Hindu-dominated unitary state. Thus, for the Muslims, the political focus shifted back to the centre and revived the fortunes of the AIML and Jinnah as protectors of Muslim interests at the all-India level. Their revival was aided by the Congress' Quit India campaign and the encouragement that Jinnah received from the Raj as a counterweight to the Congress' perceived threat to the war effort. Initially Jinnah was only able to win over the élites of the Muslim minority provinces by playing the anti-Congress card. Among the urban masses he was less successful, and was forced to play second fiddle to Mashriqi until the mid-1940s when the Khaksar star waned. By 1944 the Muslim League was influential among the urban population throughout India, particularly in the Muslim minority provinces. The League then tried to widen its popularity by using community consciousness to pull the regional parties into its orbit. The élites of the Muslim minority provinces funded the pro-Pakistan publicity generated by intellectuals and helped establish the hegemony of the Pakistan idea, despite its many contradictions.

Muslim nationalism acquired greater influence in the provinces, thanks to Jinnah's enhanced all-India status and the Pakistan slogan. The regional parties, however, remained strong. In the Punjab, Khizr, backed by the British, strongly resisted the League's advance. In Bengal it was transformed into a mass organization because it was taken over by elements concerned primarily with Muslim regional interests. But in Sind and Sarhad, Jinnah and Pakistan had hardly any influence at all. Thus, by 1944, the League had achieved partial unity in the subcontinent's Muslim politics but still faced strong challenges in the provinces.

However, the end of the war in Europe was followed by constitutional negotiations that generated political uncertainties. The League capitalized on the anxieties of the Muslim-majority provinces and welcomed deserters from the provincial parties into its fold. It was helped by the emergence of economic nationalism which gave Muslim nationalism a mass base. The Congress had lost much of its support among the Muslims by the late 1940s. The incarceration of its leaders and cadres after 1942 had left the League free to take full advantage of the declining popularity of the Congress. Thus, when it returned to the negotiating table only weeks after the leaders were released, the Congress stood no chance of catching up with the League.

On the basis of his enhanced authority, Jinnah was able to extract the maximum constitutional concessions from the British and the Congress. However, the weakness of the unifying impulse was at the root of Muslim ideological confusion. Jinnah's understanding of Pakistan changed because of pressures from within the party, and he had to accommodate the different interpretations so as to avoid a revolt against his leadership. The problem was compounded by the League's lack of strong party structure needed to control and enforce discipline over the regional supporters. Jinnah's personal authority was of limited value at the periphery. There were some instances where the central leadership could enforce their authority (for instance, the expulsion of Khizr and Sayed, and the reorganization of the NWFP League). The AIML, however, was virtually bereft of any constructive capacity. It was dependent on the provincial leaders for repairing any damage and advancing the party's cause.

Moreover, strong regional concerns and identifications had penetrated Muslim nationalism, as in the case of Bengal and the Punjab. In the Sarhad and Sind, the matter was complicated by the emergence of Pakhtun and Sindi ethnicity as a counter to the Pakistan ideology. However, opposition to the Muslim League collapsed almost overnight owing to contingent circumstances. The Civil Disobedience Movement mounted by the League, at an extremely tense moment in the history of the subcontinent, triggered off a communal explosion which engulfed northern India. The ferocity of the violence caused the support for anti-League parties in the Muslim majority provinces to collapse, and their fate was sealed when the Congress demanded partition. Ineluctably, Pakistan came into existence through political exigencies that became powerful influences during the negotiations for the transfer of power. Hence there were difficulties, many unforeseen, which confronted the Muslim League leadership in their efforts to establish their authority in the new state. The League had to remove the confusion surrounding the idea of Pakistan itself, harmonize the strong currents of regional interest with the aims of the leadership and set up a new centre.

The leadership's perception of potential threats from India left it in no doubt that a strong centre was crucial if Pakistan was to survive as an independent state. This was the one area where there was an agreement, in principle, between the Punjabi and Bengali groups in the cabinet. However, the fact that centralization was to be achieved by aligning with the United States was the source of some of the differences within the cabinet and party and with the emerging opposition. Rather than reaching a broad consensus, the leadership dealt harshly with all potential opposition and anybody who suggested alternatives to the government's strategy. They made examples of hapless small groups, such as the People's Organization, the Communist Party of Pakistan and the Jinnah Awami Muslim League. Internal dissent within the provincial Leagues was crushed equally robustly. Executive fiats and party discipline were deployed to subdue recalcitrant chief ministers and replace them with pliant supporters, with varying degrees of success. However, continuous intervention by the military-bureaucratic oligarchy had serious long-term implications. It retarded the emergence of an alternative leadership, broke up the Muslim League into numerous opposition parties and ultimately prepared the ground for the Governor-General's assault on parliamentary democracy itself.

Nazimuddin's downfall was due to at least two separate intrigues against his government. The Prime Minister's attempt to diffuse the opposition to Karachi, that was building up in East Bengal, through constitutional concessions, was expressed in the Final Report. The possibility that, through the political process, Bengal could dominate Pakistan set alarm-bells ringing in the military-bureaucratic camp and among the provincial politicians in the Punjab. Daultana turned the anti-Ahmadiyya agitation against the premier to depose him. Ghulam Mohammad, aware of this manoeuvre, allowed Daultana to mortally wound Nazimuddin so that neither could resist him when he staged his takeover bid. The fact that the Bengali group was prepared to placate the religious opposition by sacrificing Zafrullah (the architect of Pakistan's pro-western foreign policy) increased the urgency for the Governor-General to rid himself of Nazimuddin and his supporters.

The emergence of the Punjabi-dominated military-bureaucratic combine as the dominant force in the country caused a major shift in the politics of Pakistan. The usurpers had only limited political support in Lahore, and were surrounded by strong currents of anti-centre politics emanating from East Bengal, the NWFP and Sind. As a result, the political configuration established by Muslim nationalism was restructured, and Muslim politics was again marked by strong centrifugal tendencies as it was in the 1930s and early 1940s. The Punjab's position, however, changed from being a major advocate of provincial autonomy to becoming the greatest enthusiast for a strong centre. Ghulam Mohammad's dismissal of Nazimuddin destroyed the fragile unity wrought by Muslim nationalism and reactivated the strong regional concerns in Pakistan's politics.

The military-bureaucratic oligarchy's determination not to concede ground to the opposition and reach a political solution only aggravated the political instability. The compromise formula of Mohammad Ali Bogra was a dead letter even before it had been completed. Khwaja Nazimuddin's legislative coup caught Ghulam Mohammad's cohort by surprise and led directly to the counter-coup. When their actions became entangled with the courts, the consensus in Ghulam Mohammad's camp was that if the verdict went against them they would resort to military rule. Time was on the side of the centre. John Foster Dulles decided to support the military-bureaucratic camp in recognition of their service in bringing Pakistan into the western alliance.

The objective of the Punjabi group was to establish a strong centre with One Unit as its hub. The constitution, however, was not a product of any consensus or accommodation but was achieved with brute force, and there lay its fundamental flaw. The military-bureaucratic oligarchy could only sustain its control over the opposition by holding on ruthlessly to the reins of power. The brittle unity in Pakistan's politics was broken up by President Mirza in his quest for new, loyal coalitions. As a result, the political processes became so volatile that they began slipping out of the Punjabi cohort's control. It was in this situation that a military takeover was contemplated. For Mirza and Ayub this had always been the preferred option, but they had been dissuaded by US influence. Consequently, there was an assumption behind Mirza's manipulation of the political process that if it got out of control they would be justified in taking authoritarian action.

As expected, the arbitrary actions of the junta led to the revival of anti-centre politics. The Republican Party was in disarray. The rump of the Muslim League's influence, led by Qaiyum Khan, was limited to the

Punjab, but it was still expected to form the largest grouping in the West Pakistan Assembly. In the former minority provinces of West Pakistan, the opposition cut across party lines to form the Anti-One Unit Front which had the support of members of the Muslim League, the Replication Party and the National Awami Party. The opposition to One Unit could also count on support from the East Pakistan National Awami Party. Undoubtedly, the Awami League was the only party with all-Pakistan pretensions, and was expected to do well in the elections, mainly in East Pakistan. It was likely that it would form a coalition with the Muslim League and accommodate the demands of the Anti-One Unit Front if it was to form the government. Such a coalition almost certainly would have had to scrap One Unit.

It was precisely for this reason that Mirza and Ayub imposed martial law. They feared that the anti-centre forces would capture political power and dismantle the constitutional structures used to keep the Punjabi group in power. However, Mirza was also ousted from power. He had become too closely associated with the political turmoil to be tolerated. His rash attempt to remove Ayub only confirmed his image as a trouble-maker who had to be got out of the way. Ayub Khan pursued an uncompromising line, refusing to accommodate the demands of the opposition. His efforts to concentrate all power in the hands of a central oligarchy maximized the possibility of conflict, both internally and externally. Some State Department officials noted that his strategy increased the chances of confrontation with India and secessionist movements within Pakistan. It simply reinforced the emerging trend in Pakistan's politics: a Punjabi dominated centre imposing control on the rest of the country. The fundamental tension between an autocratic centre and regional interests was at the root of the discontent that led to the emergence of Bangladesh. Under different circumstances it was also the ultimate cause for the Baluchistan rebellion of the 1970s, the uprising in Sind in the 1980s and the recent emergence of Muhajir ethnicity. This tension between inept efforts at centralization and the assertion of regional autonomy that can be traced back to the colonial period remains the basic problem underlying the politics of Pakistan even today.

GLOSSARY

abwab	Illegal exaction
alim	Scholar versed in Islamic knowledge
anjuman	Association, society pl. *ulama*
anna	Indian currency, sixteenth of a Rupee
ajlaf	Of the lower orders (sing. *jalaf*)
ashura	Voluntary fast-day which is observed on the 10th of *Muharram*
ashraf	Muslims of respectable status (sing. *sharif*).
assalam alaikum	Peace be with you
atta	Flour
azad	Free, independent
bania	Hindu trader or moneylender
barawafat	The 12th day of the month *Rabi al-awwal*. It is observed as a holy day in commemoration of the death of Prophet Mohammad
bhadralok	'Respectable people,' refers particularly to the high caste Hindu élite of Bengal
biraderi	Patrilineal kinship group
chehlum	Funeral observance forty days after death. The Shiahs observe a ritual anniversary for the death of the sons of Ali
crore	Ten million
darbar	Court of a king or great saint
dars-i-nizamia	Traditional curriculum emphasising Arabic, philosophy and jurisprudence which is used in most Muslim seminaries
dal-bhat	Literally rice and pulses, used to signify basic subsistence
fatwa	An opinion on a point of law concerning civil or religious matters by a Muslim divine
firman	Royal proclamation
gaddi	Throne or seat of authority
hari	Sharecropper without occupancy rights, or landless labourer
hijrat	Flight, act of migration from religious persecution
inam	Tax-free land grant
izzat	Prestige, honour

jagirdar	A landholder who has a revenue-free land grant
jirga	Tribal council, body of tribesmen representing a tribe *vis-à-vis* the government
jotedar	Peasant farmer, usually one with large holdings
jukta	United
kafir	Unbeliever, non-Muslim
kamin	Village menial, artisan
khan	Chief, landlord
khatib	One who delivers the sermon in a mosque
khel	Subdivision of a tribe
kisan	Peasant
korbani	Sacrifice, an offering
krishak	Peasant
lambardar	Village headman
lasker	Tribal war party
lakh	Hundred thousand
lunghi	Allowance given by the government to individuals (lit. a cloth used as a wrap)
madh-i-sahabah	Praises recited in honour of the first four Caliphs by Sunnis
madrasa	A secondary school or college for Muslims
maktab	School for teaching children elementary knowledge of the Koran
maulana	A title generally used for an *alim*
maulvi	A title equivalent to *maulana*
mir	A Baluchi tribal chief or leader in Sind
mofussil	The rural districts
muhalla	A ward or quarter
muhajir	Literally a refugee, commonly used to signify the Urdu-speaking minorities in Pakistan
muharram	The month in which Hussain, grandson of Prophet Mohammad, was assassinated
mujtahid	In the UP usually applied to the Shiah *ulama*
mullah	A preacher, usually attached to a mosque
murid	The disciple of a spiritual mentor or *pir*
namasudra	Agricultural castes in Bengal
pakhtunwali	Pakhtun social code
pir	Spiritual guide
proja	Tenant
purba	Eastern
rabani	A Muslim who believes in an egalitarian Islamic state
rais	A notable patron or prominent person
ramazan	The Muslim month of fasting
rupee	Currency of India and Pakistan
sabha	An association or society
sajjada nashin	Custodian of a *sufi* shrine
samiti	Party or association
sangathan	A movement aimed at unifying Hindus

sarhad	The North West Frontier Province
satyagraha	Non-violent civil disobedience
satyagrahi	A satyagraha practitioner
sayed	Descendent of the Prophet
sharia	Islamic law derived from the Koran and *Sunna*
shuddhi	'Purification,' the reconversion to Hinduism of those who had embraced other faiths
sufi	Muslim mystic
sunna	Teachings of Prophet Mohammad
swaraj	Self-government
tabarra	Comminations or curses against the first three caliphs whom the the Shiahs consider usurpers of Ali's rightful succession
tabligh	Proselytizing Muslim group
talimat	Education
talukder	In UP a superior landholder engaged by the state to collect revenue
tanzim	A movement aimed at unifying Muslims and improving them educationally
tarburwali	Rivalry between close kin
ummah	The Muslim world
vakil	Pleader, also used to denote an advocate or representative
wadera	Landlord in Sind
waqf	Muslim religious trust (pl. *auqafs*)
zaildar	Semi-official functionary in charge of an administrative subdivision in the Punjab

BIBLIOGRAPHY

Primary Sources

Manuscripts

India Office Records and Library, London

Dow Collection, Mss. Eur. E 372.
Fazl-i-Husain Collection, Mss. Eur. E 352.
Haig Collection, Mss. Eur. F 115.
India, Pakistan and Burma Association, Mss. Eur. F 158.
Lambrick Collection, Mss. Eur. F 208.
Linlithgow Collection, Mss. Eur. F 125.
Mudié Collection, Mss. Eur. F 164.

Quaid-i-Azam Academy, Karachi

All-India Muslim League Records.
Sardar Abdur Rub Nishtar Collection, PC-ARN.
Shamsul Hasan Collection.

National Archives of Pakistan, Islamabad

Quaid-i-Azam Papers.

Nehru Memorial Museum and Library, New Delhi

K. M. Munshi Papers, Microfilm No 31.
Mirza Ismail Papers, Microfilm No 26.
Rajagopalachari Papers, Microfilm No 34.

Government Records

India Office Records and Library, London

Records of the Public and Judicial Department, L/P&J/7, L/P&J/8.

Public Record Office, London

Dominion Office Papers: DO35 and DO134.
Foreign Office Papers: FO371.

National Archives, Washington, D.C.

Records of the Department of State. Internal Affairs of Pakistan, 1945-49, RG 59, Decimal File 845 F, Microfilm Roll 1-6.
Records of the Department of State. Relating to Internal Affairs of Pakistan, 1950-59, record series 790D.00, Group 59, Box 2561, 2562, 3859-3868, 3871, 3875, 3876.25, 4144-4148.

National Document Centre, Lahore

CID record series, S 160, S 247-248, S 358-361, S 387, S 390-396, S 400-426, S 428-435.

Official Publications

The Assassination of Mr Liaquat Ali Khan: Report of the Commission of Enquiry, Karachi, 1951.
Bureau of Statistics, Planning and Development Department, Government of West Pakistan, *Census of West Pakistan Government Employees, 1962*, Lahore, n.d.
Census of India, 1931, NWFP, xv, Peshawar, 1933.
The Constituent Assembly of Pakistan, Debates, 1947-1954, Karachi.
The Constituent Assembly (Legislature) of Pakistan, Debates, 1948-1954, Karachi.
Federal Court of Pakistan, Judgement in the Case of Federation of Pakistan and Others versus Molvi Tamizuddin Khan, Lahore, 1955.
Government of India Act, 1935, Government of Burma Act, 1935, Draft, Cmd 5181, London, 1936.
Government of India Act, 1935: Indian Financial Enquiry, Cmd 5163, London, 1936.
Hughes, A.W. *A Gazetteer of the Province of Sind*, London, 1874.
India Constitutional Reforms: Government of India's Despatch on the Proposal for Constitutional Reforms, Cmd 3700, London, 1930.
Indian Franchise Committee: Report, i, Cmd 4086, i-v, London, 1932.
Indian Round Table Conference: Proceedings of Sub-Committee, London, 1931.
Indian Round Table Conference, Cmd 3778, London, 1931.
Indian Round Table Conference, Cmd 3997 (second session), London, 1932.
Indian Round Table Conference, (third session), Cmd 4238, London, 1933.
Indian Statutory Commission, i-xvii, Cmd 3568, 3569, 3572, London, 1930.
Minutes and Debates of the Legislative Council of India and its Successors, 1935, London.
National Assembly of Pakistan, Debates, 1956-58, Karachi.

Pakistan Economic Survey, 1972-73, Islamabad, 1973.

Parliamentary Papers, 1918, xviii, Cmd 9178, London.

Report on Indian Constitutional Reforms (Montagu-Chelmsford Report), Cmd 9109, London, 1918.

Report of the Court of Inquiry Appointed Under Section 3 of the Sind Public Inquiries Act to Enquire into the Riots which Occurred at Sukkor in 1939, Karachi, 1940.

Report of the Court of Inquiry Constituted Under the Punjab Act II of 1954 to Enquire into the Punjab Disturbances of 1953, Lahore, 1954.

Report of the Basic Principles Committee (as presented to the Constituent Assembly), Karachi, n.d.

Return Showing the Results of Elections in India, 1921, Cmd 1261, London, 1921.

Return Showing the Results of Elections in India, 1937, Cmd 5589, London, 1937.

Return Showing the Results of Elections of the Central Legislative Assembly and the Provincial Legislatures in 1945-46, New Delhi, 1948.

Published Sources

Ahmad, W. *Diary and Notes of Mian Fazl-i-Husain*, Lahore, 1976.

————. *Letters of Mian Fazl-i-Husain*, Lahore, 1976.

Arif, K. *America-Pakistan Relations: Documents*, i, Lahore, 1984.

Aziz, K.K. ed. *The All India Muslim Conference, 1928-1935: A Documentary Record*, Karachi, 1972.

Bamford, P.C. *Histories of the Non-Co-operation and Khilafat Movements*, Delhi, 1925 (reprinted 1974).

Chopra, P.N. ed. *Towards Freedom*, i, New Delhi, 1985.

Choudhary, Valmika, ed. *Dr Rajendra Prasad: Correspondence and Select Documents*, i-ix, New Delhi, 1984.

Choudhry, G.W. ed. *Documents and Speeches on the Constitution of Pakistan*, Dacca, 1967.

Hasan, Mushirul, ed. *Muslims and the Congress: Select Correspondence of Dr M.A. Ansari, 1912-1935*, New Delhi, 1979.

Khuro, Hamida. *Documents on the Separation of Sind from the Bombay Presidency*, i, Islamabad, 1982.

Malik, Abdullah Malik, ed. *Selected Speeches and Statements: Mian Iftikharuddin*, Lahore, 1971.

Mansergh, Nicholas, ed. *The Transfer of Power, 1942-47*, i- xii, London, 1970-83.

Moon, P. ed. *Wavell: The Viceroy's Journal*, London, 1973.

Nehru, J. *A Bunch of Old Letters*, London, 1960.

Pandey, B.N. ed. *The Indian Nationalist Movement, 1885-1947: Select Documents*, London, 1979.

Petria, Sir David. *Communism in India, 1924-27*, Calcutta, 1972.

Pirzada, S. Sharifuddin, ed. *Foundations of Pakistan*, i- ii, Karachi, 1970.

Pradhan, Sudhi, ed. *Marxist Cultural Movement in India: Chronicles and Documents*, Calcutta, 1985.

Rahman, Hasan Hafizur, ed. *History of the Bangladesh War of Independence*, i-xv (Bengali), Dhaka, 1982.

Rowlands, Sir A. *Report of the Bengal Administration Enquiry Committee*, Alipore, 1945.
Sadullah, Mian Muhammad, ed. *The Partition of the Punjab, 1947*, i-iv, Lahore, 1983.
Williamson, Sir Horace. *India and Communism*, Calcutta, Reprint 1976.
Zaheer, S.S. 'A Note on the Progressive Writers' Association', in Sindhi Pradhan, ed, *Markist Cultural Movement in India: Chronicles and Documents*, Calcutta, 1985.
Zaidi, A.M. ed. *Evolution of Muslim Political Thought in India*, Delhi, 1979.
Zaidi, Z.H. ed. *M.A. Jinnah: Ispahani Correspondence, 1936-48*, Karachi, 1976.

Newspapers

Bombay Chronicle, Bombay.
Dawn, Karachi.
Pakistan News (later renamed the *Weekly Pakistan News*), London.
Pakistan Observer, Dacca.

Annuals

Indian Annual Register, ed. N.N. Mitra, Calcutta.
The Pakistan Year Book and Who's Who, 1949: A Historical and Statistical Annual, ed. S.A.R. Bilgrami, Karachi, 1949.
The Muslim Year Book of India and Who's Who, With Complete Information on Pakistan, 1948-49, ed. S.M. Jamil, Bombay.
The Indian and Pakistan Year Book and Who's Who, 1949, xxxv, ed. I.S. Jehu, Bombay.

Secondary Sources

Theses

Chatterji, Joya. 'Communal Politics and the Partition of Bengal,' Cambridge Univ. Ph.D. thesis, 1990.
Cheesman, David. 'Rural Power and Debt in Sind in the Late 19th Century, 1865-1901,' London Univ. Ph.D. thesis, 1980.
Husain, Imdad. 'The Failure of Parliamentary Politics in Pakistan, 1953-58,' Oxford Univ. D.Phil thesis, 1966.
Jones, A.K. 'Muslim Politics and the Growth of the Muslim League in Sind, 1935-41,' Duke Univ. Ph.D. thesis, 1977.
Long, Roger Douglas. 'Liaquat Ali Khan: From National Agriculturist Party to Muslim League,' Univ. of California Ph.D. thesis, 1985.
Mitra, Chandan Souran. 'Political Mobilization and the Nationalist Movement in Eastern Uttar Pradesh and Bihar, 1937- 1942,' Oxford Univ. D.Phil, 1983.
Murshid, Tazeem Mahnaz. 'The Bengal Muslim Intelligentsia, 1937-77: The Tension Between the Religious and the Secular,' Oxford Univ. D.Phil thesis, 1985.
Shah, Sayed Wiqar Ali. 'Muslim League in the NWFP, 1936-47,' Peshawar Univ. M. Phil thesis, 1986.
Ziring, Lawrence. 'The Failure of Democracy in Pakistan: East Pakistan and the Central Government, 1947-1958,' Columbia Univ. Ph.D. thesis, 1962.

Published Works

Afzal, M. Rafique. *Malik Barkat Ali. His Life and Writings*, Lahore, 1969.
———. *Political Parties in Pakistan, 1947-1958*, Islamabad, 1986.
Ahmad, A. Khan. *The Founder of Pakistan: Through Trial to Triumph*, 1942.
Ahmad, Aziz. *Islamic Modernism in India and Pakistan, 1857-1964*, London, 1967.
Ahmad Mushtaq. *Government and Politics in Pakistan*, Karachi, 1970.
———. *Politics Without Social Change*, Karachi, 1971.
Ahmad, Syed Nur, ed. by Craig Baxter. *From Martial Law to Martial Law: Politics in the Punjab, 1919-58*, Colorado, 1985.
Ahmed, Abul Mansur. *Fifty Years of Politics As I Saw it* (in Bengali), Dhaka, 1975.
Ahmed, Akbar S. *Religion and Politics in Muslim Society*, Cambridge, 1983.
Ahmed, Raffiuddin. *The Bengal Muslims, 1871-1906: A Quest for Identity*, Delhi, 1981.
Alavi, H. 'Authoritarianism and Legitimation of State Power in Pakistan', in S. Mitra, ed, *The Post-Colonial State in Asia*, London, 1990.
———. 'The Origins and Significance of the Pakistan–US Military Alliance', in S. Kumar, ed, *Yearbook on India's Foreign Policy*' New Delhi, 1991.
Alavi, Hamza and **Teodor Shanin**. *Introduction to the Sociology of 'Developing Societies,'* London, 1982.
Ali, Chaudhri Muhammad. *The Emergence of Pakistan*, New York, 1967.
Ali, Choudhary Rahmat. *The Millat and the Mission*, Cambridge, 1942.
———. *What Does the Pakistan Movement Stand For?*, Cambridge, 3rd ed.,1942.
———. *India: The Continent of Dinia or the Country of Doom*, Cambridge, 3rd ed., 1946.
———. *Pakistan: The Fatherland of the Pak Nation*, Cambridge, 3rd ed., 1947.
Ali, Imran. 'Malign Growth? Agricultural Colonization and the Roots of Backwardness in the Punjab,' *Past and Present*, 114, February 1987.
Ali, Tariq. *Pakistan: Military Rule or People's Power?*, London, 1970.
Anderson, Benedict. *Imagined Communities: Reflections on the Origin and Spread of Nationalism*, London, 1983.
Ansari, Khizar H. *The Emergence of Muslim Socialists in North India, 1917-47*, Lahore, 1990.
Ansari, Sarah F.D. *Sufi Saints and State Power: The Pirs of Sind, 1843-1947*, Cambridge, 1922.
Ansari, Shaukatullah. *Pakistan: The Problem of India*, Lahore, 1944.
Azad, Maulana Abul Kalam. *India Wins Freedom*, Calcutta, 1959.
Azam, Ghulam. *Islam Movement*, Dacca, 1968.
Aziz, K.K. *Party Politics in Pakistan, 1947-1958*, Islamabad, 1976.
———. *A History of the Idea Of Pakistan*, i-iv, Lahore, 1987.
———. *Rahmat Ali: A Biography*, Lahore, 1987.
Bahadur, Kalim. *The Jama'at-i-Islami of Pakistan*, New Delhi, 1977.
Banuazizi, Ali and **Myron, Weiner**, eds. *The State, Religion and Ethnic Politics: Pakistan, Iran and Afghanistan*, Lahore, 1987.
Baxter, Craig. 'The People's Party versus the Panjab "Fendalists" ', in J.H. Korson, ed, *Contemporary Problems of Pakistan*, Leiden, 1974.
Bayly, C.A. 'Local Control in Indian Towns: The Case of Allahabad, 1880-1920,' *Modern Asian Studies*, 5, 4, 1971.
———. *The Local Roots of Indian Politics: Allahabad 1880-1920*, Oxford, 1975.
Binder, Leonard. *Religion and Politics in Pakistan*, Berkeley, 1961.

Bose, Sugata. *Agrarian Bengal: Economy, Social Structure and Politics, 1919-1947*, Cambridge, 1986.

Braibanti, R. *Asian Bureaucratic Traditions Emergent from the British Imperial Tradition*, Durham, 1966.

————. *Research on the Bureaucracy of Pakistan*, Durham, 1966.

Brands, H.W. 'India and Pakistan in American Strategic Planning, 1947-54: Commonwealth as Collaborators', *Journal of Imperial and Commonwealth History*, 15, 1, 1986.

Brass, P.R. *Language, Religion and Politics in North India*, Cambridge, 1974.

Broomfield, J.H. *Elite Conflict in a Plural Society: Twentieth Century Bengal*, Berkeley, 1968.

Buzan, B. and **G. Rizvi**. *South Asian Insecurity and the Great Powers*, Basingstoke, 1986.

Callard, Keith. *Pakistan: A Political Study*, London, 1957.

Caroe, Olaf. *The Pathans, 550 BC-AD 1957*, London, 1958.

Chakrabarty, Dipesh and **Ranajit Das Gupta**. 'Some Aspects of Labour History of Bengal in the Nineteenth Century: Two Views,' *Occasional Paper 40*, Centre for Social Sciences, Calcutta, 1981.

————. *Bengal, 1920-47: The Land Question*, Calcutta, 1984.

Chatterjee, Partha. *Agrarian Structure in Pre-Partition Bengal*, Calcutta, 1982.

Clapham, Christopher and **George Philips**, eds. *The Political Dilemmas of Military Regimes*, London, 1985.

Cohen, S.P. *The Pakistan Army*, Berkeley, 1984.

Council of the Bengal Provincial Muslim League. *Annual Meeting, 1944*, Calcutta, n.d.

Coupland, R. *Report on the Constitutional Problem in India*, i-iii, London, 1944.

Das, Suranjan, *Communal Riots in Bengal, 1905-1947*, Delhi, 1991.

East Pakistan Renaissance Society. *Eastern Pakistan: Its Population, Delimitation and Economy*, Calcutta, 1944.

Faruqi, Ziya-ul-Hasan. *The Deoband School and the Demand for Pakistan*, Bombay, 1963.

Gallagher, John. *The Decline, Revival and Fall of the British Empire*, Cambridge, 1982.

Gankovsky, Y.V. and **L.R. Gordon-Polonskya.** *A History of Pakistan, 1947-58*, Lahore, 1974.

Gardezi, H. and **J. Rashid**, eds. *Pakistan: The Roots of Dictatorship: The Political Economy of a Praetorian State*, London, 1983.

Gilmartin, David. 'Religious Leadership and the Pakistan Movement in the Punjab,' *Modern Asian Studies*, 13, 3, 1979.

————. *Empire and Islam: Punjab and the Making of Pakistan*, London, 1988.

Gordon, Leonard A. *Bengal: The Nationalist Movement, 1876-1940*, New York, 1974.

Gupta, Amit Kumar, ed. *Myth and Reality: The Struggle for Freedom in India, 1945-47*, New Delhi, 1987.

Hardy, Peter. *The Muslims of British India*, Cambridge, 1972.

Hasan, Mushirul. *Nationalism and Communal Politics in India, 1916-28*, New Delhi, 1979.

————, ed. *Muslims and the Congress: Select Correspondence of Dr M.A. Ansari, 1912-1935*, New Delhi, 1979.

————. *Communal and Pan-Islamic Trends in Colonial India*, New Delhi, 1981.

————. 'The Muslim Mass Contact Campaign: An Attempt at Political Mobilization,' *Occasional Papers on History and Society*, 14, Nehru Memorial Museum and Library, n.d.

Hashim, Abul. *In Retrospection*, Dacca, 1974.

Huq, Fazlul A.K. *Muslim Sufferings Under Congress Rule*, Calcutta, 1939.

Husain Azim. *Fazl-i-Husain: A Political Biography*, Bombay, 1946.

Jahan, Rounaq. *Pakistan: Failure in National Integration*, New York, 1972.

————. *Bangladesh Politics: Problems and Issues*, Dhaka, 1980.

Jain, N.K. *Muslims in India: Biographical Dictionary*, i-ii, New Delhi, 1979.

Jalal, A. 'Inheriting the Raj: Jinnah and the Governor-Generalship Issue,' *Modern Asian Studies*, 19, 1, 1985.

————. *The Sole Spokesman: Jinnah, the Muslim League and the Demand for Pakistan*, Cambridge, 1985.

————. *The State of Martial Law*, Cambridge, 1990.

Jalal A. and A. Seal. 'Alternative to Partition: Muslim Politics Between the Wars,' *Modern Asian Studies*, 15, 3, 1981.

Jamaluddin, Syed. 'The Bareloos and the Khilafat Movement', in Mushirul Hasan, ed, *Communal and Pan-Islamic Trends in Colonial India*, New Delhi, 1981.

Jansson, E. *India, Pakistan or Pakhtunistan: The Nationalist Movements in the North West Frontier Province, 1937-47*, Stockholm, 1981.

Kamanev, Sergei. *The Economic Growth of Pakistan*, Lahore, 1985.

Kennedy, Charles H. *Bureaucracy in Pakistan*, Karachi, 1987.

Khaliquzzaman, Choudhry. *Pathway to Pakistan*, Lahore, 1961.

Khan, Abdul Rashid. *A Report on the Transfer and Concentration of Muslim Population in Other States, Provinces and Central Compact Blocks*, Lucknow, 1946.

Khan, Ayub. *Friends Not Masters: A Political Biography*, Karachi, 1967.

Khan, Bazlur Rahman. *Politics in Bengal, 1927-1936*, Dhaka, 1987.

Khan, Major-General Muqeem. *The Story of the Pakistan Army*, Karachi, 1963.

Khan, Nawabzada Liaquat Ali. *Muslim Educational Problems*, Lahore, 2nd ed., 1952.

Khan, Sikander Hayat. *Outlines of a Scheme of Indian Federation*, Lahore, n.d.

Khan, Tahawar Ali Khan. *Biographical Research Institute, Pakistan*, Lahore, n.d.

Khan, Wali. *Facts are Facts: The Untold Story of India's Partition*, New Delhi, 1988.

Kheira, Muhammad Abdus Sattar. *National States and National Minorities: Committee of Writers of the AIML*, Lahore, 2nd ed., 1947.

Kochanek, Stanley A. *Business and Politics in India*, Berkeley, 1974.

————. *Interest Groups and Development: Business and Politics in Pakistan*, Delhi, 1983.

Korson, J.H. ed. *Contemporary Problems of Pakistan*, Leiden, 1974.

Kumar, S. ed. *Year Book on India's Foreign Policy*, New Delhi, 1991.

Latif, Syed Abdul. *A Federation of Cultural Zones for India*, Hyderabad, 1938.

————. *The Cultural Future of India*, Bombay, 1938.

Leigh, M.S. *The Punjab and the War*, Lahore, 1922.

Low, D.A. ed. *Soundings in Modern Asian History*, London, 1968.

————. *Congress and the Raj*, London, 1977.

————. *The Indian National Congress: Centenary Hindsight*, Delhi, 1988.

————. *The Political Inheritance of Pakistan*, Basingstoke, 1991.

Mahmood, Safdar. *Pakistan Divided*, Lahore, 1984.

Malik, Iftikhar Haider. *Sikander Hayat Khan, 1892-1942: A Political Biography*, Islamabad, 1985.

Maniruzzaman, Talukder. *The Politics of Development: The Case of Pakistan, 1947-1958*, Dacca, 1971.

Mcpherson, Kenneth. *The Muslim Microcosm: Calcutta, 1918 to 1935*, Wiesbaden, 1974.

Minault, Gail. *The Khilafat Movement: Religious Symbolism and Political Mobilization in India*, New York, 1982.

Mirza, Sarfaz Hussain. *Muslim Women's Role in the Pakistan Movement*, Lahore, 1969.

Mitra, S. ed. *The Post-Colonial State in Asia*, London, 1990.

Momen, Humaira. *Muslim Politics in Bengal: A Study of the Krishak Proja Party and the 1937 Elections*, Dacca, 1972.

Moore, R.J. *Churchill, Cripps and India, 1939-1945*, Oxford, 1979.

———. *Endgames of Empire: Studies of Britain's Indian Problem*, Delhi, 1988.

MRT. *Pakistan and Muslim India*, Delhi, 1942.

Muhammad, Shan. *Khaksar Movement in India*, Meerut, 1973.

Mujahid, M.M. Shareef ed. *Federation Souvenir*, Madras, 1947.

Mujahid, Sharif al. *Quaid-i-Azam Jinnah*, Karachi, 1981.

Musa, General Mohammad. *Jawan to General: Recollections of a Pakistani Soldier*, Karachi, 1984.

Page, David. *Prelude to Partition: The Indian Muslims and the Imperial System of Control, 1920-32*, New Delhi, 1982.

Pandey, Gyanendra. *The Ascendancy of the Congress in Uttar Pradesh, 1926-34: A Study in Imperfect Mobilization*, Delhi, 1978.

Philips, C.H. and **M.D. Wainwright.** *The Partition of India: Policies and Perspective, 1935-47*, London, 1970.

Ponomarev, Yuri. *The Muslim League of Pakistan, 1947-1977*, Lahore, 1986.

Prasad, Rajendra. *India Divided*, Bombay, 1947.

Punjabi, A. *A Confederacy of India*, Lahore, 1939.

Qaiyum, Abdul. *Gold and Guns on the Pathan Frontier*, Bombay, 1945.

Rab, A.S.M. Abdur. *A.K. Fazlul Huq: Life and Achievements*, Lahore, 1966.

Rahman, Anisur. *Pakistan and Mussalmans*, Bombay, n.d.

Rashid, Harun-or. *The Foreshadowing of Bangladesh*, Dhaka, 1987.

Rahman, Inamur. *Public Opinion and Political Development in Pakistan, 1947-58*, Karachi, 1982.

Reeves, P.D. 'Landlords and Party Politics in the United Provinces, 1934-37', in D.A. Low, ed, *Soundings in Modern Asia History*, London, 1968.

Rittenberg, Stephen A. *Ethnicity, Nationalism and the Pakhtuns: The Independence Movement in India's North West Frontier Province*, Durham, 1988.

Rizvi, Gowher. *Linlithgow and India: A Study of British Policy and the Political Impasse in India, 1936-43*, London, 1978.

———. 'Pakistan: The Domestic Dimensions of Security', in B. Buzan and G. Rizvi, eds, *South Asian Insecurity and the Great Powers,* Basingstoke, 1986.

Robinson, Francis. *Separatism Among Indian Muslims: The Politics of the United Provinces' Muslims, 1860-1923*, Cambridge, 1974.

Roy, Asim. *The Islamic Syncretistic Tradition in Bengal*, Princeton, 1983.

Sayed, G.M. *Struggle for New Sind. A Brief Narrative of the Working of Provincial Autonomy in Sind*, Karachi, 1949.

Sayeed, Khalid Bin. *Pakistan: The Formative Phase, 1857-1948*, London, 1963.

———. *The Political System of Pakistan*, Boston, 1967.

———. *Politics in Pakistan: The Nature and Direction of Change*, New York, 1984.

Sen, Rangalal. *Political Elites in Bangladesh*, New Delhi, 1987.

Shah, Ikram Ali. 'Economic Justification of Pakistan,' *The Contemporary Review*, October 1943.

Shah, Sirdar Ikbal Ali. *Pakistan: A Plan for India*, London, 1944.

Shaikh, Farzana. 'Muslims and Political Representation in Colonial India: The Making of Pakistan,' *Modern Asian Studies*, 20, 3, 1986.

———. *Community and Consensus in Islam: Muslim Representation in Colonial India, 1860-1947*, Cambridge, 1989.

Shareef, S.M. *A Study on the Lahore Resolution: Popularly Known as Pakistan*, Patna, 1940.

———. *Report of the Publicity Committee of the Bihar Provincial Muslim League on Grievances of the Muslims, 1938-39*, Patna, n.d.

Singh, Anita Inder. *The Origins of the Partition of India, 1936-47*, Delhi, 1987.

Smith, Wilfred Cantwell. *Modern Islam in India*, Lahore, 1943.

Stephens, Ian. *Pakistan*, London, 1967.

Symond, Richard. *The Making of Pakistan*, London, 3rd ed., 1951.

Talbot, Ian. 'The 1946 Punjab Election,' *Modern Asian Studies*, 14, 1, 1980.

———. *Punjab and the Raj, 1849-1947*, Delhi, 1988.

———. *Provincial Politics and the Pakistan Movement: The Growth of the Muslim League in North West and North East India, 1937-47*, Karachi, 1988.

Talukdar, Mohammad H.R. ed. *Memoirs of Huseyn Shaheed Suhrawardy with a Brief Account of his Life and Work*, Dhaka, 1987.

Taylor, David and **Malcom Yapp.** *Political Identity in South Asia*, London, 1979.

Tucker, Sir Francis. *While Memory Serves*, London, 1950.

Venkataramani, M.S. *The American Role in Pakistan*, Lahore, 1984.

Wheeler, R.S. *The Politics of Pakistan: A Constitutional Quest*, New York, 1970.

Wilcox, Wayne. *Pakistan: The Consolidation of a Nation*, New York, 1963.

Wolpert, Stanley. *Jinnah of Pakistan*, Oxford, 1984.

Zaman, Mukhtar. *Students' Role in the Pakistan Movement*, Karachi, 1978.

Ziring, L. *Pakistan, The Enigma of Political Development*, Kent, 1980.

Ziring, L., R. Braibanti and **W.H. Wriggins.** *Pakistan: The Long View*, Durham, 1977.

INDEX